Elena Mukhina

# The Diary of Lena Mukhina

· · · · · · · · · · · · · · · · · · · · · · · · · · · · · · · · ·

Edited and with a Foreword by
VALENTIN KOVALCHUK, ALEKSANDR RUPASOV
and ALEKSANDR CHISTIKOV

Translated by
AMANDA LOVE DARRAGH

MACMILLAN

First published 2015 by Macmillan
an imprint of Pan Macmillan, a division of Macmillan Publishers Limited
Pan Macmillan, 20 New Wharf Road, London N1 9RR
Basingstoke and Oxford
Associated companies throughout the world
www.panmacmillan.com

ISBN 978-1-4472-6987-8 HB
ISBN 978-1-4472-8435-2 TPB

The publishers would like to thank T. S. Musina for the use of photographs
from the family archive, the Central State Archive of Historical-Political
Documents in St Petersburg and the State Hermitage Museum.

1 3 5 7 9 8 6 4 2

A CIP catalogue record for this book is available from the British Library.

Printed and bound by CPI Group (UK) Ltd, Croydon, CR0 4YY

# Foreword

The Siege of Leningrad, also known as the Leningrad Blockade, was the most terrible and tragic period in the history of the city now known as St Petersburg. On that summer's day when Nazi Germany invaded the USSR, 22 June 1941, none of the city's residents could have imagined that in less than six months' time death would be such a part of their lives.

This diary, written by sixteen-year-old Leningrad schoolgirl Elena (Lena) Mukhina and miraculously preserved from that dreadful era, gives us a human insight into the last days of peace and the first days of war. With astonishing candour and a mix of childish naivety and adult wisdom, it paints a picture of a city reeling from the impact of war and the struggle of its innocent, defenceless inhabitants for survival. The obvious talent of the writer captures our attention from the very first pages, swiftly drawing us in and holding us in a constant state of suspense as we experience the tragedy and heroism of ordinary, everyday people, on whom nations are built and by whom history is both made and recorded.

First we must give a brief account of what befell Leningrad and its inhabitants during the first year of war, including the winter of 1941–2 – the deadliest and most devastating period of the entire siege. This historical background will help to put the events experienced by Lena Mukhina, her classmates, her family and friends into context.

The city's appearance began to change from the very first days of the war. In a matter of weeks Leningrad was covered by a network of trenches and crevices for people to hide in during bombing raids. It was strange to see gas masks being carried around in bags, by civilians as well as military personnel. Shop windows and many of the city's monuments were boarded up or covered with piles of sandbags. Clodt's famous horses[1] abandoned their pedestals and found shelter in the grounds of the Pioneers' Palace.[2] Strips of white or dark-blue paper were pasted crosswise onto the windows of homes and offices. At this early stage the city resembled an agitated anthill, with queues at the shops and banks, queues of conscripts and volunteers at the military recruitment offices and crowds of evacuees at the train stations.

While battles were being fought some distance from the city, around half a million Leningraders, Lena Mukhina among them, were constructing defensive works in the west of the region. But by the beginning of September 1941, despite fierce resistance from Soviet troops, Germany's Army Group North under the command of Field Marshal General Wilhelm Leeb had reached the city's southern and south-western suburbs. Together with

---

1 Four statues of rearing horses being held by their riders, collectively known as the Horse Tamers. These were designed by the Russian sculptor Baron Peter Clodt von Jürgensburg (known in Russian as Pyotr Karlovich Klodt) and installed on pedestals at the corners of the Anichkov Bridge in 1851.

2 At the intersection of Nevsky Prospekt and the Fontanka. Formerly the Anichkov Palace.

Finnish forces advancing from the north, the Germans closed a siege ring around Leningrad on 8 September 1941, thereby condemning more than two and a half million people to slow but certain death. The last remaining link between the besieged city and the rest of the country was Lake Ladoga; the legendary 'ice road' across its frozen surface became known as the Road of Life.

On 5 September Hitler had announced: 'from now on the region of Leningrad will be a secondary theatre of operations'. In other words he had decided not to waste military resources occupying the city, since its downfall was predetermined. On 29 September German naval command issued a directive entitled 'On the future of the city of Petersburg', which stated:

> The intention is to encircle the city and level it to the ground by means of artillery fire, using shells of all calibre, and continual aerial bombardment. Any requests for surrender arising as a result of this action will be categorically rejected, since the problem of maintaining and feeding the population cannot and should not be solved by us. In this war . . . we have no interest in saving any part of the civilian population of this large city.

The city authorities still feared that German troops might invade Leningrad, and with this eventuality in mind they developed their so-called 'Plan D': the proposed destruction of 58,510 strategic targets to stop them falling into enemy hands. As a further pre-emptive measure in case of German occupation the Leningrad Party City Committee established an underground party organization to coordinate resistance efforts.

At first the inhabitants of Leningrad didn't realize that the circle around them had closed. They knew, of course, that German divisions had reached the southern outskirts of the city – they could virtually see them with their own eyes. But there seemed to be less of a threat from the Finnish troops, who had stopped 30–40 km north of the city and possessed no long-range artillery equipment. During artillery attacks it was considerably less dangerous in the northern districts of Leningrad than in the southern and central districts, so people didn't really believe that the city was surrounded. Only at the beginning of November, when food supplies were almost exhausted, did the authorities finally tell Leningraders the truth.

No one could possibly have known that the city would remain in the grip of siege for 872 days and nights. But Leningrad's citizens had begun to feel the breath of war as early as September. Daily air raids and artillery bombardment of residential neighbourhoods drove the city's inhabitants into bomb shelters, several times a day and for hours at a time. People's initial curiosity in the aftermath of the first bomb attacks soon gave way to fear and then – in conditions of appalling hunger and cold – to apathy. Leningraders welcomed inclement weather for the reduced visibility it brought. They came to dread sunny days and moonlit nights, when the Germans would be sure to bomb their city. Cloud cover, however, offered no protection from artillery fire: in just over six months from the start of the siege there were only thirty-two days when shells did not explode on the city's streets.

Hunger soon set in. Between September and November 1941 the bread rations that had been announced in July were reduced five times, reaching their lowest point on 20 November: 125 'blockade grams' for children, dependants and white-collar workers and 250g for manual workers, technicians and engineers. Rations of meat, butter, sugar and other food items were severely reduced. The summer months and the beginning of autumn, when it was still possible to buy food without ration cards in ordinary shops and canteens, were no more than a distant memory.

Even these limited quantities of food were not always easy to come by. People would start queuing outside shops in the early hours of the morning, but when the bread arrived there was sometimes only enough for the first twenty or thirty lucky individuals out of the hundreds standing in line. And you could hardly call it bread: up to 40 per cent of the flour was replaced by additives such as bran, oil-cake,[3] wallpaper dust and wood cellulose. Leningraders grew accustomed to new dishes, such as *khryapa* (made from the green outer leaves of a head of cabbage) and a kind of soy protein made from crushed soybean husks, both of which had been used as cattle feed prior to the war. People ate crows, pigeons, cats and dogs. They boiled up 'meat' jelly from carpenter's glue and made flatbreads out of foraged pine nuts. One of the factories tried to bake bread rolls using dextrin – a by-product of starch, used as industrial glue. The resulting rolls and biscuits stuck people's teeth together, but they soon discovered a way to get round this unfortunate side-effect: sprinkling a spoonful of powdered dextrin directly into their mouths and washing it down with water.

Hunger drove some to cannibalism – both *trupoedstvo* (eating the flesh of those who had died of natural causes) and *lyudoedstvo* (killing others for this purpose). Human flesh was cut from corpses and either eaten or sold on the black market. Some people murdered not only strangers but family members too, even their own children. Cannibals were considered to be guilty of 'banditry' and as such were subject to strictly enforced penalties: over 2,000 arrests were made in the city between the

---

3  Oil-cake (*duranda*, also *zhmykh*) was a food substitute consisting of the compressed husks of the seeds of oil-yielding plants once the oil had been extracted from them.

autumn of 1941 and the end of 1942. Later, when food supplies improved significantly, both forms of cannibalism disappeared.

The symptoms of starvation and 'dystrophy' (extreme malnutrition) were shocking. 'It would change a person's face, their whole appearance, turning them into a walking corpse. And, as everybody knows, a dead body is never a pleasant sight,' recalled one siege survivor.

Those yellow faces were absolutely terrifying, and they wore such a glazed expression. It was nothing like the pain people suffer when they hurt an arm or a leg. In this case the entire body was afflicted, and more often than not mental faculties were impaired as well. Their face would turn yellow, their eyes would glaze over, their voice would fade away – you couldn't even tell from someone's quavering voice whether they were a man or a woman. They were ageless, sexless beings.

Death could strike anywhere and at any time. At the end of 1941, between 6 and 13 December alone, 841 people dropped dead in the street. At the beginning of 1942, 101,583 Leningraders died in January, 107,477 in February, 98,966 in March and 79,769 in April. During these months, an average of 110 to 160 of the city's inhabitants were dying every hour. The logistics of burying so many bodies presented a serious problem. On some days in February 1942 there were as many as 20,000–25,000 corpses awaiting burial at the Piskarevskoye cemetery. They were stacked along the central path in rows 180–200 metres long and up to 2 metres high. As an emergency measure, the authorities gave orders for some of the corpses to be burned in the furnaces at the Izhorsky and Pervy brick factories.

On 25 December 1941, bread rations were increased by

75–100g, making it a memorable day for many Leningraders. 'What joy, what joy!' begins Lena Mukhina's diary entry for the day. However, it was impossible to survive on rations alone. The city's inhabitants sought additional sustenance by fair means and foul: they bought extra food or bartered valuables and other possessions for it, they were given food in exchange for donating blood, they were sent food by relatives elsewhere in Russia or at the front, and some were able to regain their strength in special recuperation clinics[4] set up by the authorities. Some resorted to theft, others tried to use forged coupons. Quite simply, as one siege survivor put it: 'Those who ate more survived, those who ate less died.'

According to another contemporary: 'Hunger and cold – that was our psychological impression of the blockade.' Winter came early that year and was especially severe. The first snow fell on the streets of Leningrad in the middle of October. News that the siege now encircled the city led to fears that buildings would be left without heating, given that Leningrad had always been dependent on outside supplies of firewood and coal. These fears were soon realized. Despite official orders for wooden houses, fences, market stalls and stadium benches to be used for fuel, the city's central heating stopped working at the very beginning of winter. Residents set about constructing

---

4   Residential recuperation clinics (*statsionary*), offering food and medical treatment, were set up throughout Leningrad on the basis of a resolution passed by the Executive Committee of the Leningrad City Council on 29 December 1941. Many organizations and establishments ran their own clinics, and there was one in every district. The city's main recuperation clinic in the Hotel Astoria was for party leaders, senior Soviet officials, industrial managers, Stakhanovites and prominent figures in the fields of science and culture. According to Leningrad's department of trade, '60,000 people were treated at recuperation clinics' between January and April 1942. These clinics were subsequently replaced by special canteens serving food high in calories or other nutritional properties.

temporary metal stoves in their rooms, feeding them with anything that would burn, such as furniture, books, shelves and doors from abandoned apartments.

The city's water supply and sewerage system began to fail next, leading to the closure of public baths and hairdressing salons. Leningraders were forced to abandon the pride they had always taken in their appearance. They had less energy and fewer opportunities to attend to their personal hygiene; washing had become a tortuous procedure, requiring enormous effort. People relieved themselves in abandoned rooms and dark stairwells. Cesspits and makeshift latrines were constructed in some courtyards, but not all residents had the energy or the desire to make it that far.

In the middle of November the city was plunged into darkness. Electric lighting was available only in certain institutions, and light bulbs of the lowest available wattage were permitted for use in guard rooms. But in other rooms, where the curtains were pulled shut to keep out the cold and the walls were covered with hoarfrost, the only light came from the faint flickering of the modest flames of icon lamps and home-made oil lamps.

The silence was broken by air-raid sirens, missile explosions, the sound of distant gunfire and the rhythmic, round-the-clock ticking of the metronome from the city's loudspeakers, interrupted only by Leningrad Radio broadcasts and bulletins from the front line.[5]

During the winter of 1941–2, the city was transformed again. Dozens of trams and trolleybuses stood motionless in the

---

5  Throughout the siege, the radio broadcast of a ticking metronome was the means by which Leningrad's citizens were alerted to air raids. In the first months of the siege 1,500 loudspeakers were installed in the streets. If the tempo was fast, an air raid was imminent; if slow, the threat was over.

snow-covered streets, abandoned mid-journey when the electricity supply was cut off. The snow itself was unusually white and clean, since the city's factories and manufacturing plants had been evacuated or ceased production. The hunched figures of Leningraders trudged along the winding paths that crisscrossed the streets, rivers and canals.

An acute sense of despair led many to contemplate the futility of the struggle for survival. People were overcome by apathy, so much so that they no longer even mourned the loss of their loved ones. But they were outnumbered by those who wanted to survive. This desire was an astonishing stimulus – giving rise to ingenuity and bringing out the highest moral qualities in some, while in others manifesting itself in a willingness to sacrifice fellow citizens, including their own flesh and blood, for personal gain. Nevertheless, in spite of everything, the majority of Leningraders 'kept their humanity'.

It is almost incomprehensible, but even in these truly inhuman conditions workers still repaired weapons, some schoolchildren and students carried on going to classes, and hospitals remained open. Lena Mukhina even attended an organized New Year's party with some of her classmates. These parties – with dancing around decorated fir trees, theatrical performances and, most importantly, food – appear to have made a lasting impression on all schoolchildren in the besieged city. Academic life continued. Even at the beginning of January 1942 Leningrad's cinemas were still screening feature and documentary films, and theatres continued to stage performances.

Lena Mukhina planned to leave Leningrad in the late spring of 1942, just as the city – cleared by its inhabitants of corpses and sewage and thereby spared the otherwise inevitable epidemics – was experiencing something of a rebirth. Hunger had already released its grip. The trams were running again, and public parks and flowerbeds had been turned into temporary allotments. Boys who had survived the winter ventured out to play football. Some people even made the most of the fine weather by sunbathing. Eyewitnesses noted that women were trying to dress as elegantly as circumstances permitted. By no means did all Leningraders want to leave; some were convinced that the worst was over and had to be evacuated almost by force. But the war was never very far away. The city continued to strengthen its defences and, mindful of the tragedy of the first siege winter, stocked up on firewood. Bursts of artillery fire continued and bombing resumed, taking hundreds of civilian lives.

It would be eight long months until the blockade was broken, and a further year until the victory salute that marked Leningrad's final liberation from the siege.

How many lives did the siege claim? It is impossible to give a precise figure, but most historians believe that the final death toll came to at least 800,000.

Lena Mukhina was doubly lucky: she found a way to escape the besieged city and, unlike many other evacuees, she survived the journey. Ultimately, however, her experiences in Leningrad during the siege cast a shadow over the rest of her life. She dreamed of being happy. To all intents and purposes, this dream remained unfulfilled.

As soon as the last page of Lena Mukhina's diary is turned, the reader is left with several questions. Did she leave or did she stay? Did she die or did she manage, against the odds, to survive? If so, then what happened to her?

First of all, we had to establish what we already knew. Which was not a lot, as it turned out: she was a pupil at Leningrad's School No. 30 and she lived somewhere in the vicinity of Zagorodny Prospekt, Vladimirskaya (formerly Nakhimson)

Square, Sotsialisticheskaya Street or Razyezzhaya Street, with Mama and Aka (a nanny, a grandmother?). She had extended family in Gorky (now Nizhny Novgorod); the address is even given in the diary. And we knew her date of birth. But we didn't know her patronymic, or her address in Leningrad.

We decided to pursue several lines of inquiry at the same time. We contacted the St Petersburg Civil Registry Office, hoping that if Lena had been born in Leningrad they would be able to give us her exact address, so that by consulting the house register we could at least find out whether or not she had left the city. At the same time we contacted the Central State Archive of Historico-Political Documents, St Petersburg, where the original diary is kept, to ask when and how it came to be there. The response was not particularly enlightening. The diary had arrived at the archive in 1962 along with various other documents, about which nobody could tell us anything. However, the archivists did have some good news for us. A recently published anthology about the siege included several pages from the diary of Lena Mukhina with this postscript: 'Elena Mukhina was evacuated from Leningrad a few days later. Her subsequent fate is unknown.' 'How do you know this?' we asked the author, G. I. Lisovskaya. She replied: 'A long-serving member of staff at the archive mentioned it.' We were unable to find out who or when. But Lena had survived – and we were keen to find further evidence to prove it.

At this point we heard back from the Civil Registry Office. There was no record of Lena Mukhina having been born in Leningrad. The calls we made to Nizhny Novgorod, using telephone numbers we found on the internet, didn't lead to anything either. We didn't seem to be getting anywhere.

We had to turn to the diary again in the hope of finding new clues. This time, close scrutiny of the original yielded further information. On one of the blank pages at the back of the notebook there was a note in pencil, which had clearly been written by somebody else: 'E. N. Bernatskaya, Apt 6, 26 Zagorodny, tel. 5.62.15'. This immediately brought to mind a phrase from the diary: 'I'm writing in Mama's notebook.' Could E. N. Bernatskaya be 'Mama Lena'? This possibility was confirmed when we consulted the *Kniga pamyati*, or Memorial Book, for the siege and discovered an entry dated February 1942 relating to the death of Elena Nikolaevna Bernatskaya, who lived at the address indicated in the diary.

But why did they have different surnames and the same forenames? And why did Lena frequently refer to her mother not just as Mama but as Mama Lena? And what explanation could there be for the two diary entries about the death of her mother, when she is referred to immediately afterwards as though she were still alive? Perhaps Bernatskaya was her adoptive mother, and it was her birth mother who died in July 1941. This seemed to make sense, but we were still just guessing.

For the time being, our main question – the fate of Lena herself – remained unanswered. Our next approach was to search for clues in documents relating to the Leningrad artist Vera Vladimirovna Milyutina, whom Lena mentions a number of times in the spring of 1942 and who, as is clear from the diary, played the most active role in arranging Lena's evacuation.

The personal archive of V. V. Milyutina and her husband, the musicologist Aleksandr Semenovich Rozanov, is kept in the Central State Archive of Literature and Art, St Petersburg. A quick glance through the inventory, which listed more than 700 acts by name . . . and suddenly, there it was: File No.315 – letters to V. V. Milyutina from Elena Vladimirovna Mukhina, artist! Seven letters, twenty-four pages in all, covering the period 1942–84. Could it be her?

A thin file containing letters and postcards was delivered to us a week later, and it became immediately obvious that it was indeed her. There were too many correlations between the letters to V. V. Milyutina and the diary for it to be a coincidence. We had found the answer to our main question: Lena Mukhina was evacuated from Leningrad in June 1942 and four decades later she was living in Moscow.

As well as letters the file contained envelopes, on which she had written her address, and anecdotal information about her relatives, some of whom had been mentioned in the diary. Could she still be alive? A certain amount of apprehension preceded our telephone call to Moscow: were we calling the right people, and how would they respond to our questions? The initial response at the other end of the line was confusion: Yes, we know Elena Vladimirova Mukhina. What diary? She wrote it during the siege? She never mentioned it.

Nevertheless, it soon became clear that we were speaking about the same person. Elena Vladimirovna was no longer alive, but her niece Tatyana Sergeevna Musina and her husband, Rashid Maratovich, were more than happy to help us in our quest. An album they had kept containing photographs and letters from Elena Vladimirovna, her mother and Mama Lena, together with the archive materials that we had already been able to unearth, not only provided answers to the rest of our questions but also enabled us to build up a more accurate picture of the life story of the Leningrad schoolgirl Lena Mukhina.

Elena Vladimirovna Mukhina was born on 21 November 1924 in Ufa but moved to Leningrad with her mother, Mariya Nikolaevna Mukhina, at the beginning of the 1930s. When Mariya Nikolaevna became seriously ill Lena went to live with her mother's sister, Elena Nikolaevna Mukhina (married name Bernatskaya, referred to by Lena as 'Mama Lena' and also simply 'Mama'). We must digress slightly at this point to give a little background information on the Mukhina family. Mariya and Elena had two brothers, Nikolai and Vladimir, and a sister, Evgeniya (known as Zhenya, married name Zhurkova). Their mother, Sofiya Polikarpovna, worked as a schoolteacher in the village of Durykino near Moscow. According to family legend, Sofiya Polikarpovna was a *narodnitsa* – a member of the *raznochinets* intelligentsia and an active participant in the populist *narodnik* movement. Her husband Nikolai worked as an accountant at the Moscow city government offices. Elena Nikolaevna Bernatskaya had enjoyed riding since she was a child, and her love of equestrian sports stayed with her throughout her life. This passion changed Bernatskaya's life dramatically, however, when a fall from a horse ended her career as a ballet dancer. But Bernatskaya maintained her links with the theatrical world, later becoming a set designer at Leningrad's Maly Opera Theatre. Lena Mukhina's diary attests to her familiarity with her aunt's professional environment and acquaintances – the opera singer Grigory Filippovich Bolshakov, the artist Vera Vladimirovna Milyutina, the scenic artist Sergei Viktorovich Senatorsky and his wife Lyubov (Kisa), and also Kira Nikolaevna Lipkhart, who worked in the literary department of Leningrad's Maly Opera Theatre, amongst others.

Unfortunately, her theatre work was not rewarded with material prosperity. Nor did financial affairs take a significant turn for the better when Bernatskaya began making copies of sketches. 'At the moment, as I write, I don't have any work, and we don't have enough to last us more than three weeks. But I'm not too upset about it. After all I have been living like this since 1934 . . . It will be summer soon, and I don't have a single kopek set aside,' she admitted in a letter to her sister Zhenya in the spring of 1941. Lena was fully aware of the situation:

'We're not going to the dacha this year. We can't afford it,' she writes ruefully in her diary on 28 May 1941. Then she continues cheerfully: 'But it doesn't matter, in fact I'm quite pleased about it – I haven't spent the whole summer in the city for ages. I'll definitely get a job.' Alas, war broke out less than a month later.

Lena's experience of the first year of the war is detailed in her diary. But what happened next?

Lena Mukhina left Leningrad at the beginning of June 1942. A special train carrying evacuees left Leningrad for the city of Kotelnich in the Kirov Oblast, but during the course of that month Lena somehow ended up in Gorky, where she began a milling apprenticeship at the factory training school (FZU). It wasn't until the autumn of 1945 that she returned to Leningrad in order to enter the Leningrad School of Art and Industry, from which she graduated three years later with a master's degree in mosaics. After working for just over a month as a mosaic artist at SU-4 Lenotdelgrazhdanstroi Lena went back to continue her studies, but in January 1949 she started work at the Leningrad Mirror Factory. 'As well as working from sketches I also pro- duced my own designs, and some of them weren't bad,' she wrote subsequently to her aunt Zhenya. She liked the work, but she had to live in rented accommodation as she had lost her room when she was evacuated. Mass redundancy at the factory soon left her without work too.

Finding herself at something of a crossroads in her life, Lena initially considered applying to a technical college in order to train for a different career with better prospects, but not all colleges were able to offer free accommodation – and with a grant of just 140 roubles she couldn't afford to rent. She didn't want to keep asking her relatives for help either. So Lena decided to resurrect her milling career and headed for Moscow, where she applied to Glavmuka (abbreviated name for the

Chief Administration of the Flour Milling Industry of the USSR Ministry of Procurement) and was posted first to Yaroslavl, and from there to the city of Rybinsk (formerly Shcherbakov). At this point she took another decisive step to change the course of her life. In March 1950, after turning down the position of laboratory assistant at the mill, Lena Mukhina applied to work on the construction of the Southern Kuzbass thermal power station in the Kemerovo Oblast. Initially she had to work as an unskilled labourer, but by the end of the year she was working as a designer in the labour and salaries department at the Chief Administration. 'My main job is designing all the artwork relating to socialist emulation – slogans, displays, the Board of Honour and so on. My salary is over 500 roubles,' she wrote in a letter to her beloved aunt Zhenya.

She was forced to reconsider her employment options when her contract came to an end in March 1952. 'I miss Leningrad terribly – the opera, the museums. But I have nowhere to live there,' she wrote in her next letter to her aunt Zhenya. She didn't have any accommodation in Moscow either, but she did have relatives there, so Lena chose the capital. In June 1952 she was taken on at the Kuntsevo Mechanical Works, where she worked for fifteen years, primarily in the branding department. Before retiring owing to ill health Lena spent her final years of employment reproducing painted designs on fabric at the Kuntsevo Factory of Artistic Haberdashery and as a homeworker for the Soviet Army factory.

Elena Vladimirovna Mukhina died in Moscow on 5 August 1991.

VALENTIN KOVALCHUK, ALEKSANDR RUPASOV,
ALEKSANDR CHISTIKOV

# Remember My Sad Story:
## Lena Mukhina's Siege Diary

Consider any day on which you do not discover anything new or learn anything useful a lost day!

Anyone can become strong, smart and steadfast. There is only one essential requirement – will power!

Will power can conquer anything.
A strong-willed person is persistent and determined.

People are not born brave, strong and smart.
These qualities must be acquired through perseverance and with determination, like the ability to read and write.

# Lena Mukhina

· · · · · · · · · · · · · · · · ·

# Diary

22 MAY 1941–25 MAY 1942

## 22 May 1941

I went to bed at five o'clock this morning, after spending all night studying my literature textbook. I got up this morning at ten o'clock and crammed more horrid literature until quarter to one. At quarter to one I went to school.

I saw Emma, Tamara, Roza and Misha Ilyashev standing by the entrance. They'd already finished their exams[1] and were so happy. They wished us luck. I said hello to Lyusya Karpova and Vova. The bell hadn't yet rung for the next group to go in, so we waited in the hall. All the boys from our class were in our group, except Vova Klyachko. I asked Vova whether he'd managed to revise everything. He said no. I wanted to say something else, but he went over to join his friends.

---

1 The Central Committee of the All-Union Communist Party (Bolsheviks) passed a resolution on 25 August 1932 introducing evaluative exams at the end of the academic year for all secondary-school students. A further resolution passed on 3 September 1935 ('Ob organizatsii uchebnoi raboty i vnutrennego poryadka v nachal'noi, nepolnoi srednei i srednei shkole') called for more comprehensive testing of students' knowledge across the whole syllabus during final and end-of-year exams.

The bell rang, and we went up the staircase and into the class-room. Everyone else was really nervous, but I felt calm, because I was so sure that I would fail: all the dates and biographies were mixed up in my head. I hadn't even managed to read through all the materials. To be honest, I was more worried for the others than I was for myself.

Lyusya and I sat at the last desk but one. Lenya and Yanya were in front of us, with Vova between them. They started to call us up. I was thinking more about Vova than about the exams. Not because I was worrying about him – actually, I rather hoped he would fail. No, I wanted to spend time with him, to talk to him, to feel him looking at me . . . to be as close to him as possible. If he failed he would be sad and miserable, and I really like seeing him like that. When he's miserable, I feel closer to him. I want to put a hand on his shoulder, to make him feel better, and for him to look into my eyes with a tender, grateful smile. He was sitting so close that I could have reached out and touched his elbow, which was resting on our desk. But I couldn't bring my-self to do it. He was too far away. The girls were sitting behind us, they would have seen me move, and his friends were right next to him. They would have noticed too and would have made something of it, and then it would all have gone wrong. But how? I don't even know. So I just sat there, leaning on the desk with my chin in my hands, secretly watching Vova so that no one would notice. I wasn't really watching him, just looking at him. I love looking at his back, his hair, his nose, the expression on his face. Vova was sitting at a slight angle, watching Dima give his answers and occasionally chatting with either Yanya or Lenya. I wished he would look in my direction, just once. Why was he looking at Yanya and Lenya and talking to them, but acting as though I didn't exist? I shouldn't expect to be included, though: Vova isn't a girl, and I'm not a boy. And anyway, what's so special about me? He doesn't exchange glances with the other girls either. I looked down at the desk for a moment, lost in thought. But then I glanced at him again, I couldn't help it . . . What was I afraid of? He was my darling Vova, looking the same as he did that time at the theatre, wearing the same suit, and his smile was exactly the same. I felt my shyness lift and thought to myself, yes, I love him more than anyone else, and I wasn't at all embarrassed about it. I moved Lyusya's notebook with the literature syllabus towards myself and wrote on the cover: 'I hope you get a 5.'[2] Nudging his elbow, I pushed it towards him. He turned round straight away and I think he was pleased, because his face lit up and he wished me the same. I mumbled something and sort of shook my head, to let him know that I was sure I would fail.

Then it was my turn to be called up to the front. I sat at the second desk without turning round to look at my friends, so I couldn't see Vova and didn't know whether or not he was interested in how I did. I sat there knowing that my friends who hadn't been called up yet were all behind me, including Vova. I really wanted Vova to be thinking about me right then, for him to be nervous on my behalf. Maybe he was. I honestly don't know. It wasn't long before he was called up too, and he sat at the desk in front of me.

I got a dreadful set of questions, and I didn't know the answers to either of the first two. I decided to wait a while and swap my paper for a different one. I didn't really have a choice. Vova was sitting with his shoulders hunched up, looking nervous. He tore up the piece of paper he'd been writing on and fiddled with the

---

2 Academic exams in Russia are graded according to a five-point system, from 5 (distinction) down to 1 (fail). A mark of 3 is considered 'satisfactory', the minimum pass mark; a mark of 2 is considered 'unsatisfactory'.

scraps. He started running his hands through his hair, then he grew thoughtful and started writing again. He turned round a couple of times, and once our eyes met. He looked at me help-lessly. I tried to ask him with my eyes: do you know it? He shook his head vaguely. Then he started writing again . . .

I took another exam paper, and as soon as I read it I knew that all was not lost:

1. Motifs in Pushkin's lyric poetry;
2. Sentimentalism;
3. The narrative structure of A Hero of Our Time.[3]

I knew the second one well, and the third. I had to think a little more about the first, but I already knew that I'd passed literature. Vova had prepared his answers and was sitting at the very end of the desk. He kept looking round. I didn't look at him. I was concentrating on trying to remember Pushkin's lyrics. But I could tell that Vova was concerned about me. He couldn't have helped noticing that I was on my second paper, and I must have looked pretty miserable too. But this is the terrible thing . . . When I get what I want and someone starts paying me atten-tion, I try as hard as I can to make myself invisible because I'm afraid that other people will notice. Silly, isn't it? But that's the way it is. Vova managed to ask with a look (he always looks straight into your eyes when he talks, which is something I find difficult): did I know the answers? I nodded, and he seemed to relax.

After Grisha, it was his turn. He spoke readily, and his answers were clear and precise. They interrupted him before

---

3  A Hero of Our Time, written by Mikhail Lermontov between 1838 and 1840, is widely regarded as the first great Russian novel.

he'd finished and let him go without asking any further questions. I went up to answer. Vova left the classroom. I immediately forgot all about him. Maybe he looked back through the door to see how I got on, or maybe he was so pleased it was over that he forgot about me and went to find his friends. He can't spend all his time thinking about me, can he?

So, that's two exams over and done with.

Today: I spent the whole day doing nothing. I feel a lot calmer now. I've got three days ahead of me, plenty of time. It's always the same – as soon as I start to relax a little I find it difficult to get back into a routine, and the day just slips away. I listened to some German ballads on the radio. I love ballads. After the broadcast I read all of Pushkin's ballads one after the other. It is a good thing that evil spirits don't really exist, or they would never leave us in peace.

It's about ten o'clock now. I promised Mama that I would go to bed at nine. She could come in at any moment and then she'll see that I haven't kept my word. That would be a blow to my pride. I do feel guilty, but I can't stop writing. I'm so caught up in it.

I've decided to write my diary more neatly. I'll want to read it again myself one day. Goodness, Aka[4] has come in and I'm

---

4  Azaliya Konstantinovna (Aka) was a friend of Lena Mukhina's family, who lived with them. According to family legend Aka, an Englishwoman by birth, had come to Russia before the 1917 Russian Revolution to work as a governess for a family of Russian landowners. By the 1930s it appears that she was sharing a room in a communal apartment with Lena Mukhina and 'Mama Lena'. One of the volumes of the Memorial Book, which lists the victims of the Leningrad Blockade, refers to a Rozaliya Karlovna Krumz-Strauss, who lived at the same address as Lena Mukhina and died in January 1942. (*Blokada 1941–1944, Leningrad: Kniga pamyati* (Memorial Book), St Petersburg, 2005, vol. 16.) It is possible that Rozaliya Karlovna was known within the family as Azaliya Konstantinovna or Aka.

not in bed yet. 'You promised, you're supposed to be in bed*'[5]
'I am, I am,' I said. But I'm still writing (Aka has left the room).
I want to record all my worries in my diary, every single one of
them, like Pechorin[6] did. His diary is so interesting. But I've done
something dreadful – I'm writing in Mama's notebook, and she
might be angry with me. Well, never mind, I'll talk her round
somehow, but for now I'll put it back where it belongs.

---

5  Single asterisks are used throughout to indicate unclear and illegible words in the
   original diary.

6  Pechorin is the main character in Lermontov's *A Hero of Our Time*.

## 23 May 1941

Damn, nobody woke me. I woke up at ten o'clock. I haven't done my exercises again. I listened to a children's programme on the radio called *Amundsen's Youth*.[1] He had such determination. Whenever he set a goal for himself, he made sure he achieved it. If I were a boy, I would probably want to be like Roald. But I've never heard of a girl setting herself such goals. And it's quite daunting, the idea of being the first.

I wish Vova would dream of becoming a polar explorer, a traveller or a mountaineer, but he doesn't seem to be interested in that kind of thing. He doesn't want to end up smashing his head in a crevasse. I ought to ask him about it. But when will I get the chance? Maybe I'll go and visit him at his dacha and we can talk then – about the ninth grade, about his future and mine. If he wants to talk to me, that is. Maybe I've got it wrong, maybe he doesn't like me at all. No, that can't be true . . . He must like me, even if it's only a little bit.

---

1   This refers to a radio broadcast about the Norwegian explorer Roald Amundsen (1872–1928), who was the first to cross by the Northwest Passage from Greenland to Alaska (1903–6) and the first to reach the South Pole in December 1911.

Right, time to study. I need to do some German revision.

It's already ten o'clock at night. I'm back, pen in hand. I went round to see Lyusya Karpova. And I found out the exam results. Vova, Grisha, Misha Ilyashev, Leva, Lenya, Yanya, Emma, Tamara, Lyusya, Beba, Zoya and Roza all got a 5. Dima, Misha Tsypkin and a few others got a 4. The rest of us got a 3: Kira, me, Lyusya, Lida Klementieva, Lida Solovieva and Yasya Barkan.

I haven't done much at all today. I only started working properly in the evening. I studied Chapter 4. Lyusya and I went for a walk in the little garden[2] earlier. It was full of people. Like an anthill. But Vika wasn't there.

It feels as though something's missing all the time. I feel empty inside. Lyusya and I went for a walk, then we went back to her place, but something wasn't quite right. I don't really enjoy spending time with Lyusya, but I don't have anyone else. I'm particularly aware of it at the moment, when we're supposed to be revising. I prefer to revise with a partner. Especially for German. Lyusya wants to revise by herself. Lyusya and I aren't really that close, to be honest. I've known that for some time. I'm so envious of the others in our class. Emma and Tamara study together, so do Roza and Beba, and the other Lyusya has a study partner. The other girls have all paired off too. The boys in our class are always in touch with one another. Vova prefers to study by himself, but if he gets bored of being alone he's immediately surrounded by friends. And not just Vova – they're all like that. But I'm completely alone. I don't have a best friend or a boyfriend.

Mama sometimes wants me to kiss her and be affectionate with her, but I'm sad all the time because of the unhappy thoughts

---

2   A small square situated between nos. 15 and 17 Zagorodny Prospekt and opposite no. 26, where Lena Mukhina lived.

in my head. I just want to burst into tears, to scream and shout. I act as though everything's fine, but inside it's unbearable. I always feel as though something's missing. Whenever Mama's out, I want her to come home, but when she's here I can't stand the sight of her or the sound of her voice. I'm sick of them. Both Mama and Aka.

I want new faces, new people, new experiences. Something, anything new. But nothing is ever new, and I can't bear it. Right now I feel like running somewhere far, far away, where I won't have to see or hear anyone. Not a single person. No. I want to go and be with my best friend, who loves me, and to tell her my sorrows. That's all I want. And then I'll feel better. But I don't have anyone. I'm all alone. And I can't tell anyone how I feel. I could tell Mama. She would kiss me, cuddle me and say: 'It doesn't matter.' She thinks the reason I don't have any close friends is because I'm better than all of them, because they're not as good as me. But that's nonsense. There are many things she doesn't understand. So many things. I'm completely ordinary. I'm no different from the others. I might have more thoughts in my head – but that's not an advantage, it's a curse. Thinking constantly, and more specifically analysing every step I take, picking over the bones – is that not a curse? If only I could just think less, not take things too much to heart, life would be a lot easier.

Anyway, time for bed.

## 28 May 1941

The German exams are over. Everything went well. Thirteen of us got a 5. Vova got a 4. I don't know why – he barely deserved a 3, but he had a really easy set of questions. I've got algebra tomorrow. Soon, soon I will be free. And I've got so many plans!

We're not going to the dacha this year. We can't afford it. But it doesn't matter, in fact I'm quite pleased about it – I haven't spent the whole summer in the city for ages. I'll definitely get a job. And buy myself some clothes. I'm already sixteen and I don't have anything smart or 'fashionable' to wear. I'm also going to study German every day starting from 7 June so that I'll be top of the class in the ninth grade and not have to hear the words 'could do better'. I'm ashamed of myself for only scraping a 3 in chemistry. I used to see Anna Nikiforovna and her Adka so often . . . No, I absolutely have to get top marks in chemistry next year. There are chemistry exams at the end of the ninth grade. I'll have to study hard all year and get a 5 in the exams. And in order to do this**[1]

---

[1]  Double asterisks are used throughout to indicate where sentences are left unfinished in the original diary.

## 30 May 1941

The weather is good, but still my heart aches. Today is Mama's birthday, and we have nothing. Mama has gone to work to try and earn a bit of money. We're not exactly starving, but that's hardly any consolation. We've been living on other people's money for some time now. Mama keeps borrowing more and more. It's becoming embarrassing to show our faces in the apartment, because we owe everyone money. We've never lived like this before.

We had our algebra exam yesterday. Vova got a 4, I got a 5, Lyusya got a 3. I don't know about any of the others. I went round to Vova's the day before yesterday. Vova, Dima and I spent the whole evening solving equations and answering algebra questions, but mainly just chatting. Vova can be very funny. We're getting on better now than we did last winter. He always greets me like a good friend these days, which feels really nice. The more time I spend with him, or rather at his place, the less I think about my feelings for him. But if I go a long time without seeing him I begin to love him again. Some of us were planning to go and visit him for the day at some point this summer. But then we changed our minds, decided it was unnecessary. Actually, it will be better if I don't see him all summer. Then when we meet again in the autumn, I'll greet him like an old friend and we'll be even closer. I must ask him to give me a photo before we part for the summer, and I'll ask him for another one when we meet again in the autumn. It will be interesting for both of us to see how much he's changed over the whole summer. I'd like Dima's photo too, which he's already promised me, and one from Misha Ilyashev, and also from Emma, Lyusya Ivanova, Tamara Artemieva and Beba, but it will be harder to get photos from them.

I've got geometry tomorrow. Then there are only two exams left: anatomy and physics. I'm not worried about anatomy, but I'm really worried about physics. Only two days until the physics exam. That's not long at all. The other bad thing about it is that our group has to be there by nine o'clock in the morning. At that hour the physics teacher will be wide awake and very demanding. Better to be in the second group, when he's already tired and starting to nod off. Then it's easy to answer the questions.

Vova is a nice boy, he really is. I wish he could be our class president[1] in the ninth grade. But I know I'm just daydreaming. He probably doesn't even want to think about it yet. Well, that's up to him.

The one place where I feel completely at ease is with Vova's family. After spending time with them I always feel happy and cheerful, and somehow the river of life seems no more daunting than a knee-deep stream.

When our algebra revision class was over, everyone gathered around Vera Nikitichna. Vova and the other boys stood by the

---

1  President of the class council, a self-governing student body.

window. I walked over to the blackboard, leaned against it and called to Vova. He turned round immediately and walked over to me. Lenya came with him.

'Have you solved the equations?'

'No. I don't feel like it.'

'Come on, let's work on them for a bit.'

'Ah Lena, I really don't feel like it.'

'You know, Vova,' I said, scribbling on the board with a piece of chalk, 'I've completely forgotten how to solve some of them. I might fail tomorrow because of it.'

'Don't be silly, they'll be easy equations tomorrow.'

'Even so. I'm coming round to yours, all right?'

He nodded and turned to Lenya. 'Come with us, back to my place. I don't get the synthetic methods. Shall we try solving a couple?'

'No, Vova, I can't right now.'

The boys all left school together. I walked along beside Vova, then with Yanya. I asked: 'Vova, why didn't you do better in the German exam?' Vova didn't say anything. Yanya answered for him: 'He didn't do that badly. He got a 4.'

'I don't mean the actual mark. I just think he could have done better.'

'Like you did, you mean?'

'It doesn't matter what I got. I'm talking about Vova, not myself.'

'Lenochka, you wouldn't say that if you'd seen him before the exam. He was like a dying Hamlet.'

I've just been out to the garden. I saw Genya Nikolaev on the way. We said hello and talked for a bit. But I'm as much of a fool as I always was. There were so many things I could have asked him. Instead, fool that I am, I just said a couple of words and was ready to say goodbye. He gave me a big smile and asked: 'Well, how are things? What marks have you been getting?'

Fool that I am, I quickly babbled something in response. I didn't even shake his hand when we said goodbye, but ran away from him without a backward glance. I expect he turned around and thought: 'What a strange girl.' I'm such a fool. A complete idiot. I saw Genya and I couldn't even talk to him properly. Well, next time I see him I'll apologize for my awkwardness and ask him how he is, how he's planning to spend the summer. There are so many things I could ask him about. I could ask him for his photo, for a start.

## 31 May 1941

Today is the last day of May. It'll be June tomorrow – summer. I got a 4 in geometry. I know I've been lucky, I keep getting such easy exam papers. The only ones left now are anatomy and physics.

To tell the truth, I only spent three hours studying geometry: two hours yesterday and an hour this morning. But it would have been impossible to fail. Lida Solovieva didn't know the answers to any of the questions on either her first paper or her second, and she still got a 3. If I'd been in her shoes I would have managed to come up with something, at least. But she didn't have a clue.

I can't go and visit Vova any more, because I don't have an excuse. It's too awkward. I wish I could say to him: 'You know, Vova, it's a pity I'm not a boy. Then I could come to your place more often. I really like your family. Studying algebra or geometry used to be my excuse for coming round to see you, but now I haven't got a reason it just feels awkward.' Only I'm afraid he would get angry and say: 'You've got it all worked out, haven't you? But as far as I'm concerned boys and girls are just the same.' Or something like that.

Anyway, I'm off to study anatomy.

## 2 June 1941

I got a 5 in anatomy. Nearly everyone got a 5.

The weather has been awful today. First there was hail, then big flakes of snow. The cold wind blows right through you. From time to time the sun appears and then disappears again.

The only exam I have left is physics. Time is flying by. Summer will soon be here. There are so many things I need to do. This summer mustn't be even the slightest bit like last year's. Last summer was a complete waste of time. This summer will be different, I give my word of honour as a Soviet student. It shouldn't be too difficult. I just need to remain disciplined. The thing is, for students the exam period is like one big exercise in moral discipline: you know you have to keep revising and working hard enough to pass, but after the last exam you feel a kind of emptiness. It seems as though everything is over, that only emptiness lies ahead. And this is the point at which some give in, they surrender themselves and . . . and then everything is so easy. Wandering the streets, going to the cinema, reading one book a month, getting up at ten o'clock, going to bed at midnight. The entire summer is spent like that. Day after day, the same thing over and over, until all of a sudden it's time to go back to school.

But the summer can be spent quite differently, as long as you don't give in to laziness. Laziness, what is laziness? Laziness is a quality unworthy of a Soviet student. So laziness must be defeated.

This is how my life is going to be:

Get up at seven o'clock. Do my exercises along with the programme on the radio.

To begin with, I'll be going to Pushkin with Mama and working there. I'll go for a walk in my lunch break. I'll leave there at five o'clock, and by seven o'clock I'll already be at home. I'll study German from half past seven to half past eight, then I'll have a cup of tea and listen to the radio or read. At half past ten I'll wash and do my exercises, then I'll go to bed at eleven, switching off the radio when it's at its most interesting.

Later, once Mama has finished working at Pushkin and we're working on the sketches together, this is how I plan to spend my time:

Get up at seven o'clock. Do my exercises along with the radio. Start work at nine o'clock. Finish at four o'clock. Go for a walk. Have a cup of tea when I get home. Spend one hour studying German with Aka. Then read and listen to the radio.

## 4 June 1941

It's the physics exam tomorrow. I'm in the first group. So I won't have any time in the morning – but I'm so undisciplined, and this is a sign of my cowardice. It's embarrassing to admit it, but I just can't pull myself together. After all, it's the last exam: one final effort and I will be free. Am I really going to give up and admit defeat so close to the end? No, no, I can't let that happen. I'm going to start revising now, and even if I have to keep studying until one o'clock in the morning I will pass that exam tomorrow. Not passing tomorrow would be a joke, because it would mean I had strained every last nerve in vain.

It's the last exam. Draw on whatever strength you have left, Lena, and tomorrow, tomorrow you will be free! Free, do you understand? Free.

I'm not a coward. I'm going to pass physics tomorrow!

## 5 June 1941

Well, I'm free. I got a 4 in physics. So it was worth sitting up all night revising after all. Now I have a well-earned break to look forward to. The holidays have begun. Hello, freedom.

## 6 June 1941

I woke up at ten o'clock. They took pity on me and decided not to wake me earlier. Aka brought me a cup of tea in bed. I was about to drink it when the doorbell rang twice. Mama went to open it. I heard voices: Mama's and a man's voice. I immediately assumed that it was someone bringing something for Mama, a base for one of her architectural models[1] or something. I quickly turned out the light, took my glasses off and wrapped myself up in the blanket. I heard Mama say to someone: 'Wait a minute.' Then she came into my room and said: 'Vova is here to collect some books. Can he come in?'

'Vova? Of course he can.'

'Sorry it's so early, but I'm here for your books.'

'Give him my books, Mama, they're on the shelf. I was going to bring them to you myself.'

'Well, it looks like I beat you to it,' he said, with a little laugh. Mama started rummaging about on the shelf.

---

1    In this context the author is referring to scale models of the theatre stage, including the proscenium arch, set on a board base and featuring hatches, supports for hanging decorations, lighting equipment and so on.

'Here you go, Vova, she's already read this one,' she said, showing him a book by Levine.[2]

'No, I don't mean those books. I need your textbooks.'

Then I remembered. Vova had been given the responsibility for returning all the textbooks to school.[3]

Mama started gathering up my textbooks. 'Sit down, Vova,' she kept saying.

'I'm fine, thanks. The lads are waiting for me outside.'

Mama asked him where he was going for the summer. He said that he didn't know yet.

'Vova, why don't you come to the Volga with us? You could start saving up for it.'

'Where am I going to get that kind of money?'

Then I said to him: 'Come again soon, Vova. We can talk about the ninth grade. And other things.'

He paused before answering: 'Fine, I'll come round some time.'

---

2  This refers to the book *Evgeny Levine*, translated from the German into Russian by Elena Eikhengolts (Moscow: TsK MOPR, 1927). Eugen Leviné (1883-1919) was president of the executive council of the Bavarian Soviet Republic in April 1919, when he was court-martialled and sentenced to death by firing squad. This book contained details of the speech he gave before his trial, his memoirs and various sketches. A book by Leviné's widow, Roza, was also published in the USSR; *A Soviet Republic in Munich* (Moscow, 1926) included Eugen Leviné's biography in the appendix.

3  A resolution passed by the Council of People's Commissars of the USSR on 26 October 1940 introduced tuition fees for older secondary school pupils and students at higher-education establishments. In Leningrad the parents of children studying in the eighth, ninth and tenth grades had to pay 200 roubles per child per year. The resolution justified this measure on the basis of 'improvements in workers' welfare' and increased state expenditure on education, but the fact remained that having to find an extra 200 roubles per year led to a serious deficit in the household budget for many families (particularly if they were paying for more than one child). Some families tried to raise funds to cover this additional expense by collecting and returning old textbooks.

As he was leaving, I repeated: 'Come again, Vova, please.' He didn't reply.

'So Vova, are you just going round collecting everyone's books?'

'Yes.'

'Where else have you been?'

'Nowhere. I came to you first.'

'Why me? What about Roza and Lyusya?'

He asked for Lyusya's phone number and said he was going to see Roza next.

Later I found out that he'd been to Roza's and called Lyusya.

I went to school at one o'clock to collect my money, as Vova had told me to. Towering piles of books filled the classroom where they were collecting them, from floor to ceiling. Some of my classmates were there: Vova, Yanya, Misha Ilyashev, Asya, Tamara, Roza and Lyusya Ivanova.

We all left school together. Girls first: Roza and Tamara went off in one direction, then me, then the boys. The girls didn't say goodbye to me, as though we were strangers. I had already started walking away from school but couldn't help turning round. The boys were coming out just at that moment, and Vova bowed to me. Well it wasn't exactly a bow, more of a farewell gesture. No, I don't think he'll come and see me. I'm not going to go and see him either. We'll see each other on 9 June at the class meeting, and I'll ask him why he didn't come round, and then I'll ask him again to come and see me. Or perhaps I shouldn't? We'll see.

## 7 June 1941

Today I started the day properly. I got up at quarter past seven and did my exercises along with the radio. Then I washed, brushed my hair, made my bed and went out to the garden. No one else was there yet. The bad-tempered caretaker had almost finished tidying it. It's really nice in the garden. You can hear birds singing and see them flitting between the bushes.

After the garden I came home and listened to a programme about submariners on the radio. The training and working life of our Soviet mariners are difficult and very important. For example, they have to learn how to operate the submarine in the darkness, by touch. The life of the whole ship depends on each and every individual. Duties are allocated in such a way that even the cook, for example, as well as preparing food, must rush to join his gun crew at a moment's notice. Our soldiers train like this with their commanding officers day in, day out, and when our enemies attack us – because war is inevitable, sooner or later – we will be absolutely certain of victory. We have something worth fighting for, people worth fighting for, and the means with which to fight.

A group of pilots and submariners once got together and

began discussing their respective professions. The pilots said: diving deep underwater, that's terrifying. Soaring through the sky, on the other hand, is a different matter. The submariners replied: flying over earth and sea, that's too terrifying. Swimming beneath the water like a fish, on the other hand, is a different matter.

Yesterday I bought two literature textbooks for the ninth grade. When I saw the number of books on the syllabus, I decided to start reading straight away. I started with Turgenev, as I've already got some of his.

At the moment I'm reading *Rudin*.[1]

Here are a few quotes:

'There is nothing more excruciating than the realization that one has just committed an act of stupidity.'

'It is calculated, to a certain extent: a man puts on a mask of indifference and laziness, assuming that people will believe he has squandered all his talents. But if you look at him a little more closely, you will see that he has no talents whatsoever.'

'Deny everything, and you'll pass for a clever person.'

---

1  Ivan Turgenev's first novel, published in 1856.

## 8 June 1941

Today I decided to call Tamara, then I went round to see her. On the way there I wondered what I would talk to her about, but in the event it was fine. Tamara is like me in many ways. It's already past eleven, so I don't have time to write about everything in detail.

All I will say is that I talked to her a lot about Vova. I said: 'Let's go and see Vova together tomorrow.' I would never have suggested the idea of visiting Vova to anyone but Tamara, because Vova doesn't particularly like the girls in our group. But Tamara's an exception – he gets on well with her. As soon as I suggested it to Tamara I knew she would agree, although I couldn't even have imagined this when I was on my way to see her.

At first Tamara said that it would be awkward to visit him without a good reason, but I assured her fervently that Vova is a nice boy, that he's completely different at home, etc. So she agreed.

We decided that we weren't prepared to accept the injustice of boys and girls being so separate and not visiting each other at home like real friends. We decided to go and visit Vova. We thought up an excuse: Tamara will ask to borrow some books, and I will return a couple of books that he lent me. It will be interesting to see how it all goes. Perhaps it will be the start of something new. Perhaps the three of us will become close friends. There's no way of knowing just yet. But it made me feel hopeful. New aspirations, new hopes, new dreams. Perhaps the three of us won't become close, but it may well bring Tamara and me closer together. Tamara is just what I need. She could be a true friend.

Yes, there is much uncertainty ahead.

## 9 June 1941

Today's events were such that I simply can't keep them to my-self. I'll try and keep it brief.

After our class meeting, which took place in the staffroom and where we were given our school reports, we decided to go home. The boys left before us. The other girls were drag-ging their heels, so I decided to leave without them. I met the boys in the changing room. They already had their coats on and soon left, saying goodbye to me and Tamara, who had decided to go home too. The two of us put our coats on and decided to go upstairs and find out if the dancing had already started and what the other girls were planning to do. We met them on the stairs. We went outside and stopped by the entrance. Emma said: 'Oh girls, I really don't want to go home. I feel like dancing.' Soon all the girls – and there were quite a few of them: Tamara, Beba, Emma, Roza, Zoya, Nadya, Dysya – decided that they des-perately wanted to go dancing, not at school and not alone, but in someone's apartment, with the boys. The curses began – the devils, the scoundrels, the cheek of them – all of it directed at the boys, for going off and leaving us to suffer here without them. Someone suggested that if we simply told the boys that we felt

like dancing, they would join us without hesitation. Then someone else said: 'Let's teach them a lesson, girls!' And so a plan was
formed. One of us would call either Dima or Misha or Grisha
and say that we had a marvellous idea, and that they should
meet us at school in five minutes. Meanwhile we would hide
in the main entrance* of the building opposite the school and
laugh at them. We decided to put our plan into action without
further delay.

We went to the post office, intending to call from there. It
was very busy. Nadya and Zoya went to call, while the rest of us
waited for them outside under the scaffolding. They soon came
back. Neither Grisha nor Misha was at home, and Dima put the
phone down on them. So our little joke had backfired.

We stood there for a long time, wondering what to do next.
We needed the boys more than ever at that point, like travellers
thirsting for water in the desert. We peered at every boy that
walked past and looked all around, but to no avail. We were
almost dying of disappointment, of anger, of outrage, but the
boys simply wouldn't appear. We felt like the most unfortunate
creatures in the world, and the longer we hesitated, the more
passionately we burned with the desire to see them.

In the end we decided that we would just start walking and
keep going until we ran into them. We just knew that our boys
were out there somewhere, and we were determined to find
them if it killed us. We had just set off, when suddenly one of the
girls cried out: 'There they are.' We all turned in the direction
Nadya was pointing and saw them, our long-lost boys. They
saw us too and stopped, waved and crossed the street towards us. We started chatting, and I immediately noticed that
although the girls had been desperate to see the boys they were
now acting aloof and indifferent. I suppose they thought they
were preserving their dignity by behaving this way. We didn't

talk for long. After a little while we parted and went our separate ways. But when the boys were already some distance from
us, we realized that we'd made a mistake.

'What are we doing, girls? Why did we let them go? We
wanted to dance with them.'

'Come on then, let's go!'

'Where?'

'After them!'

'Let's go.'

We all turned round and started following the boys. Faster
and faster, until we were practically running. We didn't really
know what we were doing or what we wanted from the boys.
We just wanted to catch up with them, to make sure we didn't
let them out of our sight.

The distance between us soon decreased. We were giggling,
we couldn't help it. We got closer and closer until we were no
more than ten paces from the boys – so close that they must
have been able to hear us. Looking over their shoulders, they
quickened their pace. There was the post office. Suddenly the
boys ducked into the entrance of the post office and hid, choking
with laughter. We carried on, turned into Razyezzhaya and just
kept walking. We reached Misha's building, then decided that
we should head back. 'If we see them, girls, let's ignore them.'
We turned around and started walking. When we reached
Vera Prokofieva's building we saw the boys walking along the
opposite side of the street. When they saw us they bowed, and
Misha Ilyashev made a great performance out of it. We walked
a little further, stopped and looked at them. They were standing
there chatting amongst themselves, laughing and looking at us.
Then they went off to Kira Krutyakov's place. Only then did we
come to our senses. What had we done? We were burning with
shame. They wouldn't let us live it down (but, as it turned out,

the boys were so well mannered that they didn't even mention it the following day, and it was as though nothing had happened).

A bitter argument broke out between me and the other girls. They were criticizing the boys, and I was defending them. Gradually I began to give in. They won the battle. I conceded every point except one: I simply wouldn't agree that Vova was the worst of the boys, even though they attacked me on this more than any other point, particularly Roza. The way she described Vova, I didn't even know how to respond. 'He's arrogant and conceited and thinks everyone else is worthless! He looks down on everyone and makes the other boys dance to his tune. They all just copy him. Who was the first to start talking to us? Vova! Who was the first to play that stupid game, asking us who we liked? Vova! Who was the first to start making a performance out of giving girls their coats? Vova. And you're so convinced that he's such a nice boy, Lena. Well, I'm sure,' continued Roza, 'that when Misha Ilyashev was making fun of you in front of all the boys, Vova wasn't far away.'

'Do you think he was making fun of me as well?' I asked.

'Of course,' Roza answered confidently.

I didn't say anything. There was no point in arguing with her. She was so convinced she was right. I found it strange because I could clearly picture Vova at home, and at school, and at parties . . . and these images had nothing in common.

Vova doesn't even realize that the other boys follow him. He just doesn't realize it. He thinks that's the way it should be. No, no and no again. Roza is lying. She doesn't know what he's really like. Either that or she wants to take him away from me. She probably thinks that he's in love with me and has forgotten her. It's all nonsense.

## 22 June 1941

At quarter past twelve the entire country heard Comrade Molotov's speech·

He announced that at four o'clock this morning, without any formal declaration of war, the German army launched an attack along the western border. Their aeroplanes bombed Kiev, Zhytomyr, Odessa, Kaunas and other cities, leaving 200 people dead.

At five o'clock the German consul announced on behalf of his government that our countries are at war – in other words, that they have declared war on us. So, what we dreaded more than anything has come to pass.[1]

---

1 The USSR People's Commissar for Foreign Affairs, Vyacheslav Molotov, gave a speech at midday on 22 June 1941, in which he officially informed the Soviet people of Germany's 'perfidious' attack on the Soviet Union and announced the beginning of the Second World War. Radio announcer Yuri Levitan read the speech out nine times that day. The actual text read by Levitan was published by the Communist Party newspaper *Pravda*, but not until 24 June. This delay, and the fact that the published text differed in several places from Molotov's original text, suggests the possibility that it may have been edited by Stalin himself. The surviving recording of Molotov's speech appears to have been a later version, which corresponds to the published text. In it, Molotov mentioned the bombing of Zhytomyr, Kiev, Sevastopol

We will win, but victory will not come easily. It won't be like Finland.[2] This war will be savage and cruel.

Chemical weapons may not have been used yet in this war, but there is no doubt that when they attack us**

It's already half past eleven in the evening, and there hasn't been any more news. On the radio they are broadcasting an almost endless succession of war songs, poems and announcements about martial law and mobilization. Meanwhile there are planes flying overhead, circling above the city, and even though we know that our Soviet pilots are at the controls it's still unsettling.

The engines of enemy bombers will sound exactly the same. This is awful. Aren't they going to update us? If we had won even the slightest victory they would announce it, but it's probably too early for good news. Yes, they must be fighting hard on the front line.

People coming in from outside say that there are mobilized troops in the streets. They're singing, and their wives, children and girlfriends are there to see them off.[3]

Victory will be ours, comrades!

---

and Kaunas, amongst other cities and gave a figure of over 200 for Soviet casualties, both dead and injured. He also referred to the announcement made by the German ambassador to the Soviet Union, Friedrich Werner von der Schulenburg, at 5.30 in the morning of 22 June, regarding the state of war between the two countries.

2 Lena is referring to the Soviet–Finnish war of 1939–40.

3 Lena is mistaken. Volunteers began signing up at the city's military recruitment offices on 22 June 1941. A decree was issued by the Presidium of the Supreme Soviet of the USSR on 22 June 1941 stating that mobilization would start on 23 June. Those liable for conscription into the army and navy included all men born between 1905 and 1918 and resident in the following military districts: Leningrad, Baltic Special, Western Special, Kiev Special, Odessa, Kharkov, Orlov, Moscow, Arkhangelsk, Ural, Siberian, Volga, North Caucasus and Transcaucasia.

At two o'clock I was woken by the mournful wail of a siren. Mama and I got dressed quickly and went into the kitchen. It was very quiet. We couldn't hear any planes. Then we heard some distant, muffled explosions. We held each other close and thought: 'Bombs!' But we couldn't hear any planes. The noise got closer and closer, then it seemed to stop moving. It was our anti-aircraft guns. We listened: the anti-aircraft guns were firing, firing relentlessly. The siren began to wail in the courtyard, and the anti-aircraft gunfire continued. Meanwhile clouds drifted indifferently across the pale sky and stars shone here and there among them. It was terrifying. The all-clear was given half an hour later. Mama and I went to bed without getting undressed and fell asleep straight away.

## 23 June 1941

They finally issued a news bulletin this morning.

'At four o'clock in the morning on 22 June 1941 Hitler's troops crossed our border and began to infiltrate our territory. Large formations of German bombers dropped bombs on our peaceful towns and villages. However, by six o'clock the Germans had encountered the forces of the Red Army. Fierce and bloody fighting took place throughout 22 June, as a result of which German troops sustained heavy losses and were forced to retreat along the entire length of the front line. At only a limited number of points were Hitler's forces able to advance and capture small towns and settlements 30–40 km from the border.'

German bombers may have raided the towns and villages of our homeland, but they were met by our fighter planes and anti-aircraft gunfire everywhere: 65 German bombers were shot down along the entire front.

The English army and General Churchill [sic] have announced that they will do anything in their power to help Russia, and they will be supported in this by the USA. Hitler has miscalculated: he thinks that he will get the better of the Soviet Union before the onset of winter and then proceed to conquer Western Europe once and for all. Hitler believes that his enemies in the western hemisphere are weak and unable to stop him realizing his long-term plans, but he has misjudged us: we will fight the enemy day and night, with increased force. We will do all we can to defend Russia. We will do anything to save humanity from tyranny. Work began early this morning in the courtyard and the attic. They're hurrying to construct a gas-proof shelter in the courtyard, which will take up the whole of the basement, and dismantling all of the partitions in the attic because they're wooden, and if a bomb causes a fire in the attic they will be the perfect fuel.

Ivan Ivanovich has only just got back. He spent all night digging trenches in Udelnoe[1] with seventy people under his command. He didn't see any enemy aircraft, because they were flying really high in order to stay out of reach of our anti-aircraft guns. But he heard the drone of their engines and heard and saw anti-aircraft gunfire. He doesn't know about any bombs. Apparently the caretaker said that another group of planes had broken through and bombed the Bolshevik factory.[2] I don't know whether or not this is true, but I doubt the caretaker would spread false rumours. He is better informed than the rest of us.

The truth of the matter is that our apartment is not prepared for an attack. None of us knows where the first aid point is, or the dressing station, or the air-raid shelter, or the air defence

---

1  Udelnoe was a suburban district to the north-west of Leningrad (now within the city boundary of St Petersburg).

2  The Germans carried out their first aerial bombardment of Leningrad on 6 September 1941.

headquarters.[3] Or what to do if we're hit by an incendiary or high-explosive bomb. I know you're supposed to sprinkle them with sand, but we haven't got any sand in our apartment. I think we should (as I saw at the cinema) stick paper bags together, fill them with sand and pile them up at the door of every room and in the corridor.

Mama and I went to the Field of Mars.[4] There are six anti-aircraft guns in the central square, with heavy boxes of artillery shells stacked up alongside them. They aren't letting people anywhere near the guns.

As of today the city has started to look different.

---

3  This probably refers to the local headquarters of the Civil Air Defence Organization, since the headquarters of the Northern division of the Air Defence Forces (PVO) (commander: Major General F. Kryukov; Chief of Staff: Colonel K. Chumak) was situated on Dvortsovaya Square, and the headquarters of the 2nd Air Defence Corps, which was directly responsible for the defence of Leningrad, was at Baskov Lane 16.

4  Known from 1918 to 1944 as Zhertv Revolyutsii (Victims of the Revolution) Square.

## 24 June 1941

We slept calmly last night.

I went out for a walk this afternoon. Taking up the entire width of the round garden near Chernyshev Bridge[1] was a silvery barrage balloon,[2] which looked like a fish lying on its side. It was being held down by ropes. A heap of gas cylinders lay on the ground nearby. Deep trenches, about a metre wide and the depth of an average person, are being dug as a matter of urgency in the gardens on Ostrovsky Square and around the Pioneers' Palace. Many of the workers are from the intelligentsia.

There are building materials piled up in nearly every

---

1  Now Lomonosov Bridge.

2  During the war barrage balloons were used to help defend Leningrad from German aircraft attacks, while observation balloons were used to track German artillery. By 22 June, 328 barrage balloon posts (three regiments) had been deployed in chessboard formation in the sky above Leningrad. Each post consisted of two identical balloons, which were raised either singly or in tandem, depending on the circumstances, by extending a cable from an automobile winch (mines were attached to each cable). Single balloons usually rose to a height of 2–2.5 km, and the highest balloon in a tandem rose to 4–4.5 km.

courtyard, for the construction of gas-proof shelters. Sand has been delivered to many courtyards too.

Today there was a message from school, telling me to be there at five o'clock.

By five o'clock I was in the blue assembly hall at school. There were between sixty and seventy of us. Mostly girls. The headmaster told us, in short, that our help would be required. From our class there were Misha Ilyashev, Yanya, Vova Klyachko, Tamara, Bella Katsman, Galya Virok [sic], Lida Solovieva and Zoya Belkina.

We quickly split into teams: two teams of boys, five teams of girls. We all ended up in the same team. Our team leader was Maya Chebotareva. We will carry out all instructions from headquarters.

I'm going to bed now. Who knows what tonight will be like!

## 25 June 1941

The night was calm. There were two air-raid warnings this afternoon. During both of them I ended up in the school air-raid shelter with some of the other girls. Maya had called this morning to say that we had been instructed to paper over the school windows, so that's what we were doing. There were about twenty of us, all girls. From our class: Maya, Tamara, Lida Solovieva and Nina Aleksandrova. After the second all-clear I went home, telling the others that I would have something to eat and then go back. But I didn't go back. There weren't many windows left to cover – no more than two or three classrooms. I decided that they could manage without me and found a different, more useful job to do. I worked with a team of women from our building, dragging planks of wood from the attic into the basement. We worked quickly, as a human chain, for forty minutes without a break. I went home to rest, then went back to work at six o'clock. The work was very hard. It was men's work, really. Nevertheless we managed it, with two of us lifting the heavier planks between us.

At eight o'clock this evening there was a meeting at the

*zhakt*[1] for all residents of our apartment block. The meeting was addressed by an official from the district Party Committee, then the most pressing issues were discussed. Mama joined the voluntary medical unit for our building.[2] There are just six of them in the unit altogether.

Tomorrow is going to be another busy day. But now I need to check the apartment and go to bed.

What will tonight be like?

---

1   From the acronym ZhAKT (*zhilishchno-arendnoe kooperativnoe tovarishchestvo*), mean-
    ing cooperative rented housing association, or house management office. These
    organizations were abolished in October 1937 and the management of individual
    apartment blocks was handed over to local councils and state enterprises, but Lena
    Mukhina continues to use the old name out of habit.

2   Voluntary associations were formed by the residents of individual apartment
    blocks in order to offer first aid in everyday situations, as well as treatment for bullet
    wounds and other injuries, gas poisoning, frostbite, fainting and so on. Volunteers
    were required to have completed at least a basic medical training course.

## 25 June 1941[1]

This morning I was summoned to school. We were divided into teams. I signed up to the fire team. We had to haul sand up into the attic. Then I went home because I was completely worn out. I must have overdone it yesterday.

A Sovinformbyuro news bulletin is broadcast every day at six o'clock in the morning.[2] Fierce fighting is continuing on the front line. The odds are in our favour. German soldiers are going into battle drunk. Nazi artillery is in position at the rear of the Romanian soldiers, yet enemy soldiers are still giving themselves up at the first opportunity. Germany's economic situation is worsening by the day. In order to provide for their army and industrial workers at home, the Nazis are appropriating the last remaining food reserves from their occupied

---

1 Lena mistakenly dated this entry in her diary as 25 June 1941.

2 The Soviet Information Bureau (Sovinformbyuro) was created by the Council of People's Commissars of the USSR on 24 June 1941 and reported directly to the Central Committee of the All-Union Communist Party (Bolsheviks). Aleksandr Shcherbakov was appointed director. Broadcasts were made from Sverdlovsk (now Ekaterinburg) until 1943.

territories. In Holland, Belgium, Yugoslavia, Bulgaria, France, Romania, Norway, Denmark and elsewhere there are signs of increasingly widespread discontent and mounting hostility towards these bloodthirsty monsters. Despite the threat of repercussions, despite the fact that a single word or a questionable smile can lead to prison, a concentration camp or the firing squad, these enslaved nations are expressing their hostility openly and with increasing frequency. The most dangerous adversary the Germans have is not on the battle front but at home – the hungry masses of their countrymen, driven to despair by the Nazi regime. And the Nazis themselves know this only too well. This attack on the Soviet Union is the desperate attempt of a drowning man to grasp something to keep himself afloat, the desperate attempt of a suffocating man to fill his lungs with air.

In the deluded belief that their army is invincible, the Nazis are attacking the Soviet Union in order to improve their economy by seizing Ukraine, Belorussia and other regions of our homeland. But our enemies have miscalculated. Even if their army were considerably better armed than ours we would still defeat them, because the Nazi army lacks unity: their soldiers are being forced to fight against their will, they're exhausted, they're worried about their families, they don't want to fight the Soviet Union. Not only regular soldiers but also Nazi pilots, tank drivers and others are keen to surrender. These people have no strength left to fight, either physically or mentally.

In air-to-air combat between two planes – both brand new, with identical flight capabilities – the one flown by our pilot always wins. This is simply because the shattered nerves of the enemy pilot are the first to give way, and just one moment of hesitation is enough for the pilot with stronger nerves to assert his mastery of the air. The latter is almost always the Soviet pilot, because he is defending his homeland, his family and his friends, because he is sure of victory and can rely on his comrades, in the knowledge that any one of them would rush to help him in his hour of need. Meanwhile the enemy pilot is uncertain of the successful outcome of the battle, unsure of victory and unable to rely on his 'comrades', because he knows that at the critical moment each of them will save himself, his own plane, his own life. He is unsure of victory because he doesn't even know what he's fighting for.

Only experienced Nazi pilots are capable of fighting more confidently, to our detriment, but even they cannot hold out for long against the resolve and composure of a nation of people in possession of attributes such as heroism, unity and the readiness to sacrifice their own life at any given moment, as well as first-class training, optimum fitness, steady nerves, common sense, calculated risk, resourcefulness and self-assurance.

The enemy will be defeated by our Soviet motto: 'One for all, and all for one!'

## 28 June 1941

The air-raid siren went off at four o'clock this morning. We went down to the basement. Hardly anyone else from the rest of the building went – they just stayed where they were. The all-clear was given at five o'clock. We went outside, and strong, slanting rays of bright sunlight were radiating from behind the Vladimirskaya bell tower.[1] All the barrage balloons were shining brightly in the sun. It was so beautiful that I didn't feel like going home. A freight tram went past, loaded with milk churns and crates full of milk bottles. I felt such happiness, such joy in my heart. It was so peaceful.

---

1   The detached belfry of Our Lady of Vladimir Church in the centre of the city.

# 1 July 1941

They started evacuating children three days ago.[1] Every morning children aged between one and three or more are transported to the train stations by bus, from *zhakt* offices, nurseries[2] and other children's organizations. Some go to Vitebsk Station, others to Oktyabrsky.[3] Everyone is finding it very hard. There is one leader and one nanny for every hundred children. Greta, Ira and Zhenya are leaving today. Revekka Grigorievna is lucky enough to be going as a leader. There have been no air raids for two days. On the radio they are recounting military incidents, promoting vigilance and warning people of the dangers of careless talk, repeatedly reminding us that the city of Leningrad is at war, advising people on what to do in the event of an attack and giving instructions on how to extinguish incendiary bombs and incendiary strips.

---

1   The first ten special trains, carrying a total of 15,192 children, left on 29 June 1941 from the Oktyabrsky (Moscow), Vitebsk and Warsaw railway stations.

2   *Ochagi* ('hearths') were educational establishments for pre-school children in the USSR in the 1930s.

3   The name of St Petersburg's present-day Moscow (Moskovsky) Station from 1923 to the beginning of the 1930s.

Across the city the construction of air-raid shelters, ditches and trenches is nearing completion. Decrees have been issued introducing compulsory labour duty[4] and ordering the population to hand in all wireless radio devices to stop them falling into enemy hands.[5] We have enough enemies here already. Air assaults are the enemy's favourite approach. Vast numbers of paratroopers are being deployed, but thanks to the vigilance of Soviet citizens, workers and collective farm workers, the majority of them are apprehended the moment they reach the ground. The remainder are caught by special detachments made

---

4 According to a decree on martial law issued by the Presidium of the Supreme Soviet of the USSR on 22 June 1941, in areas where martial law had been declared the military authorities were permitted to recruit citizens for labour duty, which could mean constructing defensive works, defending transport networks, buildings, communication facilities, power stations and other important targets, or fighting fires, epidemics and natural disasters. Citizens were recruited for labour duty in accordance with the labour code. Anyone younger than 18 was exempted from labour duty, as were men over the age of 45 and women over the age of 40. Lena Mukhina had not yet turned 18. A resolution passed by the Council of People's Commissars of the USSR on 10 August 1942 decreed that labour duty should always be introduced by a resolution of the Council of People's Commissars – unless martial law had been declared, in which case it could also be introduced by the military authorities in accordance with the aforementioned decree on martial law issued by the Presidium of the Supreme Soviet of the USSR. This resolution also decreed that those guilty of the evasion or avoidance of labour duty, or of detaining in any way individuals working at establishments and organizations who had been recruited for labour duty, should be subject to criminal liability 'under the laws of war'. The first resolution introducing labour duty for Leningraders was passed by the Executive Committee of the Leningrad City Council on 27 June 1941.

5 The Council of People's Commissars of the USSR passed a resolution on 26 June 1941 requiring the public to surrender all radio receiving and transmitting devices within five days to the People's Commissariat for Communication. A further resolution passed on 22 August 1941 required them to surrender any binoculars in their possession within ten days to the district military recruitment offices. The Plenum of the Supreme Court of the USSR decreed on 14 July and 22 September 1941 that evasion of these duties was punishable according to the Criminal Code of the RSFSR.

up of NKVD forces and civilian workers. But many of them have not yet been caught. They are wandering the streets of our city dressed as policemen or wearing civilian clothing. These enemy paratroopers are tasked with gathering intelligence, blowing up key targets, setting fire to collective farms, spreading false rumours, sowing panic, recruiting new agents and damaging our radio, telegraph and telephone networks.

Some of them are women. All kinds of absurd rumours are circulating about these spies – for example, that two enemy aeroplanes recently landed right on Nevsky Prospekt.[6]

But we can't just pretend the problem doesn't exist. The police have detained a number of 'outsiders'.

Fierce fighting is continuing at the front. Every one of our soldiers is a hero of the motherland. The enemy is cunning and sly. For example, some of their machine gunners tried to sneak up to ours behind a cow – a real live cow. On another occasion the enemy concealed himself behind a group of soldiers disguised as women. Our soldiers respond to these tricks with intrepid valour and heroism. The enemy doesn't like to fight openly: he is sly, he sets cunning traps.

Three German Ju88s have already joined us. Many soldiers have come over to our side. And more will follow.

---

6   The public's obsession with spies reached unprecedented levels during the war. As the academician Dmitry Likhachev recalled, people 'were always on the lookout for spies. A person only had to visit a *banya* with a briefcase, and he would be detained and "checked" . . . There were a lot of rumours about spies. People talked about signals being sent to German aeroplanes from the roofs of buildings. Apparently there were automatic beacons of some kind, which would start sending signals as soon as the air raids began. According to the rumours these beacons were situated in chimneys (so they could only be seen from above), on the Field of Mars and so on. Perhaps there was some element of truth in these rumours: the Germans really did seem to know everything that was going on in the city.'

## 2 July 1941

Fierce fighting is taking place on all fronts. In many places the intrepid valour of our defenders is delaying or weakening the advance of enemy forces, which are numerically superior. The enemy is armed to the teeth. The enemy is well trained and well equipped. The Nazi command will spare no sacrifice to achieve their aims. The Nazis have a plan, they have a strategy. For the time being they are an extremely dangerous force to be reckoned with. But whatever happens, we will win.

Greta, Ira and Zhenya have just left. Ira and Zhenya are delighted that something out of the ordinary is happening.

Our troops have surrendered Lvov.

# 5 July 1941

Despite suffering heavy losses, the Germans are approaching Smolensk. A voluntary people's militia is being created in Moscow and Leningrad.[1] Stalin gave a speech on the radio recently.[2] Detachments of volunteers are already marching in the streets.

I went to see Vova yesterday. He's such a nice boy – so young, healthy and full of the joys of life. His dream is to move to the Karelian Isthmus. He's always making jokes. I love him so much.

---

1    The Military Council of the Northern Front passed a resolution on 27 June 1941 regarding the creation of a 100,000-strong voluntary army. The formation of the Leningrad People's Militia Army began on 30 June. The first divisions of a voluntary people's militia in Moscow were established at the beginning of July 1941.

2    This refers to a speech given by Iosif Stalin on 3 July 1941, in which he attempted to substantiate the reasons for the defeats of the Red Army and the success of the German approach. In particular, he claimed that the occupation of Soviet territory was 'mainly due to the fact that when Nazi Germany declared war on the USSR, circumstances favoured their troops whereas Soviet troops were at a disadvantage. Having initiated the war, Germany's troops were already completely mobilized.' Lena Mukhina conspicuously avoids referring to the subject of Stalin's speech in her diary. It is highly unlikely that she was unaware of the details.

Today I spent three hours (from twelve to three) unloading a barge of bricks. It was labour duty. Easy work. Just a pity that it's unpaid.

I'll get a proper job somewhere soon. It's about time. I need to help Mama.

Hostility towards fascism is growing in other countries, and so too is support for us, for my great motherland.

Oh, Vova! I would give anything to see you every day, all the time. Words cannot convey the feeling I have for him.

It's impossible to put it into words. I wish I could express the way I feel.

Only my heart can express it!!!!

## 11 July 1941

There have been eleven air raids since I last wrote:

7 July – four air raids;
8 July – three air raids;
10 July – three air raids;
11 July – one air raid so far.

The city is turning into a military camp. Both to and from Nevsky the road is busy with lorries carrying troops, equipment and ammunition, fuel tankers, field kitchens, and every morning there are weapons carriers, tanks and armoured cars. They're all camouflaged with foliage, so that the troops in some of the lorries look like they're in the middle of a real forest.

On 9 July I spent four hours digging trenches on Obvodny.[1]

---

1  A canal embankment within the city boundaries.

## 17 July 1941

On 12 July I was told to report to the *zhakt*. Mama went to find out what it was about. According to the latest decree, *zhakt* directives are not supposed to apply to schoolchildren. Mama soon returned, looking very worried.

'Come on Lena, get your things together, you're going away for three days. They said you had to take plenty of bread, sugar and other provisions.'

I went to the *zhakt* at twelve, with my little suitcase in one hand and a bundle containing a blanket and a pillow in the other. As well as me the *zhakt* was sending five others: two girls – Alya and Zoya, both of whom had just turned sixteen – and three boys – Yura Bekker, Petya and Akhmed.

We all went to the House of the Baking Industry[1] on Pravda Street,[2] then on to Vitebsk Station, where we boarded a train.

---

1   This refers to the House of Culture of the Union of Food Industry Workers, which was situated at Pravda Street 10 (1935–92). The same building had previously been occupied by the Railway Club (for railway engineers).

2   Pravda Street runs parallel to Zagorodny Prospekt, the street where Lena Mukhina lived.

It was a local suburban train. I sat by an open window. After travelling for five hours, we arrived in Tarkovichi.[3] It was ten o'clock in the evening. The sun had disappeared behind the forest. They told us to split into teams and take cover in the bushes for a while. We weren't to light any fires, because there could be an air raid at any moment. We promptly spread out among the bushes and began to eat some of our provisions. Our *zhakt* and another *zhakt* joined forces with a group of workers from the Glavtabak factory.[4] It was already dark when we set off again. Walking was difficult because of the spade I was carrying. It was a nuisance, because without it I would have been able to carry my things in both hands. We moved quickly (that way the mosquitoes didn't bite so much).

We passed through a large village, crossed a steep gully and came out onto a railway track. We crossed the railway line and went deeper into the forest. The path took us uphill then down again, twisting and turning like a snake. There seemed to be no end to this torment. We gradually began to make our way up the hill, though progress was slow and tiring. We were stumbling from exhaustion, and our feet kept getting stuck in the soft sand at the side of the path. People were walking in small groups or alone, trying not to make any noise. Our nerves were extremely on edge. We all knew about the air assaults. What if the enemy were hiding in this very forest? A machine gun could start firing at any moment, and the nocturnal silence would resonate with

---

3  Railway station and rural locality 35.6 km to the south of St Petersburg in the Luzhsky District, Leningrad Oblast.

4  This refers to either the Uritsky Tobacco Factory or the Clara Zetkin Leningrad Tobacco Factory, both under the jurisdiction of the Chief Administration of the Tobacco Industry of the People's Commissariat for the Food Manufacturing Industry of the USSR (Glavtabak).

cries and moans. Who would come to our rescue out here, in the back of beyond?

The path turned again, and a fine view opened up before us. We were standing right at the top of a hill that sloped down towards the river. The smooth, calm surface of the wide river shone silver in the peaceful moonlight. Suddenly we heard the sound of an engine, and the black silhouette of a plane emerged from the darkness. We looked at one another, all thinking the same thing: ours or theirs? The plane was flying fairly low over the river. It was really frightening* Then it flew past us, almost directly overhead. It was a twin-engine plane – a medium bomber, by the look of it. It began heading away from us. Little white and yellow lights suddenly began flashing on its wings and tail. We stood there for a long time, just staring at those flashing lights.

The sound of the engines faded away, and we set off again. Up, down, left and right. I didn't have the strength to walk any further. I gave my spade to someone. We had already begun to suspect that they were dragging us all this way in order to wear us out before abandoning us when we saw the outlines of some huts up ahead. We would soon be inside, in the warm, drinking hot tea and getting ready for bed . . . But our hopes were soon dashed. We entered the village and started walking down the main road. There were people lying everywhere – at the foot of fences, in the courtyards – and we realized that the same fate awaited us. We were told that there was no room for us in the village, that we would have to go outside the village to find somewhere to sleep. We carried on walking, but no matter how far we walked there seemed to be no end to the village. The road turned a corner, and more endless huts stretched out before us. There were people everywhere, lying side by side. Someone told us that there were already 8,000 Leningraders in the village. Eventually we reached the last hut, a kind of wooden shack, and the village came to an end. We trudged off to one side and began to unpack our belongings and settle down on the grass. The grass was wet, but there was nothing we could do about it. Suddenly I noticed something white lying on the ground. It was a battered old roof. I lay on it. At least it was drier than the wet grass. I wrapped myself up in my blanket from head to toe, stretched out and fell asleep. I slept like a log. When I woke up, the sun had just risen. The grass was sparkling in the early-morning sunlight, and the birds were singing all around. We soon learned that we were free until six o'clock that evening.

It turned out that I was in a large village on a high bank of the Oredezh River. Such a beautiful place. There was a small sandy beach. We swam and sunbathed. We learned that there wasn't any food but that there would be soon.

At six o'clock our team leader gathered us all together, and we set to work.

We worked from six o'clock in the evening to six o'clock in the morning: fifty minutes of work followed by a ten-minute rest, with a lunch break from twelve to one.

Once during a break (at nine o'clock in the evening) I heard a familiar**

## 25 August 1941

I'm home again. Got back just now.

Nelya Klenochevskaya, Krasnoarmeiskaya Telephone Station
  2-16-42
Kira Zamyshlyaeva, Apt 20, Podolskaya 23
Vitya Rokhman, Krasnoarmeiskaya Telephone Station 2-34-63

Our school and other schools have been digging just outside Duderhof.[1]

I took the suburban commuter train with Natalya Alekseevna, Valya Korobkova, Leva Libman, Yura Tserekovsky and everyone else, arriving in Duderhof at 12 o'clock. We met Tamara and her mother on the way there. Eventually we got to the school we were staying at, and an hour later we were already on the highway. That was the start of my life in a small Finnish village on one of the hills, full of Finnish people. I spent about

---

1  Village located on the eastern bank of the Duderhof Lake at the foot of the Orekhovaya and Voronya Hills, near the historic settlement of Krasnoye Selo in the Krasnoselsky District of Leningrad (St Petersburg). Renamed Mozhaisky in 1950.

eighteen days there. It was all quite calm to begin with. We got up at seven o'clock in the morning, and by eight o'clock we were already on the highway. We worked for fifty minutes then had ten minutes' rest. During breaks we lay in the shade beneath an enormous haystack. At twelve o'clock an orderly brought us lunch. Then we worked until six o'clock in the evening. We were back at base by quarter past six.

The school we were staying at was visible from some distance away. It was a large, single-storey wooden building, right at the top of the hill. In front of the building was a narrow ravine, bordered on both sides by low sloping hills. There was a rough track across the middle of the ravine. The building was no more than half a kilometre from the highway. The school building consisted of two classrooms, a corridor and an entrance hall. One room was supposed to be for girls, the other for boys. The girls in our room were from School No. 15. We didn't know any of the boys in the room next door. I particularly liked two of the girls from School No. 15: Zoya and Valya. Zoya was sixteen but looked about thirteen or fourteen. She had such a childish, innocent face. She was short and slim, with two light-brown plaits. Zoya had a very pretty face. It was oval-shaped, with a high forehead, grey eyes, arched eyebrows, a pretty nose and a wide, unattractive mouth. This mouth gave her whole face a chaste, innocent and slightly sad expression.

Valya was a tall, slim, delicate-looking girl, with short dark-brown hair and mischievous hazel eyes. She had a broad face, with high cheekbones and slightly slanted eyes.

Her face was by no means pretty, but she had an attractive, cheerful look about her. One evening we all ended up sitting together, and they told us about their love lives. It turned out that Zoya was far from the innocent girl she had seemed at first glance – on the contrary, she was rather 'corrupt'. She told us that many boys had loved her, that she had loved them back for the fun of it, and that she'd been kissed three times: on her forehead, the back of her neck and her cheek.

'So, last year I was at a health resort in the Crimea,' said Zoya, 'and one lad took a fancy to me. Seryozha, his name was. He was so in love with me, so completely besotted, it was unbelievable. I grew quite fond of him too. Anyway, once I became ill and was taken to an isolation ward, and Seryozha stayed with me the whole time. I had a really high temperature. I was lying there, semi-conscious, and I opened one eye to find him still sitting on a chair at my bedside, all morose, wearing a white robe and looking at me with such tenderness . . .'

Zoya closed her eyes for a moment, then shook herself irritably.

'And sometimes, girls, it was so awkward, simply dreadful. I needed to go, you know, and there he was, it was so awkward . . .' she said, with an embarrassed smile.

'But later . . . I'd fully recovered, and at the health resort there were separate accommodation blocks for girls and boys . . . So, one time I was in our room, and suddenly the girls called: "Zoya, Seryozha's asking for you." I ran out onto the veranda, and there he was, waiting for me. "I came to say goodbye, Zoya. I'm leaving. We probably won't see each other again. Goodbye!" He stood there for a moment in silence, then all of a sudden he put his hands on either side of my head, pulled me towards him and kissed my forehead. Oh girls, the way he held me and kissed me so gently, so tenderly . . . Then he turned and ran off, and I never saw him again.'

These girls left after a few days. Then Vova, Misha, Yanya and Kira Krutyakov came for three days. I didn't see much of them. I didn't get a chance to talk to Vova at all. I was too nervous, I couldn't bring myself to go and talk to him, and they didn't approach me either. So Vova and I behaved like strangers. I met him by chance in the corridor before he left and asked him to call in at home, to tell them how I was and to give Mama a postcard from me. For a brief moment, he was once again my dear, trusted friend. We shook hands firmly, he wished me all the best and then he left. I walked to the highway, and when I got back later that evening and went into our room I didn't recognize it at all: it was full of big, strapping lads, and they were all smoking. It was unbearably noisy.

This was the start of my acquaintance with School No. 15. There were sixteen of them: one teacher, thirteen boys and two girls. One of the girls turned out to be an old acquaintance. Nelya Klenochevskaya used to go to our school. She used to be in our class, then she moved and now she goes to School No. 15. The other girl was her friend, Kira Zamyshlyaeva. The same evening, although it was quite dark, by surreptitiously looking and listening I noticed one of the boys who really stood out from the others.

His friends all had deep voices and looked like they were seventeen or eighteen years old, but he – his name was Andrei – was of medium height, shorter than the rest of them, and had an impulsive, boyish demeanour and a high, boyish voice. Andrei looked like a boy of fifteen, at most. I assumed that the new law permitting fifteen-year-olds to be drafted had already come into force.[2]

----

2  Lena Mukhina is referring to a resolution passed by the Executive Committee of the Leningrad City Council on 9 August 1941 ('O poryadke privlecheniya naseleniya k trudovoi povinnosti'), according to which the age limits for eligibility for labour duty were extended to include men between the ages of fifteen and fifty-five and women between the ages of sixteen and fifty. Manual workers, white-collar workers and students were all to be mobilized, as were older schoolchildren and factory-school pupils. Women with children under eight were also now deemed eligible

One by one the boys started smoking. Andrei just sat there, chatting to the boy next to him. I thought: at least he doesn't smoke, that's something. But just at that moment Andrei stood up, took a flat box out of his coat pocket, stuck a *papirosa* in his mouth, struck a match on the sole of his boot in one skilful movement and lit up. This enabled me to see his face for the first time, and I liked what I saw.

Someone called: 'Andryusha, chuck us the matches.' He nodded and walked unsteadily across the room towards the door.

'Oops!'

'Damn, you could have burned me!'

'Oh! What's your name, fair beauty?'

'You'll find out soon enough. Can't you see I'm carrying boiling water?'

This was how Andrei met Valya Korobkova. When they'd finished their tea all the boys went outside. We girls were already falling asleep when two of them came back into the room: Andrei and Zorya. They lit cigarettes.

'Don't smoke in the room, boys, it's too stuffy,' said Valya.

'Where, may I ask, is that whining noise coming from?' said Zorya.

'I'm not whining, I'm speaking in a normal voice. Don't be so rude,' replied Valya.

One of them walked up to Valya, leaned over her and lit a match right under her nose, lighting up her face.

---

for labour duty; their children were to be accommodated in boarding houses. The city authorities considered the working population of the city on 1 August 1941 to be 1.45 million people. With a view to ensuring a steady supply of labour, the commission charged with the construction of fortified zones announced a plan to mobilize more than 602,000 people.

Valya blew it out.

'Ah, so that's who it is,' said Andrei. Then he lit a match under my nose.

I said: 'We're trying to sleep.'

'Andrei! You idiot, what are you lighting matches for? Put it out!'

'We're getting to know the girls,' said Zorka.

'Well, is that any way to go about it? Please forgive him, girls. Everyone knows he's got no manners.'

'Keep your hair on, Sasha,' replied Andrei. 'Everything's fine now. We just didn't know what kind of girls they were . . . They might have stabbed us while we slept.'

Someone burst noisily into the room.

'I tell you, we took that city, you bastard!'

'A little decorum, please, there are ladies present,' said Andrei. 'Come on, lads, no swearing in front of the girls.'

'The girls are probably fast asleep, dead to the world.'

'Girls, you're not asleep are you?'

Silence.

'Gi-irls, are you asleep?'

We said nothing. A match was struck, the room was lit.

'They're asleep.'

That's what life was like. It was fun. Noisy. Crazy.

Another day Andrei and Valya were left on duty together. By the time the rest of us got back they already had water on to boil, the room was tidy and the dishes had been washed. Everyone began to shower them with praise.

Andrei said: 'Valya's no ordinary girl, she's a real treasure.'

'She'd make a good wife, that's for sure.'

'Let's marry them, let's marry them,' everyone began to shout.

'What can I say, lads, but of course . . . The groom agrees.'

'Did the bride say yes?'

'Brides have no say in the matter,' said Andrei. 'Whatever next!'

'There's no point asking her, lads. She's so overcome with joy she can't speak!'

Valya defended herself from the boys as best she could.

'Go to hell, the lot of you! Have you lost your minds?'

'Leave her alone,' ordered Andrei. 'You don't know how to behave around women. Women require a very particular approach.'

Valya was choking with laughter. So was everyone else.

'Valya's a clever girl, isn't she,' said Andrei and turned to Valya, taking her by the hand. 'You'll be my wife forever, won't you? Yes?'

'Yes! Yes! Yes! Yes! Just leave me alone. Stop pestering me.'

'She said yes, she said yes,' everyone howled. 'Congratulations, Andryusha, on your new acquisition.'

Andrei laughed. 'Thank you, thank you, and now we will celebrate!'

The boys tumbled out of the room. Valya fell heavily onto her blanket. Blushing, laughing, she looked around at the rest of us with happy eyes.

'The beasts. Pestering me like that!'

Then she turned her back to us and lay with her face buried into her pillow.

Andrei appeared at the door.

'Valya, dear Valechka, come and help us. We can't do anything without you.'

Valya didn't move. Andrei walked over to her. Valya covered her face with her hands. Andrei looked at her and squatted down beside her.

'Come on, Valya, what's the matter?

He moved closer to her. I heard him whisper.

'Valya, what is it – are you offended? Oh Valechka, we were only joking around. Did we upset you? Did we, Valya? Answer me. Forgive us, it was a stupid joke. Do you forgive us? We won't do it again.'

'Leave me alone, Andrei!'

Andrei stood up immediately and drew himself to his full height.

'I see . . . it's like that, is it? Well, to hell with you. She's so high and mighty, she can't even take a joke!'

Andrei walked towards the door.

'Valya, I'll ask you one more time, will you come and help us?'

Valya looked up sharply.

'Help you with what?'

Andrei said: 'Well, the thing is, we want to make some coffee.'

'But there's nothing to it. Do you really not know how?'

'No one's ever taught us,' answered Andrei.

'You're all useless.'

Valya jumped up.

'There, you see? You should have done that straight away, instead of acting all high and mighty. I can't stand it when girls behave like that . . .' And then with a grin he added: 'Especially my wife.'

'I'm not your wife!'

She ran out. Andrei took his mug from the windowsill and followed her, singing: 'We'll be married, my dear, you and I.'

I spent nearly all my free time with Tamara. We would walk up the hill opposite the school and sing whichever songs came into our head. Or we would talk about the meaning of love, or what the word naivety actually means.

Once after work I was lying on the hillside, daydreaming about various things and various people. It was about seven o'clock. It was a pleasant evening, and I could feel the gentle warmth of the sun. The faces of people I knew were drifting through my mind. Suddenly I clearly heard in my head the words: 'We'll be married, my dear, you and I!' An image of Andrei came into my mind. Slim and handsome, with a lock of wavy hair falling onto his high forehead. The look on his face was bold, almost impudent. My God, I thought, why doesn't Vova look like him? And with this an image of Vova came into my mind. There he was – tall, slim, such a nice boy. Why doesn't he love me like I want him to? I wish he would love me like Seryozha loved Zoya. How is Zoya any better than me?

We're at the theatre. Sitting next to each other, watching *The Glass of Water*.[3] I'm stealing glances at him. He's right next to me, so familiar yet such a stranger. I just want to put my hand on his. But he's not paying any attention to me. He's engrossed in what's happening onstage.

Now he's wearing a threadbare embroidered cap over his tousled hair. He's lying on his stomach with his cheeks resting in the palms of his hands, lost in thought. The train is rushing along. The large freight wagons are making a noise like thunder. We're travelling to the city. I'm quite comfortable lying on my side on the wooden boards of the top bunk. Vova is lying on the opposite bunk, with Misha Ilyashev asleep on the next bunk.

Now he's turning towards me, and his pensive face breaks into a smile. A happy, heartfelt smile. He doesn't say anything, just looks at me with this open, friendly smile. It's the smile of someone who wants to show his friend what he is feeling inside. I look into his bright, happy eyes and smile back in the same way. Vova isn't in this kind of mood very often. We look at one another for a long time in mutual, unspoken understanding.

---

3   A play written by Eugène Scribe (1791–1861) in 1840.

Now he's standing on a street corner with his friends. Dressed all in white, eating an ice cream. So calm and indifferent to everything, as though nothing in the world can bother him.

And now we're in the headmaster's office at our old school. I'm standing by the stove, and Vova is sitting on the sofa next to Mama. We're looking at one another, and he's wearing the same smile, and the meaning of this smile is unclear. Either he's feeling happy again, or he's pleased to see an 'old friend', or perhaps there's another reason . . .

My thoughts were interrupted by the droning of aircraft engines. I returned to reality. The boys from School No. 15, a noisy crowd of them, were coming down the next hill along. They were singing a song with a chorus that included the words 'stamp your feet, sta-amp your feet!' They were heading towards the bottom of my hill. I could hear the words they were singing. It was a crude, smutty song. They might have been a gang of hooligans from Ligovka.[4] Then they started singing a different song. This one was better. In fact, I rather liked it. I can remember some of it:

Sail on, our daredevil boat! Ha ha![5]
Where is the current taking you?
It's a thieving life for us! Ha ha!
Once a thief, always a thief.

· · · · · · · · · · · · · · · · · ·

---

4  The area around Ligovskaya Street (from 1956 onwards Ligovsky Prospekt) from Nevsky Prospekt to the Volkov cemetery had been considered one of the most disreputable districts in Petersburg/Leningrad since the early 1900s. The term 'Ligovka' was used to designate any gathering place for petty criminals, prostitutes, drug addicts and other antisocial elements.

5  One version of a thieves' song from the 1930s.

A robber will never be a laundress! Ha ha!
A thief will never be hired as a cook.
Getting our hands dirty with a wheelbarrow? Ha ha!
That's no work for a thief.

We live on a boat with no roof over our heads! Ha ha!
And the current takes us where she will.
Money, women and vodka! Ha ha!
That's what we hold in the highest esteem!

. . . . . . . . . . . . . . . . . .

A thief will never be a laundress! Ha ha!
This is the only life for us!
Get our hands dirty with a wheelbarrow? Ha ha!
We'll smoke our way through it somehow.

They were all there: Sasha, Zorka, Andrei, Zhenka, Nader, Igor and Levka.

About Nader . . . That's his real name, not a nickname. His full name is Nader Avshar. He's Persian. He could pass for eighteen or even nineteen, but in fact he's only just turned sixteen. He's tall, strong and well built. He has an angular, dark-skinned face. A large, slightly hooked nose, dark oriental eyes and black curly hair. Nader nearly always wears a beret, and it suits him better than anyone else. Nader is very handsome. He looks Spanish. I found out later from Nelya (they're in the same class) that he's a nice person, too. Decent and sincere. He's sometimes a bit vulgar with his friends, but not very often.

There was the sound of shouting, and the boys drew back. A fight was breaking out. It was Zorka and Zhenka. About Zorka . . . He's Jewish. Tall, slim and reasonably attractive. Absolutely full of his own self-importance. No sense of shame, no conscience. Arrogant and impudent with the girls. When he talks, he fires his words out like bullets from a gun.

I don't like the shifty, shrewd, imperious look in his eyes, or his fleshy lips. And what's more, Zorka brought his gramophone all the way from home and spent a whole evening playing one record after another. He loves jazz and is mad about all the singers – Klavdiya Shulzhenko, Edit Utesova and so on. He loves showing off in front of the girls, but drives them away with his arrogance.

It was a serious fight. Neither of them would back down. They spent a long time rolling around on top of one another. Eventually Zhenka won.

What can I say about Zhenka . . . Just an ordinary boy. Nothing special about him. A nice enough face. Snub nose. Good-natured and agile. Loved showing off in front of the girls. An excellent dancer, he always gave a little bow at the end of every dance. Expert at blowing smoke rings. Wore a dark blue beret.

At this point they all started shouting and making a racket. Zhenka held his hand out to Zorka and helped him to his feet. Andrei rolled up an old tyre that he'd found somewhere, and the boys started to play football. Andrei was in goal. Zorka was the other goalkeeper. Andrei limped to the side and took his trousers off, and I saw that he had a bandage on his left leg.

Andrei took up position by the tyre and called out: 'Hey, what are you doing? The goalie's getting worried over here!' He began to do a rather convincing impression of an impatient goalkeeper. Spreading his legs and tensing his body, he stuck his head forward and jumped from side to side.

The game began. Zorka turned out to be a dreadful goalkeeper – he didn't save a single ball. Andrei, on the other hand, played really well. He didn't let a single ball in. Being short and agile, he darted about under the other players' feet, rescued the ball and kicked it away, deftly dodging every tackle. He also used a lot of bad language. His clear voice could be heard swearing more frequently than any of the others. I got tired of watching and left.

That evening I went to fetch milk. As I was walking back with the bottle I saw two people coming towards me, talking to one another. I stood to one side to let them pass, and when I looked more closely I saw that it was none other than Andrei, hand in hand with Valya Korobkova. He looked so smart. His trousers were on the outside of his boots, and he was wearing a nice wool sweater. Valya was wearing Andrei's raincoat around her shoulders and a brand-new white hat. They were the same height. Andrei was telling her something as they strolled along. He was so calm, so quiet. It was impossible to believe that this was the same Andrei who had recently been kicking a football about and swearing with such abandon. A sharp needle of jealousy pricked me. I glanced back at the two receding figures, then continued on my way. When I reached the school it was already quite dark, even though it was not yet ten. Valya and Andrei didn't get back until after eleven, by which time most people were asleep. After that, the two of them took to going out for a walk every evening. I found it rather strange at first but soon got used to it. Sometimes it was very late when they got back. I no longer envied them. They're both eighteen, whereas I'm only sixteen. I'll start dating too when my time comes.

Having said that, Zoya is only sixteen and she's already dating boys. And kissing.

I would love to be dating like Valya at my age, to the envy of the other girls.

But enough about that.

Before we had the gramophone, the boys would put on their own jazz concerts for us every evening. They sang in tune and rather well, all in bass apart from Andrei, whose high, soft voice stood out among the others. They used their voices to make the music too – howling, clicking their tongues, crowing like cockerels – and it sounded really good. Their favourite songs were 'Tanyusha'[6] and 'In the Caucasus There Is a Mountain'.[7] Here are the words:

Karapet fell in love with the beauty Tamara,
But he was no match for her.
(*Andrei sings Tamara's part:*)
'Oh, leave me alone, you old dwarf!
I'm married to young Akhmed,
And when he hears what you're saying
He will chop off your head.'
(*Chorus:*)
In the Caucasus there is a mountain. The greatest one of all.
And beneath it flows the turbulent Kura.
Anyone who climbs the mountain and jumps from it
Has a high chance of parting with life.
In the evening Karapet comes to Akhmed.
(*One voice:*)
'Oh, Akhmed, you want lots of money,
And in return you will give me Tamara.
We will go to Tbilisi and be married there.'

---

6  Lena Mukhina is referring to a song performed by Pyotr Leshchenko, which was actually called 'Tatyana' (lyrics and music by Mark Maryanovsky (1889–1944)).

7  Song written by the composer Oskar Strok (1893–1975) and Mark Maryanovsky at the beginning of the 1930s to help launch the singing career of Pyotr Leshchenko.

(*All:*) Akhmed replies:
(*One voice:*) 'How can I refuse?
Women are plentiful, but money is not.
Take my wife, and let us drink wine.
I have lost one, but I'll find five more.'
(*All:*)
In the Caucasus there is a mountain . . .

We people from the Caucasus,
We love wine and caresses.
But if the caresses betray us, ohhhhh!
We'll stay with the evil one
And sharpen our daggers.
And then we will slit her throat,
So that she cannot run away.

———————————

I don't know anything,[8]
Nor do I want to.
All I know
Is that I love you.
Tell me, my darling
Can you understand
How hard it is to suffer in love?
(*With more feeling:*)
I suffer all day,
I can't sleep at night.
I don't know anything,

———————————

8  Incorrect and incomplete reproduction of lyrics to the song 'I Don't Know
   Anything' (music by Henryk Wars, lyrics by Feliks Konarski). A recording of Evgeny
   Bodo performing this foxtrot was released just before war broke out in 1941.

Nor do I want to.
But I won't be able
To forget your smile.
And now I don't know
How I am going to live without you.

———————————

Bevochka, understand me!
Bevochka, don't torment me.
Bevochka, I'm sad without you.
You are my heart, my joy.

———————————

I don't want to cause you any pain.
Let it remain a secret
That I have begun to miss you,
And to think of our chance meeting.

———————————

I live in a musical apartment.[9]
We have a piano and a saxophone,
Four loudspeakers
And a gramophone in every room.

I have a little gramophone of my own.
Only I don't play it,
Because it'll be the end of me.
I'm so crazy about music.

———————————

9  Distorted lyrics to the song 'Jazz Fan' by Leonid Utesov (composer unknown, lyrics
   by Vasily Lebedev-Kumach).

Who did I take after?
We are an unusual family.
As soon as I hear a song,
I can sing it straight away.

Who did I take after?
It's difficult for me, being the way I am.
As soon as I fall in love with a girl,
She's already with someone else.

What dreadful stuff!

Everyone would gather in front of the school in the evenings. It was noisy and fun. Zorka's gramophone would be playing. I'm not in the mood. I walk away from the noise and follow the path down the hill. The jazz music, the shouts and laughter all fade away.

It's quiet here, at the bottom of the hill. I look all around me. Such a marvellous evening. Large stars are looking down at me from way up high. It's surprisingly warm and quiet. A soft, warm breeze stirs my hair. My heart gradually fills with sadness. I start feeling sorry for myself. I sit on the warm hay, just thinking and thinking. Sad thoughts come into my head. Here I am, completely alone, and no one cares about me. Everyone has their own concerns, their sorrows and their joys. Andrei and Valya are out walking together somewhere right now. Valya is happy. Why don't I have any happiness of my own? Why? Tamara's probably asleep right now. She's happy too. She probably doesn't ever think about such silly things. Or maybe she does, who knows . . .

Why don't I have anyone by my side? On a lovely evening like this. It's such a pity. Such a waste of an evening. I don't want to be alone, but I don't want to be with a crowd of people either. I want to be with someone I love and who loves me. But nobody loves me. I love someone, but it doesn't make any difference. It's just pointless suffering, because he doesn't love me and doesn't even know that I love him. Why should I tell him, when I know that it won't be reciprocated? Yes, it's a crying shame to be living such a barren life at sixteen. Someone will fall in love with me one day, of course they will. It's bound to happen sooner or later. But that's all in the future, and I want it to happen now, right now. At the age of sixteen, I want to know how it feels to be loved.

How dismal it is to be alone on such a marvellous evening. Vova is asleep in Leningrad, no doubt, or perhaps he's on duty in the attic. But I should stop thinking about him. Damn them, all these hard-hearted boys.

I slowly walk back towards the school. I stop near the gramophone. There's a tango playing. Andrei is gathering up the records. The tango comes to an end. Andrei prepares to close the gramophone. The girls run up to him:

'Put another one on, Andrei!'

'No, girls, that's enough for today. Everything in moderation.'

'Please, Andryusha, just the other side . . .'

He pulled out one of the records.

'What is it, Andrei?'

'Dance, girls! One final waltz!'

A waltz began to play. Andrei invited one of the girls to dance. He seized her deftly by the waist and led her smoothly and gently, swaying from side to side, then he spun her round quickly, skilfully, beautifully . . . The record stopped. Andrei thanked his partner then went over to the gramophone, removed the record and put it back in the box.

'Go on, Andrei! One more won't hurt.'

As he detached the winding handle, Andrei said: 'No, girls, I can't be persuaded today.'

'But it's not even eleven!'

'Still, it's time for us all to go to bed, girls. You're too young to be up so late at night.'

## 29 August 1941

Today Mama Lena revealed some terrible news . . . she finally brought herself to tell me that my mother is no longer alive.[1] I still can't believe it. It hasn't fully sunk in. But already I feel the emptiness of loneliness descending upon me. The love we felt for one another cannot be put into words. Such love can only exist between a mother and daughter.

> You are my bright star!
> You are my wild flower!
> You are so beautiful,
> My dear little fledgling.
> No comparison can do justice
> To my dear Lenusya.
> There is no other girl in the world
> Better than my Lenusya.

---

1  Lena is referring to the death of her birth mother, Mariya Nikolaevna Mukhina. Because her mother suffered from a serious, long-term illness Lena lived with her aunt Elena Nikolaevna Bernatskaya (Mama Lena), her mother's sister.

My hand is shaking. My heart is pounding in my chest. She died on 1 July.

---

You died on 1 July 1941 during our savage war with Germany in the forty-fourth year of your life, and I don't even know the details of your death.

Mother, my beloved, precious mother. You are no longer alive. How will I get through this? My heart is breaking. This is it, the first blow that fate has struck upon me. I'm shaking. I'm scared. I'm going to run to Tamara.

I feel like running to Vova. I don't want to stay at home. I can't bear it here.

---

The Germans have occupied Dnepropetrovsk.[2] The word is that they're approaching Gatchina. They're building pillboxes in the city. Leningrad is turning into a fortress.

How I wish I had someone to love, so that in this terrible time we could promise one another that if we were still alive in a few years we would join our lives forever.

Oh, if only! I'm in agony. Now my own mother is no longer in the world, how I wish that somebody loved me.

I'm in so much pain. I'm trembling all over. This is it, the first blow. I'm still only sixteen, and I've already been dealt the first blow. What else does fate have in store for me? I don't know.

Thousands of people are dying on the frontline and some of them are sixteen-year-old boys, the same age as me.

---

2   Dnepropetrovsk (Dnipropetrovsk) was surrendered by Soviet troops on 25 August 1941.

According to a new order issued by Voroshilov, as of today I am exempted from labour duty.[3] Because I'm sixteen, and according to the new law they're only recruiting girls from eighteen years of age, and boys from sixteen years of age. Tamara came to see me today. We had a nice time. She told me lots of interesting things. Then I read aloud Turgenev's short story 'The Dog'.

Now for some memories of the past . . .

Someone burst into our room one evening and shouted:

'Look out of the window, some planes are on fire!'

Naturally we all ran outside. There were three gigantic fires blazing away on the field and thick black smoke rising into the air. There really were three planes on fire. It later transpired that one of them was ours and the other two were German bombers. Those three strange bonfires burned all night. Their remains were still smoking the following morning. This marked the end of our peaceful life. After about four days we had already got used to it all: the aerial battles taking place right above us, planes circling like crazy, different kinds of machine-gun fire. Artillery shells from the anti-aircraft guns whistle over our heads, and you can see them exploding up in the sky: first there's a fiery explosion then a little white cloud, which looks like an open parachute. Then this cloud gradually melts. The anti-aircraft guns fire in different ways: some rumble, some roar and others making a thudding sound. Sometimes they all start firing at once, like a kind of anti-aircraft concerto, and that's really frightening. The whole area is filled with deafening thunder, roaring and rumbling, all of it cut through

---

3   This refers to a resolution passed by by the Military Council for the Defence of Leningrad on 29 August 1941 ('O privlechenii naseleniya k vypolneniyu v poryadke trudpovinnosti rabot po oborone Leningrada').

by a piercing new sound – the high-pitched whistle of artillery shells. Boom, boom – whee-phtt. Crack, boom – whee-phtt. Bang, boom, bang – whee-phtt.

Added to all of this is the barely audible but insistent and ominous drone of enemy aircraft. They're barely visible, these enemy planes. They're usually either small white dots in the clear blue sky or black dots against a backdrop of clouds. There they are, the enemy, nine of them. The anti-aircraft guns are firing at them furiously but they keep flying, insistently, obstinately, flying to where my beloved Leningrad lies spread out in a haze of blue smoke. Can't the anti-aircraft guns reach them? Apparently not. Now the nine planes are falling into a line. They're turning, they're climbing even higher, they're hiding behind the clouds, they're flying towards the sun. Suddenly one of them breaks away from its chain, the engine audibly cuts out, and it starts flying lower and lower. It's surrounded by a series of explosions, which are immediately replaced with little white clouds. Suddenly a grey cloud appears behind the plane and follows it persistently.

'It's on fire! Look, it's on fire,' someone shouts nearby.

'Where?'

'There, can you see that grey cloud behind it?'

'Yes. Does that mean it's on fire?'

'Of course.'

I keep my eyes fixed on the doomed plane. It's coming down, very slowly, but it's definitely coming down. The grey cloud has grown larger. It's about to go smoothly down behind a hill, but then it suddenly begins to fall more sharply and disappears almost vertically behind the hill.

'Well, that's that!' said someone.

---

Now I'm going to write about the distant past. When I was sent to Tarkovichi by the *zhakt*, I worked there for three days. We worked from six in the evening to six in the morning. It was like torture. By the end I was in a very weak state. I only just had enough energy to drag myself home. Our heads were spinning, and we could barely stand up. We lay on the wooden floor all day, completely spent, until six o'clock in the evening. We were so exhausted that we didn't even get the chance to recover before we had to go back to work again. Where were we supposed to get our energy from? They hardly fed us. On the first day they didn't give us anything at all. On the second day they gave us 100g of bread each and a bowl of millet *kasha* at about three o'clock. But it wasn't normal *kasha*. Even though I was really hungry I had trouble forcing it down and had to make a great effort not to be sick.

A barge carrying food supplies arrived that day, and at five o'clock we were each given 50g of salami, 100g of cheese and some bread. They also had meat pies, jars of 'peas and ham' and an enormous number of bottles of lemonade. But you had to pay for those.

The fourth day of digging began. Straight after work I lay down on the floor and wrapped myself in my blanket, and in less than a minute I was sound asleep. Some time later, half awake, I became aware of the sound of quiet voices.

'The team leader wants a list of all sixteen-year-olds. Apparently they're going to send them home.'

A woman's voice said: 'Yes, that would be the right thing to do. The poor things are completely worn out.'

On hearing this, I woke up properly and raised myself up on my elbow. Zoya was already making the list, and my name would be on it. At first, I was worried that I might be dreaming. I couldn't believe my ears. I was so afraid that they would suddenly change their minds about sending us home. The others were all looking enviously at us.

'You girls are so lucky to be leaving,' they said, all talking at once.

One seventeen-year-old girl was particularly annoyed: 'God, I wish I was still sixteen.'

'Oh, my dears,' said one woman, 'when will we see Leningrad again? Maybe we never will.'

I lay there thinking. Was fate really taking pity on me? Would I really escape from this hell?

Our team leader arrived. I will never forget him, he was such a remarkable man. Anyway, he came to talk to us when it was already almost six.

'Get your things together, girls, and take this list to headquarters. I'll meet you there. The rest of us,' he said to the others, 'are going to work, comrades.'

'When will it be our turn to go home?'

'I don't know, comrades, I'm afraid I can't tell you. All I know is that the sooner we finish, the sooner we'll be leaving.'

We hurriedly gathered our things and said goodbye to the others. It's hard to describe how envious they were.

We arrived at the headquarters. There were already a lot of people there. It turned out that they were all sick and injured. We settled down to wait. It wasn't long before we were pestered by gypsies. Then they all left, except one gypsy girl about the same age as us who came up and offered to tell our fortunes. We all declined, but she pestered us until we eventually agreed. She told everyone's fortune in exchange for sugar. I couldn't resist.

'And here is what I see written* for you, my lady. Some time in the near future you will meet with your king. And this meeting will be unexpected and fortuitous, and it will bring untold joy to your heart.'

She spoke rapidly, in a sing-song voice, glancing up at me then back at her little mirror.

'Ahead of you lies a happy path. Through your beloved white king, great joy awaits you on this path.'

'How do you know,' I asked, 'that my king is white and not black?'

'Because, my lady, it is shown in my mirror.'

'You're lying,' said someone. 'That's just an ordinary mirror.'

'An ordinary mirror would tell a different story,' she said, her eyes flashing with anger. But her sugary smile soon returned.

I said: 'So tell me, please, if your mirror is so special, what is my king's name?'

She looked offended and rather displeased.

The others chimed in: 'Yes, we want to know too.'

'Vova,' she murmured, and then her voice began to sing again with extraordinary emotion. 'Great happiness awaits you, my lady, through your beloved husband. You will lead a charmed life, without ever knowing misfortune.'

That was the gypsy girl's prediction for me. And an hour and a half later I really did bump into Vova when I least expected to, and through him alone my journey back to Leningrad was a happy one.

Such interesting things happen in life by chance.

## 2 September 1941

'The enemy is at the gates of Leningrad! The valiant forces of the Red Army are fighting just outside Leningrad.' So they said on the radio.

I slept through it, but apparently last night the sound of artillery fire was clearer than ever.

Rations are being reduced today. Now all our family gets is 1 kilo of bread a day.[1]

I just walked down the street. I went into a few shops. They're all so empty and depressing. Everything in Roskond[2] was always so expensive, but at least there was plenty of it. Now the counters are bare: not a single pie or cake. All the shop windows are boarded up. Two lorries went past. The first

---

1  From 2 September 1941 the daily bread ration in Leningrad was 600g for manual workers, engineers and technicians, 400g for white-collar workers and 300g for dependants and children.

2  A chain of cake and confectionery shops. There was one next to Lena Mukhina's building on Zagorodny Prospekt, between Razyezzhaya Street and Vladimirskaya Square. A contemporary account describes it as follows: 'Dark-blue silk beneath glass panels and medallions, decorated walls and counters – unprecedented luxury.'

was carrying the distorted body of a fighter plane on a trailer, covered with canvas. It was missing its propeller, and the tail-plane was damaged. The other lorry was carrying the wings, which were also damaged, but their red stars were still visible. I felt a deep sadness in my heart.

I am witnessing with my own eyes things that up until now I have only heard on the radio, read about in books and been told by my own family. This is different, though. The walls aren't resonating from artillery fire, nor are they riddled with bullet holes.

## 4 September 1941

After days without any air raids, the siren went off again yester-day at quarter past seven. The raid lasted for about an hour. There was a second air-raid warning in the middle of the night, at half past one.

The air raid this morning lasted an hour and a half.

It's only just finished, but the gunfire hasn't stopped. It's getting even closer. The air is already making the windowpanes tremble. It's a good thing I pasted muslin over them yesterday. What lies ahead?!

# 5 September 1941

Just before eight o'clock this evening, straight after the air-raid warning, which lasted three-quarters of an hour, I went to Tamara's and stayed there until half past nine. We didn't talk much, because we were listening to records on the gramophone. While we were listening to the gramophone we suddenly heard anxious voices in the corridor. Olga Antonovna went out to see what was happening. She soon returned and told us: 'A three-storey building on the corner of Predtechenskaya and Glazovskaya has been hit by a shell. The roof is intact, but two apartments on the first and second floors have been completely destroyed.' Tamara and I couldn't believe it. We won't believe it until we've seen it with our own eyes. There are also rumours that several bombs fell today not far from the Fontanka.[1] There were fatalities.

---

1 Leningrad first came under German artillery fire on 4 September 1941. Shells exploded at the Vitebsk-Sortirovochnaya railway station and the Bolshevik, Salolin and Krasny Neftyanik factories. However the first bombs were not dropped until 6 September, which suggests that the reference to bombs in the diary entry for 5 September might have been based on rumours. As a result of this first bombing

Just two days ago they were saying on the radio that, thanks to Stalin's glorious Falcons,[2] not one single bomb had been dropped on Leningrad. Not one single building had been destroyed in Leningrad. Not one single fatality had occurred in Leningrad.

And two days ago this was still true, but today a building has been destroyed, bombs have fallen and we have our first fatalities. Nazi monsters! We Leningraders hate them with such a passion. What are they trying to do to our city? The gunfire today was terrifying. And that was only one gun. What if there were twenty of them? What will become of our city? Will we survive? When I go to bed these days I only take off half my clothes. It's terrible to think that winter is coming, too. What will this winter be like? What hardships will we have to endure? If the Germans break into Leningrad and bring war to the streets of my city, I'll run away. I won't stay here. Mama and Aka can do what they like. I know what will happen to me if I stay here. Tamara and I will run away together.

---

raid no. 119, 25th October (Nevsky) Prospekt was destroyed and no. 115 on the same street was partially damaged, a water pipe was ruptured in Ligovskaya Street, and a fire broke out in part of the Pyatiletka factory. Predtechenskaya Street is now known as Chernyakhovsky Street, and Glazovskaya is Konstantin Zaslonov Street.

2   The Soviet Air Force. The term 'Stalin's Falcons' was first used in the Communist Party newspaper *Pravda* on 24 June 1936.

## 6 September 1941

Individual shots could be heard ringing out all day today. I went to see Lyusya today. It's so dull at her place. She never starts a conversation. Not like Tamara. To be honest, before I got to know Tamara she seemed rather dull and uncommunicative as well. But now we're so close we talk all the time, without even having to think of things to say. But I already know Lyusya. That's just what she's like. No, Tamara is more like a real friend. When we were walking back to my place yesterday evening, I told her how I felt:

'When are we going to see each other again, Tamara? You're my best friend.'

'And you're my best friend.'

'Really? What about Nadya? And Leva?'

Well, I never see Nadya, and as for Leva . . . I don't know. He doesn't care about me. He's busy studying at that technical college of his.'

'Haven't you seen him for a while?'

'Not since the 31st. And there's no way I'm going to start chasing him. I'd only regret it even more later.'

Tamara started laughing. 'That sounds stupid, doesn't it,' she said. 'You know,' she continued, 'maybe he never cared about me. Maybe he's just being polite when he keeps saying he wants me to come again.'

'Of course not, Tamara. He's treating you nicely, and he likes it when you visit him.'

'I don't think so. He just had nothing better to do. But it's different now he's studying. He hasn't called me for all this time. He won't come and see me, of course, but he could call if he wanted to. So he obviously doesn't want to.'

'How can you say such a thing, Tamara?'

'Quite easily! He called me before, when he wanted to. He asked me to go round. We went to the cinema together.

'So he did call you. What are you worrying about, then?'

'He did. But that was ages ago, when I'd just arrived.'

'Well, at least it's something. Which is more than I have.'

Tamara didn't really pay any attention to what I said. But I meant every word. Tamara's got a real boyfriend. He's her boyfriend because he wanted to see Tamara, he called her, he asked her out.

I've got a so-called 'boyfriend' too. But what kind of boyfriend can he be, if he's forgotten that I even exist? We haven't seen each other for such a long time, and it doesn't even bother him. People who behave like that can't be called boyfriends. He doesn't have a telephone, fair enough, but he could give Tamara a note to give to me. He could ask me to visit him or come and see me himself. Otherwise why claim to be my boyfriend?

This is what I think: he should either relinquish the role or be worthy of it. The word boyfriend is not just a meaningless sound. It carries certain obligations.

# 7 September 1941

Today is IYD.[1] Everyone's doing voluntary Sunday work, including Mama Lena. On the radio today there was a broadcast from a women's meeting in Moscow. I heard the anxious voices of Barsova, Marina Raskova, Dolores Ibárruri,[2] a German writer, a Romanian woman and many others.

Deeply worrying words!

Apparently Old Nevsky was bombed at midnight last night, and three buildings were destroyed. I'm still alive for now, but the future is uncertain.

---

1  International Youth Day, celebrated for the first time in 1915 according to a resolution passed by the International Socialist Conference of Youth, which took place that year in Bern (Switzerland). IYD was celebrated in Russia for the first time in 1917 and for the last time in 1945.

2  On 7 September 1941, a meeting entitled Women of the World in the Fight Against Fascism was held in the Column Hall of the House of Unions in Moscow. After the delegates had made their speeches, which were broadcast live on the radio, the participants issued an appeal to the women of the world. The participants included Valeria Barsova (real name Vladimirova) (1892–1967), Russian and Soviet opera singer, People's Artist of the USSR; Marina Raskova (1912–1943), Soviet navigator, Hero of the Soviet Union (1938); and Dolores Ibárruri Gómez (1895–1989), activist within the Spanish and international labour movement, leader of the Spanish Communist Party.

## 8 September 1941

There was a short air raid this morning. Yesterday I finished reading The *Story of a Childhood* by Vodovozova.[1] Lyusya has given me *Curumilla*, a novel by Gustave Aimard.[2]

Mama came home at seven o'clock this evening, as usual. She brought tomatoes and cabbage, and we sat down to dinner. We had barely eaten three spoonfuls when we heard the ominous sound of the siren. We opened the window a little and carried on eating. But before we'd eaten even two more spoonfuls we heard the first shots of the anti-aircraft guns, then more and more of them, getting closer and closer, then there was a loud rattling noise. Eventually we couldn't stay in the room any longer. Mama rushed off to find out what was happening. My eyes grew wide with fright, and I jumped up as though I'd been

---

1  Elizaveta Nikolaevna Vodovozova (1844–1923) was a Russian children's author and teacher. Her book *The Story of a Childhood* is a children's version of her memoirs *At the Dawn of Life* (1911).

2  Gustave Aimard (real name Olivier Gloux) (1818–83) was a French writer. Lena Mukhina is presumably referring to the Russian edition of his novel *Curumilla*, which was published in Moscow in 1900 by Ivan Sytin.

stung. I didn't understand was happening. There was so much thunder, so much noise, it sounded like the sky was falling down. I assumed that bombs were exploding, that the end had come. My hands were shaking but I grabbed my coat and began to put it on, then pulled on my beret and rushed down to the bomb shelter. People were scattering down the stairs like spilled peas, some carrying children, others helping old women. Something was happening outside, something terrible. I only had one thought in my head: to get downstairs as quickly as possible, to safety.

The shelter was full of people. Somehow we pushed our way through to the second room and sat down in there. Despite the noise inside the shelter, we could hear the roar of thunder outside.

Once the noise had died down, Mama went home because she was tired and hungry. Aka went home too. I stayed. Mama soon returned. Leaning towards us so that the others couldn't hear, she said that there must be an enormous fire not far away, because there was a vast column of smoke covering half the horizon. Soon after that they sounded the all-clear. I rushed outside. As I ran out into the courtyard I noticed how dark it was. Everyone was looking up, so I looked up too and was horrified by what I saw. A cloud of smoke was swirling and twisting, spreading across the sky like a storm cloud. It was ominous and threatening – an impressive sight, like a volcano erupting. I'd never seen anything like it. I ran to Ivanovskaya Street.[3] It was chaos. Everyone was rushing about, waving their arms in the air. Crowds of young boys, lads, teenagers were racing towards this terrible cloud, pushing people out of the way. There was

3   Lena Mukhina is using the old street name. From October 1918 Ivanovskaya Street was known as Sotsialisticheskaya Street.

a smell of burning in the air. I walked along Ivanovskaya, then turned into Pravda Street and walked a little further. In the gap between two buildings I saw that the base of the smoke was crimson red, and it was swirling and slowly spreading across the sky. Fire engines raced along Zvenigorodskaya, one after the other. A woman said that 'it' was behind the Alexander Nevsky Monastery, about 3 km away.

'A chemical factory's on fire.[4] Where they make varnishes and paints,' she said as she ran past.

I went home. On Ivanovskaya the lads were showing off the shrapnel that they'd gathered from anti-aircraft shells. Fire engines were racing along Zagorodny too, from the 11th Fire Brigade. Yes, the Nazis have been saving something really special for Leningrad. But how did the swine manage to force their way through? I just don't understand it.

They say that a six-storey building on Old Nevsky Prospekt has been destroyed by bombs. Apparently the place was surrounded by police and they were carrying bodies out all day today.

I'm not getting undressed tonight. I dread to think what this night will be like!

We've just had an air raid that lasted from half past ten to quarter to one. I had just gone to bed and was trying to sleep. I must have had a feeling that it would happen, because I didn't even take my boots off. As soon as the siren went off I leaped out of bed, put my coat on and left the apartment with the others.

---

4 This refers to the Koksogazovy factory (Obvodny Canal Embankment 72–4). Similar accounts are to be found elsewhere. 'It became immediately obvious that the fire was coming from the chemical coke factory on Obvodny,' reads a diary entry dated 9 September 1941 by I. D. Zelenskaya, a worker at the 7th State Electrical Power Station (I. D. Zelenskaya, 'Dnevnik. 7 iyulya 1941–6 maya 1943', 'Ya nes damsya do poslednego . . .': Zapiski iz blokadnogo Leningrada, St Petersburg, 2010, p. 22).

I ran down to the shelter. My haste was justified, because as we were going down into the basement we could already hear the roar of thunder from the street. There were even more people in the shelter than there had been during the day. The anti-aircraft guns were blasting away outside, then there was a series of explosions and the ground shook beneath us. The lights went off briefly, and everything was plunged into darkness.

We weren't in the bomb shelter for that long, only two hours or so, but towards the end we were all completely shattered. Children were crying and asking to go home, their mothers were tired of holding them, and everyone wanted to go to sleep. During the first hour people just kept coming, carrying children wrapped up in blankets. The shelter was full to bursting. And that was only two hours. What if we'd had to stay in there for six or even eight hours? How would we have coped? I didn't get enough sleep last night. I've got a splitting headache.

According to Sovinformbyuro today, several enemy divisions have been defeated near Smolensk after twenty-six days of fighting. The remnants of these divisions are hurriedly falling back.

Today for the first time they announced: 'German aircraft attack Leningrad.' It appears that a group of enemy planes managed to break through, and in the first raid they dropped incendiary bombs over various parts of the city. Fires broke out in several residential buildings and warehouses, although these were quickly extinguished. (Quickly, indeed – they were burning for five hours.)

In the second raid the enemy dropped high-explosive bombs. Buildings were destroyed. People died, others were injured. No military targets were hit.

It's not yet nine o'clock in the morning. Another short air raid has just finished. Strangely, the all-clear was given some time ago, but I could clearly hear the drone of an aeroplane and individual shots from the anti-aircraft guns.

It's still droning now. It must be a spy plane, inspecting the work of yesterday's guests.

Well, it wasn't a bad start. Yesterday they managed to burn down a gas plant, the Badaev food storage warehouses,[5] the textiles warehouses and the Vitebsk freight station. Yesterday the ground literally shook beneath our feet. The bombs were probably large calibre. Yes, Hitler's little gift to us is really something special. But we'll get our own back, we'll get our own back on 'them' for everything.

Blood for blood! A death for a death! The horrors of medieval torture chambers pale in comparison to the tortures that these animals in human form are inflicting on Soviet citizens who fall into their clutches. They cut off people's hands and feet, for example, and throw them straight into the fire while they're still alive. No, they will pay in full. For the Leningraders, Muscovites, Kievans and others who have been killed by bombs and missiles, for the tormented, maimed and injured soldiers of the Red Army, for the women and children who have been shot, torn to pieces, stabbed, hanged, buried alive, burned

---

5    Several dozen wooden storerooms on Kievskaya Street belonging to the Aleksei Badaev warehouse complex were subjected to aerial bombardment by German troops on 8 and 10 September 1941. The resulting fires destroyed a considerable proportion of the food supplies that were stored there. Several hundred tons of burnt flour and sugar were subsequently salvaged for use by the city's food manufacturing industry, and numerous contemporary accounts describe Leningraders gathering or buying charred earth that was saturated with sugar, dissolving it in hot water, filtering it and either drinking this sweetened water or using it to prepare food. Many Leningraders considered the fires at these warehouses to be one of the main causes of the brutal famine of the winter of 1941–2, though in fact, based on rations in force at the time, the food supplies lost in the fire would have lasted no more than a few days.

and suffocated. For all the women and young girls who have been raped, for the death of young Sasha, who wasn't afraid of them and wore his red neck scarf regardless,[6] for the children and mothers with babes in arms gunned down by these barbarians, sitting at the controls of their planes and hunting them just for fun. For all of this, for everything, they will pay in full.

---

6  An article was published in *Leningradskaya Pravda* the following day in which A. Janssen, a communal services worker in Tartu, Estonia, spoke about the eleven-year-old son of his neighbour Karl Vesk, who had encountered a group of enemy air-craft pilots in the local park. 'When they saw the boy's red neck scarf,' said Janssen, 'the Nazis took hold of the Young Pioneer and dragged him to a tall chestnut tree. One of the assailants fetched a rope. With sadistic composure they made a noose, put it around the boy's neck and hanged him from the tree' (*Leningradskaya Pravda*, 9 September 1941). It is possible that Lena Mukhina heard about this on the radio, but she may be referring to another, similar incident. The red neck scarf, tied in a special knot, was a symbol that identified members of the Vladimir Lenin All-Union Pioneer Organization. The three ends of the scarf symbolized the unbreakable link between three generations: communists, the Komsomol youth organization and the Young Pioneers.

## 9 September 1941

Today is 9 September. It's midnight. Today there were nine air raids, two of which lasted for over two hours. God, these frequent warnings are so exhausting. If we have nine air raids a day for ten days in a row, then I believe there will be considerably more lunatics than sane people left in the city. I say this because everyone is so agitated after only one day of it. There is chaos and confusion in the streets. People are tearing up and down the pavement as though they're possessed. They're hanging off the trams, queuing for the trolleybus. Of course it's easy enough to say that we had nine air raids. But what air raids they were: the anti-aircraft guns were blasting away, and bombs were exploding like thunder, shaking everything all around.

Every air raid carried off dozens of lives. Every air raid meant buildings destroyed, and casualties.

Nine air raids – that's hundreds of human lives, dozens of buildings destroyed, heaps of rubble, holes and craters.

The ninth air raid was horrendous. I was on duty in our housing office from nine to eleven. Mama was there too with one other woman, also a volunteer.[1] From time to time the ground shook with explosions. The droning sound of aeroplane engines continued throughout the air raid, even though the anti-aircraft guns were blasting away. It sounded as though bombs were exploding quite nearby. Each time we instinctively huddled together, because it seemed as though a bomb was about to fall on our building. But we were spared.

---

1   The term *obshchestvennitsa* was used to denote a woman actively involved in public life and engaging in community work, both on her own initiative and by employment. The social volunteer movement developed rapidly in the USSR in the 1930s, with the wives of engineers, technicians and those who had been recognized as exemplary workers, amongst others, coming forward to help lay the foundations of a new socialist way of life. The People's Commissariat for Heavy Industry even published a newspaper called *Obshchestvennitsa*, which was aimed at these female volunteers.

## 10 September 1941

It's only eleven o'clock in the morning and we've already had three air raids. I go to the air-raid shelter every time now. I dress in winter clothes, put on my overshoes and take my little suitcase. I'm going to keep it with me now until the end of the war. It contains a new notebook, a photo of Vova, money, two handkerchiefs, a flask of tea, some bread and this diary. I have written my address and telephone number on the inside lid of the suitcase, so that if anything happens to me someone will be able to let them know at home. There's no air raid at the moment, but you can still hear the anti-aircraft guns firing.

God, our city is swarming with enemies. They've caught plenty of rocket signallers already,[1] but nevertheless, as soon as the night raids begin, treacherous flares released by those who are still at large help to guide enemy bombers to their targets.

---

1  At the beginning of the war Leningrad was rife with rumours about enemy rocket signallers, who were supposedly using flares to enable the German bombers to identify targets. However, there is no documentary evidence that any of these 'rocket signallers' were ever caught. Raids were organized, for example at the Smolenskoe Cemetery in the autumn of 1941, but they proved fruitless.

Many people who were at the gates, in the attic and on the roof during yesterday's raid said that flares kept going off over the bank (on the Fontanka), Vitebsk Station and other important targets until all enemy bombs had been dropped.

Here is further proof of the enemy's audacity: during the course of the raid, right under the noses of the duty officers and courtyard caretakers, someone poured kerosene over the road and set light to it. The scoundrel in question has been arrested, but they couldn't put the fire out straight away so burning kerosene spread down the whole street.

The fourth air raid lasted about two hours. It's now five to one in the afternoon. The eighth air raid has just finished. It's now about five o'clock. The ninth air raid is over.

It's now quarter past ten. Mama and Aka are asleep. I've got a feeling that tonight's 'performance' is about to begin. But I'm going to bed as well. I wasn't wrong . . . There goes the siren. Half past ten. The all-clear was given at twenty past twelve.

There was another air-raid warning at half past twelve. It wasn't until exactly one o'clock that our souls were left in peace.

## 11 September 1941

It's half past eight. We've already had two air raids. Bombs fell during the second one as well. So people are wrong to console themselves with the thought that daytime is not so frightening, that only reconnaissance aircraft fly during the day. No, they're dropping bombs during the day now as well. It's horrendous!

The all-clear doesn't count for much these days. Even without any bombs to worry about, there are still shells. You could be killed by an artillery shell at any moment. There's no air raid at the moment, for example, but something is making a banging noise out there somewhere.

For three days now we have had no rest, day or night. People are exhausted. One air raid follows another. There were ten air raids yesterday and nine the day before. That's twenty-one air raids, in just two and a half days. How many more days like this are ahead of us?

The worker toils at his machine day and night. He spends his free time on duty. He barely manages two or three hours of rest at home before another air raid begins. One air raid follows another, and he drags himself up onto the roof, reeling with tiredness. Most people are already drifting about like sleepy flies. They're fine while they're on their feet, but as soon as they sit down their eyes close of their own accord.

At least there was some happy news from the front today. Our troops have taken Vilnius back from the enemy.[1]

I'm completely shattered. The fifth air raid lasted an hour and a quarter. Just five minutes later there was another warning: the sixth so far today. I'm not taking my coat off any more. Long-range weapons are thundering in the distance.

Difficult times are upon us. And in these times, I am so proud to be a Leningrader. Our friends throughout the world are watching us. The entire country is following our fate. Thousands and millions of Soviet citizens are ready to help us, to come to the aid of all Leningraders.

Such hardship and difficulty, so many battles still lie ahead! But German boots will never walk our streets. The enemy will not set foot in our city until the last Leningrader dies. But even the enemy is not infinite. Our nerves are strained, but so are his. The enemy will break down before we do. That's how it should be, and that's how it will be.

It's so nice to hear the bugler sound the all-clear. After all, this and the 'Internationale'[2] at eleven o'clock are the only 'music' we ever hear. They haven't played any songs or music on the radio for a long time. Only the latest news, a regular broadcast for young people (in place of the daily chronicle) and

---

1  Vilnius was seized by the Germans on 23 June 1941 and remained under occupation until 13 July 1944.

2  The 'Internationale', the workers' anthem, was created in 1888 when the French composer Pierre de Geyter set the words of the French poet Eugène Pottier to music. The Russian text was written by Arkady Kots in 1902. The 'Internationale' (three out of the six stanzas) became the national anthem of the Soviet Union from 1918 to 1944. From 1944 it was adopted as the official anthem of the All-Union Communist Party (Bolsheviks) (the Communist Party of the Soviet Union).

the occasional broadcast for older schoolchildren. And an ever greater number of encouraging and inspiring stories. The message is the same every time: 'There are many difficult ordeals and sacrifices ahead of us, but victory will be ours. We are not alone. The whole country stands with us. The entire civilized world stands with us. All eyes are on us, and everyone is certain of our victory. People of Leningrad, gather your strength. Do not allow the glorious name of our city to be defamed.'

Bombs are exploding, the ground is shaking.
There's a crimson glow, like sunrise.
Rage away, you beast, but your fury is in vain,
For you will never capture my home city.

The darkness is disturbed by an enemy flare.
We will pay him back for everything.
Blood has been spilled on Soviet soil.
Hitler will pay for this in full.

Buildings collapse, windows tremble.
Swastika-bearing pilots bomb our city.
While our anti-aircraft missiles sing.
Having dropped their load, the Nazis flee.

As dawn rises over its buildings,
The injured city is silent, apprehensive.
People are working hard, sparing no effort,
The sooner to dress its wounds.

City of mine, you are being ravaged by a hateful foe,
Who burns with a ferocious malice towards you.
But the enemy will never see with his own eyes
Your wide streets, straight as an arrow.

City of mine, bearing the name of your leader,
Great city, creation of Tsar Peter.
We stand as one, burning with the desire
To defend you, Leningrad.

## 14 September 1941

The Germans are using long-range weapons to fire at us.[1] It was our district's turn to be targeted yesterday. Our apartment block was left intact, but there were shells falling literally all around us: on Ivanovskaya, on Razyezzhaya 16, in the Vladimirsky Gardens, on Marat Street, on Pravda Street, near the Bolshoi Drama Theatre, not far from the Aleksandrinsky Theatre and in various other places. These shells either flew over our building, or fell short of us, or landed close by. But we could have been killed at any moment. Why can't our troops find and bomb those damned guns? It might have been better if they'd dropped two small 2,000 kilo bombs . . . That way 1,000 lives could have been saved. After all, everyone wants to live. Those who have already been killed wanted to live too. Among those killed were children, babes in arms, old people, young

---

1 Between 4 September and 31 December 1941 there were only twelve days when the city was not subjected to artillery fire. During this period, according to official data from the headquarters of the local civil air defence organization (MPVO), Leningrad was the target of 13,077 artillery shells, 3,493 high-explosive bombs and 55,841 incendiary bombs.

girls and boys, all of whom really wanted to live. But an artillery shell doesn't choose its victim. This sinister piece of metal is blind, it doesn't spare anyone and there is no way to hide from it. The only salvation is to spend your whole life sitting in the basement, but for many that is impossible.

I heard with my own ears the whirr of an enemy shell, then a whistle, a crack, the thunderclap of a building collapsing and the rumbling echo that followed. It was awful! Terrifying!

But there haven't been any air raids today.

Strangely, there were ten air raids on the 10th and eleven on the 11th, but only two on the twelfth: ten o'clock in the morning and ten o'clock in the evening, and the latter was not even 'announced'. On the 13th, yesterday, there was only one air raid, and it came at a time when no one was expecting it: three o'clock in the morning. Over the course of those three terrible days – 8, 9 and 10 September – we Leningraders became accustomed to the wail of the siren at more or less precisely eleven, at which everyone would rush down to the bomb shelter (those who valued their lives), and the performance would begin: rockets, the drone of aeroplanes, the thunder of high-explosive bombs, the whistle of incendiary bombs. So on the 11th many went down earlier, but the air raid only lasted half an hour. On the 12th there was intensive artillery fire, so many stayed in the shelter all night, particularly those who live on the fifth floor of the part of the building that faces the direction they were firing from.

Incidentally, this basement room shouldn't be called a bomb shelter. It's more like a missile shelter, because it certainly wouldn't withstand a bomb. Over the course of the three days of bombing in Leningrad, it became apparent that these shelters were almost always either demolished by a bomb or blocked with piles of debris. This is what happened on

5th Krasnoarmeiskaya Street, for example. A large bomb hit a solid nine-storey brick building and destroyed a large section of it, right down to the foundations. Part of the wall directly above the bomb shelter was left standing but threatened to collapse at any moment, so it was impossible to rescue those in the shelter – they had to knock the wall down, but as a consequence many lives were unfortunately lost.

## 19 September 1941

The sirens began to wail at four o'clock this afternoon. That was the fourth air-raid warning today. I put my coat on and continued reading my book, somehow persuading myself that everything would be fine because they never dropped bombs in the daytime. So I didn't go straight down, but I did get ready.

Then the anti-aircraft gunfire began. It got closer and closer. They've set up a military launchpad for anti-aircraft guns on the skating rink behind our building. It's extremely dangerous. So when the anti-aircraft guns began to roar from the launchpad, I decided that it was time to go. As I was running to the staircase I heard a terrible howl and a whistle directly overhead, or so it seemed. People were darting out of their apartments and shooting downstairs, like arrows from a bow.

'Quick, quick, the bombs are right above us,' someone shouted.

We moved with even greater haste. There was a muffled explosion, then another and another. Another whistle, a howl and another explosion. We instinctively huddled together. It felt as though the ceiling were about to cave in on us.

Finally we were in the shelter. We were all shaking. We were safe. But nobody could believe how lucky we had been. Indeed. It was simply our good fortune that the bombs fell on the road rather than on our building.

Towards evening we found out the results of the bombing. They were high-explosive bombs: three fell at the Five Corners[1] and three fell between the Five Corners and Nakhimson Square.[2] One bomb destroyed a building on Kolokolnaya, and one fell on Pravda Street. By sheer luck, our building remained intact. Even the windows. But the windows are broken in the buildings on both sides of the places where bombs fell. Oh, and I forgot to say that one of the bombs hit a tram on Nakhimson Square, but it was empty. The passengers had already got out.

Bombs have destroyed the tram lines in many places. The overhead wires are damaged, so the trams are all stranded.

Yes, today was an awful day, but there are many more ahead!

---

1  Unofficial name for the crossroads formed by the intersection of Zagorodny Prospekt and Lomonosov, Rubinshtein and Razyezzhaya streets.

2  Now Vladimirskaya Square.

## 22 September 1941

I'm still alive and able to write in my diary.

I am no longer so sure that they're not going to surrender Leningrad.

So much has been said, so many loud words and speeches: Kiev and Leningrad are unassailable fortresses! The Nazis will never set foot in the prosperous capital of Ukraine, or the northern pearl of our country – Leningrad! But now this: on the radio today they announced that after many days of fierce fighting our troops have abandoned . . . Kiev! What does this mean? Nobody understands it.

We are under fire, we are being bombed.

Tamara came round at four o'clock yesterday, and we went for a walk. The first thing we did was to go and look at the damage caused by the bombs. We didn't have to go far. One bomb fell on Bolshaya Moskovskaya, near Vera Nikitichna's apartment block, and almost demolished an entire building. You can't see the damage from the street, only from the courtyard. The windows in the neighbouring buildings, including Vera Nikitichna's, are missing. The paved surface of Nakhimson Square has been damaged in four places, as a direct result of the bombs. The windows are also missing on the side where the pet shop is, between the bend in Nakhimson Prospekt and the lane opposite the New Children's Theatre.[1] But the damage on Strelkin Lane is even worse. In one place the buildings on both sides of the lane have been completely destroyed. The lane is strewn with debris. There isn't a single window left in any of the buildings. But the most terrible sight was one of the buildings where a whole corner had been torn away and you could see everything inside – rooms, hallways and their contents. There was an oak sideboard standing against the wall in a room on the fifth floor, next to a little table, and (this looked very strange) an antique clock with a long pendulum hanging on the wall. Against the missing wall a sofa stood with its back to us, covered in a white cloth.

On the way home Tamara and I ran into Misha Ilyashev. He had an awkward smile on his face the entire time we were talking, which made us feel awkward too. We shook hands. Talked for a bit. Then shook hands again as we said goodbye. He said that he was going to a canteen to get something to eat. Again my behaviour left something to be desired. I didn't look at him properly, just kept glancing at him. I felt nervous again, for some reason. Misha has really grown up. He looks a lot stronger, and his hands are calloused, working hands. He's like a different boy.

---

1 This refers to Leningrad's Novy Teatr Yunogo Zritelya (New Theatre of the Young Spectator) or Novy TYuZ, as it was known, which operated from 1935 to 1945, first in Leningrad and subsequently in evacuation. It was founded by Boris Zon, who was both managing and artistic director. Originally located on Zhelyabova Street (now Bolshaya Konyushennaya), then on Nakhimson (now Vladimirsky) Prospekt, the theatre was evacuated in 1941 to Anzhero-Sudzhensk. (A. Belinsky, 'Khram dovoennogo detstva', from the book *Nedoskazannoe* www.theatre.spb.ru/seasons/2_2_2000/1_case/2.htm, accessed 11 March 2011).

After saying goodbye to Misha, literally five steps later we saw Grisha Khaunin. He either didn't see us or was pretending not to, I don't know, but we walked straight past him.

Tamara and I queued outside the bread shop for some sparkling water, then sat for half an hour in the air-raid shelter, then spent half an hour arguing over whose place we should go to. I won, so we went to our apartment. Tamara got stuck at ours because there was another air raid that lasted until eight o'clock. During this time she helped me write a note to Vova. The scoundrel has behaved discourteously towards me again: our whole building is painting the attic with limewash,[2] and we're supposed to pay 15 roubles to cover our share of the attic. Mama Lena and I decided that we would paint it ourselves instead. I decided to ask my boyfriend to help, particularly as he has experience of the work involved. I went round to see him, but he wasn't at home so I left a note with his father asking him to come and help us. But he didn't come. If he'd been busy, he could have called round briefly and explained. No, it's unforgivable. Even if he had only been an acquaintance (never mind a boyfriend), then he should have come out of courtesy, which is something all well-brought-up boys of his age ought to recognize. So I wrote him a very strongly worded note and gave it to Tamara to pass on to him. Tamara and I also agreed that if he wrote a reply, she would bring it to me after five o'clock today, and if I didn't hear anything I would go round to hers.

Tamara didn't come today. I didn't go to hers either, because

---

2  In order to improve their fire resistance, interior attic walls were painted with special lime paint that had been developed at the State Institute of Applied Chemistry at the end of July 1941. Throughout August and September the interiors of virtually all attic rooms in Leningrad were painted with this compound, which significantly reduced the incidence of fires.

there were so many air raids. So I don't actually know whether he has answered my note or not. It's all very strange. In my opinion, if Vova still sees us as friends and he's ashamed of his discourteous behaviour, then of course he will reply to my note. However, if he sees my note as a worthless scrap of paper and wants nothing more to do with me, there will be no reply. Though perhaps he will show my note to the other boys and they will compose a reply together. But I won't value that kind of reply at all.

# 4 October 1941

I haven't written for such a long time. But today I feel an urge to write. Dear God, what are they doing to us, to my fellow Leningraders and me?

I'm working in the hospital wing of the Clara Zetkin Institute of Maternity and Infancy Protection.[1] We hospital orderlies work twenty-four-hour shifts: I work from nine in the morning to nine the next morning, then I have a day off until nine the following morning. So I am able to sleep only every other night. It's very hard, but not unbearable. However when I don't manage to get any sleep at all, just a few moments dozing in the bomb shelter, then it's horrendous. For example, now it's quarter to seven. Between half past seven yesterday evening and six o'clock this morning there were six air raids. Of these, two lasted about three hours, two lasted two hours, and the final

---

1   This scientific institute opened on 7 January 1925. From 1928 to 1932 it was known as the Clara Zetkin Scientific Research Institute of Maternity and Infancy Protection. In 1932 it became a higher-education establishment (university teaching hospital), and in February 1935 it was renamed the Leningrad Paediatric Medical Institute. It was known as the Saint Petersburg Paediatric Medical Institute from 1992 to 1994, when it was renamed the Saint Petersburg State Paediatric Medical Academy.

two were an hour and a half and an hour. I'm working in a hospital and it's very hard work, but I'm getting used to it. On the positive side, on days when I'm working I don't go hungry and I'm entitled to a first category ration card with 400g of bread per day.

I haven't seen Tamara since we composed that note to Vova and promised to see each other the following day. Yesterday I wrote her a note and asked Rozaliya Pavlovna to give it to Osya, so that he could pass it on to Tamara. So I still don't know anything about the fate of my message to Vova. But I have no regrets about writing to him so abruptly.

During one of the air raids I somehow got talking to Ida Isaevna about friendships between men and women. You can love only one man, but at the same time it is possible to be friends with many men. Ida Isaevna told me that when she was seventeen she was friends with some of the boys she knew, and their friendship is still as strong as ever. Five of them from her class were friends – two girls and three boys.

We're also two girls – Tamara and I, and three boys – Vova, Misha and Yanya. I don't know why we aren't friends. Do the boys treat us badly? No. Are they somehow unsuitable as friends? Again no, on the contrary. They're exactly the kind of boys it's good to have as friends. So what's wrong? I don't know. But in my opinion, we don't know how to talk to one another.

It's a pity, such a pity. In these bleak wartime days we are the only five from our class left in Leningrad. We could be developing lifelong friendships. There's nobody stopping us. Dima, Emma, Roza, none of the other girls are here. But still!

Tamara and I both have fairly calm temperaments. The boys are also quite reserved. Relations between us feel somehow strained, because we're so formal with one another. Besides, Yanya is not really like the rest of us. He's so studious, it's hard to be friends with someone like that. We would become friends more easily if relations between us were simpler, more straightforward. Like normal relationships between boys and girls. If we were attracted to one another. If they made advances towards us . . . and we resisted.

## 5 October 1941

Last night was even worse than the night before. True, there were only four air raids rather than six. But they were so horrendous. The floor was shuddering continuously due to the high-explosive bombs. During the second air raid I was sitting next to two women. One young, one elderly. The younger woman spent the entire time weeping and wailing. She soon told us what they had been through during the first air raid. After getting off the tram, they ended up in one of the bomb shelters on Zagorodny Prospekt. They (mother and daughter) went inside the bomb shelter but many others, particularly the men, stayed by the entrance. Moments later a bomb exploded, causing the entrance to the bomb shelter to cave in and burying everyone who was standing there. The ceiling of the shelter sagged a little, but everyone inside was unharmed. They smashed one of the windows and climbed out through it. They saw people digging in the rubble, pulling out those who were buried. Many of them were alive but no longer of sound mind.

This is what happened during the third air raid: I was woken up by the sound of running in the hallway. The siren was already wailing. I got dressed before the others and ran downstairs. I heard loud, agitated voices coming from outside, so I glanced into the courtyard. I heard: 'It's burning, burning below the gates, in the attic.' I didn't fully understand, but I realized that something was burning in our building. I ran to our apartment and warned my family of the danger, then ran down to the bomb shelter. It was full of people, both sitting and standing. Some were half-dressed, with children and large suitcases. Just then the firing began.

## 12 October 1941

I'm going to work as an orderly at the military hospital. I'm going to help wounded soldiers. I'm very grateful to Ida Isaevna, who arranged it all. I'm going to help those thanks to whom I still have a home and a family. I will put all my energies into it. At home I will be a member of the household with equal rights. No one will be able to accuse me of sponging. Ida Isaeva says that there are a lot of girls working as orderlies. Maybe I'll become friends with one of them. And the soldiers, the wounded – they're people too. Maybe some of the wounded will be boys my age, or seventeen or eighteen. Maybe one of them will take a liking to me and I'll find a boyfriend. I didn't think twice about whether or not to accept the job.

Of course I will do the job and help my family. I will have my own money and I will have equal rights.

Begone, doubt and sorrow.
I look boldly towards tomorrow.
Soon you will see my modest efforts,
Beautiful city, Hero City.

Help, care, love for those
Whose blood has been spilled for us.
We Leningraders will give our all.
We will defend our city from the black plague.

We have been sent a brotherly greeting from London. This is their message to us: 'The Thames is a sister to the Neva. London and Leningrad are brothers in the fight against the Nazi brutes.'[1]

It's ten to four. The seventh air raid is over. My head is pounding. I want to go to sleep. The eighth air raid is over. Tamara came to see me. We talked for a while, and then there was another air-raid warning. We went to the shelter and carried on talking to our hearts' content. All-clear. I persuaded Tamara to come up to our apartment for another half an hour. But just as we went into the kitchen, the siren began to wail again. We went back downstairs again, but not for long this time. We met Kapa Lobanova in the shelter and talked to her for a while. Then Tamara left. I really like spending time with her. We chat so openly about whatever comes into our heads.

Now it's quarter to eight. There have already been ten air raids.

I was interested to learn that Tamara doesn't like young children. I adore them. Tamara can't bear it when they cry. Their crying drives her mad. It makes her want to hit the crying child over the head with something heavy. But when I see a crying child I want to put my arms around it, to make it trust me.

---

1 It is not obvious which message from England Lena is quoting here. Many English organizations sent messages of support to their Leningrad counterparts during this period. Over the course of several days *Leningradskaya Pravda* published messages from Oxford University to Leningrad State University, from the British Museum to The Saltykov-Shchedrin State Public Library, from the 7th Anti-Aircraft Division in north-east England to the defenders of Leningrad (*Leningradskaya Pravda*, 8, 10 and 11 October 1941).

## 12 October 1941

I'm already quite accustomed to my work. The patients like me. I saw my first dead person on the 8th. Two people died on our ward that day: a pregnant woman, who had been wounded in the stomach, and a man who died from gas gangrene. I'm not frightened of the dead at all. I just felt so sorry for them it made me want to cry. Especially the man, because it wasn't long since I'd seen him alive. He had been smiling like the others and smoking a *papirosa*, and he had a really nice face. He was so young and good-looking. They took him to the dressing station and kept him there for five hours. They performed all kinds of procedures on him: blood transfusions, injections and so on. Finally they wheeled him into the corridor, and I found out that they were taking him into the operating theatre to amputate his leg. He lay there smiling, then they took him off. When they brought him back he was unrecognizable: breathing heavily, groaning in agony, pale and trembling. That's how I remember him before he died. They sent me to the dispensary for oxygen, but as I was running back the doctor met me in the corridor and said: 'There's no hurry, Mukhina, the oxygen is no longer needed. He's dead.' I couldn't believe my ears and ran to my ward, but he had already been carried out of the ward and was lying there covered with a sheet. It was awful.

The longest air raid so far was on the 7th. It lasted from half past seven to half past one. Exactly six hours. Tamara and I sat in the shelter all that time. It's hard to imagine: six hours.

Apparently there were some terrible air raids yesterday (I wasn't at home). A large number of high-explosive bombs fell on our district. Many of them failed to explode and they managed to defuse them. Apparently six high-explosive bombs exploded on Yamskaya.[1]

I'm going to see Tamara tomorrow (if I live that long).

---

1  Lena Mukhina is using the old street name. Yamskaya Street was renamed Dostoevsky Street in 1915.

## 13 October 1941

It's now quarter past seven.

The air raid has only just finished. It didn't last long, but it was a particularly bad one. Zagorodny was strewn with incendiary bombs. Instead of going to the bomb shelter I decided to go straight to our housing office, because I'm on duty today from eight to eleven. When I went outside, I immediately saw that there was a tram on fire in the direction of Vitebsk Station. Little green stars, pieces of burning phosphorus, were falling from the roof. One of the buildings at the Five Corners, the one where they keep radio and electrical equipment, has a tower on top of it – and this tower was burning too.

A no. 9 tram had stopped outside our building, and one of the incendiary bombs fell on the tramline right next to the carriage. If it hadn't been for our boys, who managed to put it out, the tram would have caught fire. The young men from our building saved that tram. A high-explosive bomb fell somewhere nearby, and the entire building shook, right down to its foundations. What a life! But this afternoon Tamara and I went to the Oktyabr cinema to watch some new films. They were all short films with music in, including *Old Guard* and *The Adventures of Korzinkina.*[1] The last film was so funny and entertaining that we laughed out loud.

---

1   On 16 October 1941 *Leningradskaya Pravda* published the following announcement in their 'Cinema' column: 'Don't miss these new feature films: (1) *Violin Concerto*, by award-winning director V. Petrov, starring Bondi; (2) *Old Guard*, by award-winning director S. Gerasimov, starring B. Poslavsky and Blinov; (3) *The Adventures of Korzinkina*, starring award-winning actress Yanina Zheimo and award-winning circus artist Musin. Directed by Fridrikh Ermler and produced by the Lenfilm Studio (Order of Lenin).' However the premiere of these films had already taken place in ten of the city's cinemas on 9 October 1941. It is worth noting that the only one of these films listed in cinema repertoires was *The Adventures of Korzinkina*, although Lena Mukhina's diary implies that all three short films were screened consecutively.

## 16 October 1941

Winter is here. The first snow fell yesterday.[1] The Germans are closing in on us, surrounding us with an insurmountable wall. It's frightening to look at the map. The latest updates are disheartening. Our troops have surrendered Mariupol, Bryansk and Vyazma.[2] Tense battles are being fought on the Kalinin front. Well, this means that Kalinin has effectively fallen. It's actually terrifying, what's happening. Vyazma is 150 km from Moscow. Which means that the Germans are 150 km from Moscow. On the radio today they announced for the first time: 'The situation on the western front is serious. The Germans have amassed vast numbers of tanks and motorized infantry

---

1   Other contemporary accounts attest to the fact that the first snow fell in the middle of October 1941. 'A white coating has lain upon Leningrad since yesterday. Snow has fallen,' wrote the artist A. A. Gryaznov on 15 October (A. A. Gryaznov, 'Dnevnik 1941–1942', *Chelovek v blokade. Novye svidetel'stva*, St Petersburg, 2008, p. 35). On 21 October the Executive Committee of the Leningrad City Council decreed that the city's central heating would operate from 25 October (*Leningradskaya Pravda*, 21 October 1941).

2   The Germans occupied Bryansk on 6 October 1941. Vyazma was taken the following day, and Mariupol on 8 October.

and have broken through our defences. After suffering heavy losses our troops have retreated.' That's what they said on the radio. They've never broadcast anything like that before.

The general mood is one of despondency. It is starting to seem as though it's no longer our destiny to see brighter days. It's no longer our destiny to make it through to the bright, joyous month of May.

The Germans will probably reduce Leningrad to ruins and then occupy it. Those of us who manage to escape will live in the forests. And there we will die, or we will freeze to death, or die of starvation, or be shot.

Yes, a terrible winter has begun, and it will be cold and hungry for many thousands of people. Tamara is coming round later today, and Aka and I are going to study English. Tomorrow I will go to work again. It's no better there. Anechka and two other women have died. I spent almost all of my last shift sitting at the bedside of a dying woman.

I saw Valery in passing. It appears that he's not going to work with us after all. He was standing in the corridor without a robe, and I didn't recognize him. He said hello first. He's a nice boy. It's a pity our acquaintance was so brief.

Today, and when I was asleep yesterday afternoon, I dreamed of Vova. I dreamed that he came to me hungry, without any clothes, and I fed him and dressed him, and he was grateful to me and said that only now did he realize what it meant to have a true friend. Then someone was chasing me with a knife. It was in the garden in the autumn, and just as they were about to catch up with me I suddenly saw Vova walking with his friends. He tripped up my persecutor and saved me, and then, and then something else happened.

## 18 October 1941

Yesterday evening was really frightening. The air-raid siren went off at eight o'clock, just as we were giving the patients their supper. The anti-aircraft guns immediately began firing very close by. Then suddenly there was a huge burst of thunder and the sound of breaking glass. I was in the women's ward at the time, and the patients immediately began shouting and groaning, many of them becoming hysterical. Anisimov ran in with the duty doctor. Somehow they managed to restore calm. When it had quietened down a little I carried the plates to the canteen with another orderly. They told me I could scrape the leftover *kasha* out of the pot. I had just started eating when I became aware of a strange noise coming from outside the window – people shouting, and police whistles. I asked one of the nurses what was happening. She reacted with astonishment: 'Didn't you know? There's a fire out there, across the street. The Karl Marx factory is on fire. Go and have a look.' She took me to the bathroom and drew the curtain to one side, and I saw how bright it was outside, brighter than daylight. Great tongues of flame were shooting up into the sky, and red smoke was swirling all around. Yes, it was an enormous fire at the Karl

Marx factory, across the street from our building. I understood straight away what the noise was. It was the sound of firemen working and shouting to one another, fire engines arriving and the droning of the water pumps. They didn't manage to put the fire out until four o'clock in the morning.

Vladimirova died in the night. They brought a new patient with a head injury and a seventeen-year-old boy with a neck injury, who had been one of the firemen on the roof.

## 11 November 1941

It's already November. There's snow everywhere. It's freezing. I'm going to school[1] and studying, and it feels as though
everything I lived through in October was just a bad dream.
It's hard to imagine that only a short time ago I was getting up
at six o'clock every morning. By quarter to seven Mama and I
were already leaving the house. It was cold, it was dark. Then
the packed tram, the entrance gate, the garden with the path
trodden straight to the door. I take my coat off, and there I am
in my white robe and white headscarf . . . There are the patients,
the bedpans, the orders: Lena, do this, Lena, do that, Lena, run
to the dispensary, Lena, run to the lab, Lena, take this urine
sample for analysis. Well, it wasn't a dream, it was real. I was
earning money. But suddenly I lost my job. And now I'm back at
school. I'm studying at School No. 30, at Chernyshev Lane 30.[2]

---

1   According to a resolution passed by the Executive Committee of the Leningrad City
    Council on 26 October 1941, students in the seventh to tenth grades were to return
    to their schools for the start of the new school year on 3 November ('Vospominaniya
    L. E. Raskina', *Oborona Leningrada 1941–1944*, Leningrad, 1968, p. 747).

2   School No. 30 was in fact based at Chernyshev (now Lomonosova) Lane 13; it had

Up until yesterday there were five boys and four girls from our class: Misha I., Misha Ts., Vova I., Yanya Ya., Osya B. and Tamara A., Nadya K., Lida S. and Bella K., as well as Galya V. I saw Vova there yesterday too, but five of them were missing today. I found out from Tamara, who found out from Osya when she saw him this morning in the corridor, that Misha I., Misha Ts., Yanya and Vova Itkinson have moved to a different school – School No. 36 on Borodinskaya. Nothing in life is reliable.

We studied in the same class for eight years. We were friends, so to speak, but now they've suddenly disappeared without so much as a word to us, without even saying goodbye. Vova, how I . . . (there's no point saying it). We used to be so close. We went to the cinema together, we had such meaningful conversations, we were good friends, but now all of a sudden he, his name and his face have been erased from my life forever. I just don't understand how they can have done this. Is it really that simple, to change schools at the drop of a hat? But why? On what grounds? They haven't explained it at all. Don't they at least owe us that? Don't eight years mean anything to them? How could they have the nerve? No, it doesn't make any sense. But then again, why not? On the contrary, it's perfectly straightforward! The simplest thing in the world! I'm just too old-fashioned! I need to get used to it. That's how everything is done these days.

Loyalty! Friendship! These concepts are as far removed from us, the youth of today, as we are from the sun.

---

also been known as School No. 318 since the beginning of the year, according to a resolution passed by the Executive Committee of the Leningrad City Council on 14 January 1941. Lessons did not resume after the winter holidays, though students were able to attend School No. 319 (formerly No. 32) in the building next door (Chernyshev Lane 11) in May and June 1942.

So, it's all over. Vova, we knew each other once but now we've gone our separate ways. Everything is fading like smoke, and we will forget one another, but one day you will be looking through a photo album and you will remember Lena Mukhina, that open-hearted girl, and you will read the inscription on the reverse of the photo: 'To my Ugly Duckling, from Lena', and then you will smile. Perhaps fate will bring us together again in the future, but I will never forget you, Vova, come what may.

I will remember you for the rest of my life.

I can't help loving you.

I will never forget you.

And I will live with longing for you in my heart.

So I would even if you were the very last scoundrel on earth. A lowly beast, undeserving of attention. But no, you are my first love, you are the one who first lit something in my heart, without even knowing it yourself, and this feeling will burn inside me for as long as I live, sometimes flaring up brightly so that my whole being is consumed with the bitterness of disappointment and a lingering sense of grievance, sometimes smouldering gently. To me, you are the dearest person on earth. Be happy in your life, and may you never know trouble or sorrow.

May God grant you all the best.

Goodbye, Vova!

Goodbye.

Goodness, I feel quite unsettled. But is he really worth it? There will be other boys. There are better boys than Vova in our class. Vova Fridman, for example, and Genya K. And our youth leader, Tolka, is just like Andrei. He has the same voice and mannerisms. Genya, who sits behind me, is a nice boy too, though he seems a little meek. But never mind, there's plenty of time for us to get to know one another.

Don't lose heart, Lena. Your first love is always followed by your second.

Be brave, move on.

If I survive, everything will be just fine.

But will I survive? Every day our city receives so many unpleasant gifts by airmail. Leningrad is surrounded. The enemy is surrounding Moscow. The Germans are approaching Tula.[3] The whole of Ukraine has been taken. Donbass. The USA are helping us with weapons and food supplies. The future is uncertain. But whatever happens I want to live, and as long as I am alive I want to love, but whom? We shall see. Maybe one of the new boys in our new class will turn out to be my future boyfriend.

---

3   The Tula defensive operation ran from 24 October to 5 December 1941.

*12 November 1941*

Every day there are terrible bombings. Every day there is artillery fire.

## 16 November 1941

Another air-raid warning. Every evening at half past seven: here come the Germans, right on time.

I had a miserable day today. Aka went out to look for something to eat at nine o'clock in the morning and didn't get back until five o'clock. Mama Lena and I had already resigned ourselves to not having any dinner, when suddenly Aka appeared, and instead of being empty-handed she had brought some meat jelly – 500g of meat jelly We immediately warmed it up and ate two full bowls of hot soup each. We can just about cope with the way we're living at the moment, but if the situation gets any worse I don't know how we will survive. Up until quite recently, Mama used to be able to get soup at work without her ration card. They gave us soup at school once too. But the following day they issued a decree making it available on ration cards only.

150g of bread is clearly not enough for us.[1] Every morning

---

1   From 13 November 1941 the daily bread allowance for white-collar workers, adult dependants and children under twelve was 150g; the daily allowance for manual workers, engineers and technicians was 300g.

Aka buys bread for herself and for me. I eat almost all of mine before school and spend the rest of the day without any bread. I just don't know what else to do. Maybe this would be better: to get a main course at the school canteen using my grain ration card every other day, but not take any bread, so that on alternate days I could have 300g of bread to eat. I'll have to try it. I don't feel very well at all these days. There's a gnawing feeling in my stomach all the time. It's my birthday soon, on the 21st of this month. I'm going to be seventeen. I'll celebrate it somehow. At least it's on the first day of the third ten-day period, so we'll definitely have some sweets. I am so hungry.

When the war ends and everything's back to normal and we can buy things again, I'm going to buy a kilo of black bread, a kilo of gingerbread and half a litre of cottonseed oil. I'll crumble the bread and the gingerbread, then pour plenty of oil over the top and mash it all together, then I'll fetch a tablespoon and take great pleasure in eating my fill. Then Mama and I will bake all kinds of pies – with meat, with potato, with cabbage, with grated carrot. And then Mama and I will fry potatoes and will eat them golden and sizzling, straight from the pan. We will eat noodles with *smetana*, *pelmeni*, macaroni with tomato sauce and fried onions, and warm crusty white bread with butter and salami or cheese. The salami will have to be thick enough to really sink your teeth into it when you take a bite. Mama and I will eat buckwheat *kasha* with cold milk, and then the same *kasha* fried in a pan with onion so that it shines with butter. Finally we will eat hot buttery *blinchiki* with jam and fat, fluffy *olady*. Dear God, we're going to eat so much we'll frighten ourselves.

Tamara and I have decided to write a book about the lives of Soviet school students in the ninth and tenth grades. About fleeting passions, about first love and friendship. Essentially the kind of book we would like to read ourselves but which, unfortunately, does not yet exist.

All-clear, the air raid is over. It's quarter past eight. Time for bed. School tomorrow.

Goodbye for now.

## 21 November 1941

So my birthday has arrived. I'm seventeen today. I'm lying in bed with a temperature as I write. Aka has gone out in search of some butter, and grain or macaroni. I don't know when she'll be back. Maybe she'll come back without anything. But I'm happy anyway – this morning Aka gave me my 125g of bread[1] and 200g of sweets. I've eaten almost all of the bread already – 125g is hardly anything, just a small slice, but I have to make the sweets last for ten days. First I decided to allow myself three sweets a day, but I've already eaten nine so I decided to eat another four sweets today because it's my birthday. From tomorrow I will be strict with myself and eat only two sweets a day.

Our city is still under great strain. We're being bombed and we're under artillery fire, but that's not so bad – we have become so accustomed to it that we marvel at ourselves. What's

---

1 Bread rations in Leningrad reached their lowest point on 20 November 1941, when the daily allowance for manual workers, engineers and technicians was reduced to 250g and that for white-collar workers, adult dependants and children under 12 to just 125g.

really dreadful is the fact that the food situation is getting worse with every day. We don't have enough bread. We're grateful to England for what they are sending. Cocoa, chocolate, real coffee, coconut oil, sugar – it's all from England, and Aka is very proud of this. But bread, what about bread? Why aren't they sending us flour? Leningraders have to eat bread, otherwise their productivity will suffer. Everyone is saying, and this is all they talk about on the radio, that we will push the enemy back from Leningrad soon, that we won't have to wait much longer. And as soon as the enemy has been pushed back, vital supplies will come pouring into Leningrad. But for now we must be patient. Yes, and we are patient, but it is so hard. Sometimes you lose hope and think, no, we're all going to die like flies, it is not our destiny to see the glorious day of our victory. But these thoughts must be chased away. They are harmful thoughts. Dear God! How I hope that Aka, Mama Lena and I survive this difficult time, to live and breathe freely once again. How I wish that Mama would regain some weight and that Aka would feel better too. I'm so worried about Mama and Aka. They won't survive real starvation. What lies ahead is uncertain. Perhaps bread will be available only every two or three days, and there will be nothing in the canteens, and then what? No, they can't allow it to come to that! England and the USA will have to provide us with more food. After all, it's in their interest for the Germans to suffer defeat outside Leningrad. Victory at Leningrad would help Moscow more than anything. And a crushing defeat for the Germans outside Moscow will bring about a turning point in the course of this historic war, specifically, the retreat of the enemy. Sooner, oh how I wish it would come sooner. Every day brings hope of a breakthrough in the enemy's ring around Leningrad.

Tamara came to visit me and . . . brought nothing with her.

Yesterday I gave her my ration cards for grain and meat and asked her to collect lunch from our school canteen today, specifically two main courses on the grain ration card, and if possible two rissoles or two portions of salami on the meat ration card, whatever they had. She promised that she would.

Aka and I had placed all our hopes on what Tamara would bring us today. We had decided that Aka would make two saucepans full of nice thick soup out of the main course, whether it was *kasha* or macaroni or whatever else it might be, and since we were celebrating we would divide the rissoles into three portions and make sandwiches out of them. But oh, what a disaster! Tamara arrives empty-handed. She has brought nothing – no main course, no soup, nothing. Sullen and irritable, she swears that she will never make any promises or do anything for anyone ever again. All I can understand from her explanation is that she spent two breaks queuing and the food ran out both times. When the meat and grain ran out, she bought one portion of soup but then spilled it. I still don't understand how on earth she managed to do that. What I do know is that our situation is utterly dire.

Aka will be back soon – frozen, tired and probably empty-handed. This will finish her off. When she finds out that Tamara didn't bring anything, I don't know how she will cope. And then Mama will come – tired and hungry. She's going to try and get back earlier today, as it's my birthday and, oh God, I don't know what will happen if Aka hasn't managed to rustle something up by then. What a way to 'celebrate' my birthday. No, I'm not going to defend Tamara to Aka or Mama, but I don't want to lose my temper with her either. She was unlucky, that's all. It's the same as if we'd had our ration cards stolen or something similar. Bad luck can happen to anyone.

Of course it's disappointing, bitterly disappointing, that on my birthday of all days we will have to miss dinner and go to bed hungry, and all because of my best friend.

Never mind, now I might as well eat the piece of bread I was saving for the rissoles. And then I'll try to go to sleep, and hopefully I'll sleep right through to the morning.

My dear, darling Mamochka will come home hungry. I will clasp her in my arms, hold her tight and tell her about the sorrow that has befallen us. I don't think she will be angry. After all, she will probably have had something to eat at work. Just as long as she's not angry, as long as my special day is not spoiled. I don't ask for anything more. We will drink a glass of wine each, and then we will have tea with some sweets.

Just as long as we don't argue, as long as everything remains calm and peaceful. This is my most ardent desire.

It's already half past six, and Mama is not back yet. The anti-aircraft guns are firing away furiously outside. It's the second air raid today. Hitler is going to punish us for yesterday, and for today.

Yes, everything happened as I predicted. Aka got home at five o'clock – tired, frozen and empty-handed. She queued for vermicelli but it ran out before her turn. Aunt Sasha was ahead of her so she got some, but Aka didn't. Aunt Sasha didn't even look at Aka. What a cow! She could have let an old woman go in front of her. God, it's impossible to believe our bad luck. It's as though all the gods and devils have turned against us.

I'm so terribly hungry. There's a horrible emptiness in my stomach. I'm so desperate for bread. I want it so badly. Right now I feel as though I would give anything to fill my stomach.

When will we ever feel full? When will we stop suffering? When will we be able to eat something substantial and filling, like a whole plate of *kasha* or macaroni? You can't survive for long on liquid alone. Yet we have been eating nothing but liquid

159

slush for more than a month already. No, it's inconceivable that anyone should have to live like this. Lord, when will this suffering end! Today is my special day, my birthday, which only comes once a year. I remember how Aka always used to bake a special pie and a big pretzel. We would sit at the table, drink tea and wine, clink our glasses. There were always sweets and pastries, sometimes even a cake on the table, and sandwiches with salami and cheese. We didn't generally have guests, particularly the last few years, but the three of us made a point of celebrating the day together. No, I will never forget 21 November 1941. I will remember this day for the rest of my life. On 21 November 1942 (if I am still alive), as I cut a large slice of black bread and spread it with a thick layer of butter, I will remember this day as it was one year before, in 1941, and this thick slice of bread and butter will be a greater luxury to me than any delicacy, more delicious than all the pies, cakes and other tasty treats in the world. Oh God, what pleasure I will take in biting into this bread, this real bread, and savouring every mouthful.

Mother, my dear Mother, where are you? You are lying in the ground, you are dead. You are at peace forever. Meanwhile I am in agony, I'm suffering, suffering together with hundreds and millions of Soviet citizens, and why? Because of the delirious fantasies of a madman, who has taken it upon himself to try and conquer the whole world. It is insane, it is nonsense, yet because of this we are suffering, our stomachs are empty, and our hearts are full of anguish. Dear God, when is all this going to end? Surely it must end at some point?!

## 22 November 1941

As it happened, I celebrated yesterday's birthday this morning instead. At seven o'clock Aka went out to get chocolate, and at nine o'clock she gave me tea, my 125g of bread and 50g of chocolate – real English chocolate. The kind of chocolate you can only dream about. We've never had real foreign chocolate before. Real English chocolate – creamy, fragrant, hard, heavy and beautiful. It came in large bars, four of them for a 50g ration. So each bar must be 12½g. It's so tasty, so bittersweet – proper chocolate, in other words, all the way from India.

Even if Leningrad runs out of bread, as long as they give us chocolate instead we won't starve to death. England has sent us plenty of chocolate, and they will send more. They're giving out other English products like real sago, raisins and (*)[1] on children's ration cards too. But only on children's ration cards, the same way they give out semolina and rice.

And we have proper soup, the soup of all soups! Aka brought it from school. What a nuisance that we didn't realize this before,

---

1 A single asterisk in parentheses indicates where a word in the original diary is completely illegible. The word has therefore been omitted entirely.

because Aka could easily have gone and got lunch yesterday to save us entrusting it to Tamara.

Today Aka took two main courses, namely rice with a piece of butter on each portion. Aka gave one piece of butter to me, then put the other piece with the rice and made a marvellous soup. It was so tasty, and there was enough for each of us to have a bowlful and three extra ladles.

We're going to organize things differently from now on. I'm taking all three of our grain ration cards and working it out to make sure that we have enough grain for the whole ten-day period, and specifically for the next eight days. It would be good if it worked out as 100g of grain each per day, but at the very least we will get 75g each, which is one soup and one main course.

Instead of three large bars of chocolate, as I expected, all there is left in my glass jar is just one pitiful morsel. I will eat this soon too, because it's silly to leave such a tiny bit. And what remains of my sweets? Aka gave me a whole bag of sweets only yesterday. I counted them straight away. There were thirty-four pretty, round sweets. I swapped four of them for two soy sweets. But today there were only five pathetic sweets left. Where have the rest of them gone? That's right, I ate them all yesterday, because I didn't have any dinner. Yes, all I had to eat yesterday was bread and sweets. I ate twenty-five sweets yesterday, salving my conscience by telling myself that it was my birthday, that I would eat them today and tomorrow I wouldn't eat a single one. But 'tomorrow' is here now, and those five sorry sweets that I spared yesterday have also met their end in my shameless mouth. I'm feeling utterly ashamed of myself. I was hungry yesterday, that was a different matter. But today I had bread, chocolate, soup . . . surely I could have left those unfortunate victims in peace? They were doomed to be eaten anyway, so it wouldn't have hurt to let them live another day or two. But no, I couldn't wait. I held out for a long time but then I finally ate one, and after that I could not stop until I had devoured everything edible that I could lay my hands on. So I started eating, and I finished off all the sweets and all the chocolate. And there are still eight days left. Once again I will spend these eight days drinking tea with nothing to accompany it, thoroughly exasperated with myself for managing to eat twenty-five sweets in one day.

My chocolate bar, my beautiful bar of real English chocolate, where are you? Why did I eat you? You were so beautiful, I could have simply feasted upon you with my eyes, but instead I ate you. I'm such a pig. Now my only hope, or rather my one consolation, is that if Mama wishes to share hers then I will have one more bar. But I will not eat it. God, no, I will keep it. I will simply admire it and eat it only when Mama no longer has a single crumb of chocolate left.

I've just re-read my entire diary. My God, how shallow I have become. All I think and write about is food, but so many other things exist apart from food.

The Germans have been getting up to all kinds of mischief. They're firing at us relentlessly from their long-range weapons. Well, never mind. They will be silenced soon enough. An aeroplane has just flown overhead, quite low, in the direction that the firing is coming from.

Normal life is continuing in the city. Factories are maintaining their productivity. Shops are trading. Cinemas, theatres and the circus are all open.[2] Schoolchildren are studying. True,

---

2  According to listings information, seven theatres were still open in Leningrad on 22 November 1941: the Lensovet, Leninsky Komsomol, Comedy, Musical Comedy and Drama Theatres, and also the New Children's Theatre (see earlier footnote) and

the practicalities of life are different: the gas has been cut off, there's no kerosene for sale, people cook their meals on make-shift stoves, over firewood, over kindling. But most people are registered at the city's various canteens. Hardly anyone bothers going down to the air-raid shelter any more, as they're so exhausted from systematic malnutrition that they simply don't have the energy to walk downstairs and back up again. People just want a bit of normality. There's not really anything to buy at the moment, so the boys are carrying a lot of money about with them. They go to the cinema and theatre nearly every day, and during breaks and air-raid warnings they go to the shelter to play cards. Every break and even during some lessons they play cards for money. It's the height of debauchery. I have often watched them play. They often win 5–7 roubles at a time, and sometimes even 8. I've seen them lose all respect for money, the way they carelessly toss a 'tryoshka' – a 3-rouble note – onto the desk or 'bank' it. And they make no haste to pick up a stray rouble that falls to the floor, let alone a 20-kopek piece. At the same time many of the boys hide their winnings away greedily, whereas others, on the contrary, do so with casual nonchalance.

I looked through my postcards yesterday. They used to make such beautiful postcards, with all kinds of different landscapes, whereas the ones they make nowadays are so lacklustre. No effort goes into producing them, no care. I looked through all the postcards with messages on the back as well, the ones that Mama Lena sent me from Pyatigorsk three years ago.

And I remembered how once, not so long ago, just last winter

---

the Leningrad Theatre of Variety and Miniatures. Twenty-four different films were shown in thirty-four cinemas, clubs and Houses of Culture, and the Gostsirk (State Circus) hosted a peformance by a jazz ensemble featuring Klavdiya Shulzhenko and Vladimir Korall (*Leningradskaya Pravda*, 22 November 1941).

in fact, Mama and I dreamed of taking a ferry down the Volga. We made some inquiries and found out how much it would cost. I remember the two of us decided that we would definitely go on holiday somewhere this summer. We won't give up this dream. One day Mama and I will sit in a sleeper carriage with pale-blue curtains and lampshades, and then that happy moment will arrive when our train pulls out from the domed glass ceiling of the station and breaks free, and we speed off into the distance, heading far, far away. We will sit at the little table, eating something tasty and knowing that ahead of us lie enjoyable experiences, delicious food, new places, all of nature with its blue sky, its foliage and flowers. Anticipating the pleasures that await us, each one better than the last. And we will talk about everything, as we look back and watch Leningrad recede into the distance. The city where we went through so much, where we endured so much suffering, where we sat hungry in a cold room, listening to the thunder of the anti-aircraft guns and the drone of enemy aeroplanes. But we will brush all these memories away like a bad nightmare and turn our gaze to the future, in the direction our express train adorned with red stars is taking us, full speed ahead. Germans walked here once, when the ground was covered with snow, scarred with shell craters, trenches and earthworks and woven with barbed wire, and the cold, icy wind whistled in their ears. The railway track we're speeding along was in pieces back then. Destroyed by partisans. Carriages lay at the foot of the embankment, broken into splinters, and the embankment itself was littered with the corpses of enemy soldiers, showing up black amidst the snow. Mama and I will peer cautiously at the thick grass covering the embankment, but we will see nothing there to remind us of the war we lived through. Though still recent, they are already in the past, those historic days when the breakthrough occurred and the Germans stopped advancing, when the Germans were pushed back, when the Germans retreated, when the Germans ran, when we entered Berlin, when the last burst of gunfire, the last explosion and the last rifle shot rang out. Those days when we greeted our valiant warriors with victory – true heroes, every one of them, and deserving of a glory that will remain undiminished for centuries to come – those days have already faded away behind us, swathed in smoke along with distant, grey Leningrad. It has all disappeared behind us, receding into the background and giving way to something new, which in turn has also passed. We have already buried our glorious troops who died in battle, honouring them with eternal memory. Leningrad's wounds have already healed. We have replaced the windows and repaired the damaged buildings. Yes, all this has passed. And so has the day the gas ring on the stove in the kitchen whistled into life again, and the day the first ice cream cone appeared.

Mama and I look out of the window. God, we are so happy. Swarms of memories fill our heads, swirling around and around. We remember and at the same time rejoice in the fact that memories are all we have, that those times are over, that they will never return. We remember the sound of the bugle that gave the final all-clear and the sight of Leningrad ablaze – no, not with flames but with the bright, joyful glow of electric light. We remember shop windows sparkling like new after throwing off their burden of boards and sand, we remember trams clanking back to life, we remember cars beginning to honk their horns and flash their headlights, we remember thousands of windows lighting up happy homes across the city. Posters, banners, everything glitters and merges together on this first day of celebration . . .

## 23 November 1941

I read my fantasy story to Mama yesterday, and she really liked it. I don't want to write any more of it. This is what I'm going to do from now on: I'm going to stay behind after school in the quiet, empty classroom and study all the lessons that we've just been given so that I learn them by heart. In the timetable, the longest gap between lessons for any subject is two or three days at most. So if I sit and study today's geography lesson, for example, in an atmosphere of peace and quiet, then I'm unlikely to have forgotten it completely in three days' time – and if I do forget anything, then it won't take much revising. If I manage to stick to this plan I'll be able to get a lot more reading done at home. I must finish Dickens' *Great Expectations* as soon as possible and start something else. I want to buy a few pamphlets and set up my own 'Bolshevik bookshelf'. Yes, and I must buy a Russian grammar book and remind myself of all the rules, so that I don't spoil my literature essays with spelling mistakes. Well, that's enough rambling for now. 'Less talk, more action!' I'm going to study literature now, then my other lessons. By then Aka will have heated up the soup and we will eat, and after that I will copy out my algebra.

## 27 November 1941

I got home from school at half past one today, and that was quite early – we got home at four o'clock yesterday and five o'clock the day before. This is what has been happening recently: a few minutes before the bell is supposed to go at the end of the fifth lesson it gives a series of intermittent rings, so we quickly put our coats on (our coat hooks are in the classroom), go downstairs, run across the courtyard and go down into the school air-raid shelter. We've got a good shelter – there are five individual rooms divided by walls, and two classes fit into each room. It's light and warm inside, and the air is clean (there's a ventilation system). There are desks and benches, a blackboard and chalk. We sit on the benches, the teacher takes his place at the board, and the lesson continues. Today the headmistress came into the classroom in the middle of our literature lesson to announce that there was an artillery raid. We continued the lesson in the air-raid shelter, then it was history, and then according to the timetable it should have been literature again. But the headmistress came back and announced that the air raid was over and we should hurry home. We didn't need telling twice. None of us particularly wanted to sit in the basement until four or five o'clock, getting even hungrier, so we left straight away. But as soon as we walked out of the gates . . . another warning. We got through just in time. I'm writing this in the middle of the air raid.

Aka is heating up the soup, and we're about to have supper. Mama and I decided not to get any bread today, so that we don't have to go without at the weekend. We've still got some linseeds left. Toasted linseeds are very tasty, as it turns out. Yesterday all three of us had enough to eat, and we won't go hungry today either. After that, who knows? Incidentally, we can get chocolate and sweets on our meat ration cards at the moment. They were issuing cheese instead of butter for a while, too, but now they've only got jam.

We can still get one chocolate sweet each a day at school for thirty kopeks.[1] We used to have to go down to the canteen for it, which caused long queues and made people late for lessons, so now they do it differently. Halfway through the second lesson the headmistress comes into the classroom, accompanied by a canteen worker who is wearing a white apron tied with a big knot and carrying several plates. They count the number of students present, and the canteen worker counts out onto a plate the corresponding number of sweets, then one of the students takes this plate round the class, giving everyone one sweet each and collecting the money, which the headmistress takes away with her. After this the lesson continues, but of course no one is paying attention any more, and more than half the class are chewing sweets. None of us goes down to the canteen to drink tea – or rather hot water – any more.

I sat next to Genya Kobyshev in the air-raid shelter today. I

---

1  School rations were not given out free of charge but had to be paid for.

noticed him the first time I saw him. He seems like a modest, unassuming boy. He never expresses his opinion. He's never the first to speak.

During the break before history, in contrast to everyone around him, who was chatting away, he sat there reading *Dead Souls*.[2] I said: 'Are you enjoying *Dead Souls*?' He responded wordlessly, with that indeterminate gesture whose meaning is always understood. Then I asked: 'Which is your favourite subject?' He answered with the same vague gesture, this time with an awkward smile. But I persisted: 'Well, do you like history?' 'No.' 'Geography?' 'Geography's all right. I like maths.' 'Maths? What about natural sciences?' 'No, I don't like science.' I couldn't think of any way of continuing the conversation. He looked at me pensively for a while then turned his attention back to *Dead Souls*.

Genya is short and quite slim. In the darkness, his fair hair sticks up in a funny little quiff. There's something warm and gentle in his light-blue eyes, and his expression is innocent, almost apologetic. He has an awkward smile, which sometimes comes across as ingratiating. I wonder what he's really like.

It's already quarter past three, and the air raid is still going on. The anti-aircraft gunfire keeps dying down then flaring up again.

I'm about to start studying my lessons. Particularly literature.

The air raid was over at five to six, but then the artillery fire started up at half past six. Mama came home on foot. We've just listened to a radio broadcast by academician Orbeli, from which we learned that the Germans have plundered the treasure

2    Novel by Nikolai Gogol, published in 1842.

troves of Peterhof and Pushkin.[3] They've sawn up Samson[4] and carted him off to Germany, and they've dismantled the Amber Room at Pushkin and taken that off to Germany as well.[5] The German people will have to supply us with the amber needed to restore it, whatever the cost.

Something has been happening in my soul lately, and I don't understand it at all. I feel a lack of desire, inspiration and curiosity, yet at the same time so many thoughts, which have rolled into a ball and keep moving about so that it's impossible to untangle them. If only I could grasp the tail-end of one of them. One minute everything seems perfectly clear, and it really does feel as though I'm starting to understand everything, I mean literally everything, but the next minute it's all shrouded in mist and nothing makes any sense. And the main thing is that I have no one to share it with. Mama? She comes home, eats and goes

3 On 27 November *Leningradskaya Pravda* published an article entitled 'Nazi Vandals' by Iosif Orbeli, director of the State Hermitage: 'In Peterhof . . . the occupiers are ripping the gilded bronze statues from the fountains, sawing up the figure of Samson – one of the most wonderful sculptures to adorn any park in the world – and carting it back to their own country in bits. They have also been swaggering about the Grand Palace in Detskoye Selo [the name given to the town of Pushkin after the Revolution] . . . and yesterday we heard that their vile, loutish hands have hacked apart and devastated one of its most magnificent treasures – the Amber Room.'

4 The statue of Samson tearing open the jaws of a lion is the centrepiece of the Grand Cascade at Peterhof. The original statue was looted during the war. A replica was cast in 1947 on the basis of photographs and archive data.

5 The Amber Room at the Catherine Palace in Tsarskoye Selo was originally created by German and Danish masters for the Prussian King Friedrich I. It was later presented by his son Friedrich Wilhelm I to Peter the Great. The room was 7.8 metres long, with a floor area of approximately 100 square metres, and the walls were decorated with 86 square metres of amber panelling. It was dismantled by the Germans in the autumn of 1941 and transported to Königsberg, where it was exhibited from 1942 to 1944.

straight to bed. She's so tired these days. Tamara? But I don't know how to tell her, or what will she make of it, or how I can even put it into words. There's nothing inside me but emptiness, absolute emptiness. I don't understand anything – or rather, I understand everything but I don't know what I'm supposed to understand.

I just can't forget about Vova. I dream about him every night. Did I really love him? I can't account for my own feelings. And why can't I get to know any of the other boys from our class? They already use the affectionate name 'Galka' when they talk to Galya Viron [sic], whereas they seem to avoid me and some of them even address me formally, like a stranger. Why is that? Why do I keep wanting to start a conversation with someone, then struggle to find anything to talk about? The devil only knows! I feel like such a misfit. Nobody likes the chemistry teacher – literally everybody laughs at him, for some reason. But I like him. Goodness knows why, but to me he's a true Soviet teacher, and I would like . . . I don't even know what exactly, but I would like him to take charge of us and to start re-educating us, to reach our hearts and souls, so that we might become Soviet students and communists through and through. I would like him to broaden our minds, for us to go and listen to a symphony with him, for our eyes to be opened to the whole world, for us to see that we are living our one and only life. I would like each of us to resolve to make the most out of our lives. To grow up to replace our parents, to be better than our parents. More sophisticated, more educated. And to become the kind of parents who will raise our children to be even better than we are ourselves. On this basis a person's life can be considered happy, productive and full of joy. Thus, dying in old age, we might be glad of the life we have lived. Knowing that it has been lived with no regrets. Dear God, how I wish someone would start to re-educate my classmates.

How I wish I lived somewhere else, in a different place, with different boys and different classmates, and I wish so many other things were different. I don't even know what else. I wish Tamara were different. And I wish Vova were different. I wish they were all striving towards something pure and beautiful. Perhaps I want all boys and girls to be romantics? Maybe. Although I don't think so. No. Of course not.

I want us to live like Lenin said we should. And I want school to be different, and our living conditions to be different.

Lenin said: 'Study, study and study!'[6] In my opinion, this should be the first priority of every Soviet student! Furthermore, every Soviet student should fight against cheating at school, against cards and cigarettes. And a lot more besides.

I wonder if I'll ever find anyone else who is interested in natural sciences, geology and mineralogy. Those stones in the mineralogical museum[7] – why do I find them so exciting? I don't know. I'd like to study all of nature right down to the smallest

---

6  This slogan is frequently attributed to Vladimir Lenin. In his article 'Better Less but Better' (1923), Lenin wrote: 'In order to achieve the renovation of our state apparatus we must set ourselves a certain objective, whatever it takes: firstly – to study, secondly – to study, and thirdly – to study, and then to go over it all again, so that our learning might not remain inert or be reduced to no more than a passing fancy . . .' (V. I. Lenin, *Polnoe sobranie sochinenii*, vol. 45, p. 391). However, this expression acquired the form of a slogan in Stalin's speech at the Eighth Congress of the All-Union Leninist Young Communist League (Komsomol) on 16 May 1928: 'To acquire an education, to forge new Bolshevik recruits – specialists in all fields of knowledge, to study, study, study with the greatest diligence . . .' – this was, in Stalin's view, the main task to which young communists should apply themselves.

7  The author is referring to the Chernyshev Central Scientific Research Museum of Geological Prospecting, which was founded in 1882 and open to visitors from 1930. Affiliated to the museum was the Minerals Office, which existed until 1982.

detail, the very last atom. Every interesting aspect of it. I'd like to write a book about people. And have albums full of photos from every corner of our land. And I want to go to the mountains, yes, the mountains and the sea. Perhaps I simply want to be a tourist? Maybe.

No! No! Not just a tourist. I don't know what I want to be. Everything's all mixed up in my head. It's chaos!

## 28 November 1941

I got home from school today at quarter past five. There was an air-raid warning at twelve o'clock. Our fourth, fifth and sixth lessons took place in the shelter. Then the bombing began, and the light flickered and went out. We sat in darkness until the all-clear. Someone nearby switched a torch on, but we just sat and chatted. I don't know when I'm going to get the chance to learn my lessons.

Mama came home at five to six. She said that Nevsky is deserted and one building has been completely destroyed – it simply no longer exists.[1] Yes, five-hour air raids, that's the way things are these days. When we went into the air-raid shelter it was daytime, and when we came out it was already dark. Everyone outside is running, everyone's in a hurry. Carrying plates and bowls for dinner. Moving along the pavement like

---

1  On 28 November 1941 a high-explosive bomb destroyed the central part of the front of the Kuibyshev (now Samara) district council building on the corner of Nevsky Prospekt 68, (then called 25th October Prospekt) and Fontanka 40, near the Anichkov Bridge.

a flock of sheep, not keeping to the correct side. Pushing and shoving one another.

The city continues to live from one air-raid warning to the next!

## 29 November 1941

I got up by candlelight today, because the lights weren't working. When I got to school it was dark there too. The first lesson was physics, and we had a test. We were each given a rum sweet in the middle of the lesson. Then we had algebra, then history. During the history lesson we had a medical examination, then they came and gave us all a coupon to exchange for a portion of jelly. Three minutes before the end of the lesson there was an air-raid warning. This time we weren't in the air-raid shelter for very long. All-clear. As soon as we'd taken our coats off in the classroom we rushed to the canteen for our jelly. The corridor leading to the canteen was dark because the lights had gone out again, and there was just one kerosene lamp in the canteen. We queued for ages. Some time after the bell had rung, I wondered why they weren't hurrying us along to our lesson. It turned out that the seventh and ninth grade classes were allowed to go straight home after their jelly.

When I'd been given my jelly and had moved away to the side to wait for a spoon, they announced another air-raid warning and said that we were to eat our jelly and go straight to the shelter. I tried the jelly, and it was so tasty that I decided to take it with me to eat at home. I made a little wrap out of a piece of paper and put it in there. I went back to the classroom, put my coat on and decided that I may as well sit in the air-raid shelter for a while, seeing as they wouldn't let us go home yet. I went out into the courtyard, which was full of mud and slush, like a spring thaw. I couldn't see anyone by the gates or by the entrance to the air-raid shelter, so I just walked straight out onto the street. I couldn't tell at first whether there was an air raid going on or not. Everyone was walking about as if nothing had happened, and a queue had formed on the corner. Only the trams stood empty. I got home at quarter to one. While I was tidying our room the gunfire began, and then came the bombs. The building shook a few times. I hid under the table. Aka came home with lunch, and I crawled out from under the table. Aka had bought two days' worth of bread for both of us, so we shared it out. I ate some bread with linseed oil but I hid my jelly, and now I don't know what to do about it. Should I eat it alone or share it with Mama and Aka, as a surprise? But if I share it none of us will get much – one cup of jelly between three of us, that's hardly more than a taste. No, best not to tease them. I'll eat it alone this time, but I'll definitely take a clean jar to school with me and if they give us any more jelly then I'll do what I wanted to do with the fruit drink, i.e. collect three portions so I can treat them too.

## 1 December 1941

Today I feel full. I'm going to bed on a full stomach. Aka got some soup and two main courses at my school. In the afternoon Aka and I ate a full bowl of soup each, with one main course, and when Mama came we each had another two bowls of soup with a second main course. Mama also brought a portion of *kasha* and one rissole. So today we had a first course and a main course. And I didn't go short of bread either: both Aka and Mama gave me their share, because Mama received ration cards for herself and Aka only today, whereas I got mine yesterday evening and used it straight away to buy today's 125g of bread in advance. We shared it into three portions. I didn't go out anywhere or do anything all day yesterday. There were air raids and artillery fire all day. I was supposed to be at school by ten o'clock today, but just as I was about to leave there was an air-raid warning. So we missed our first lesson, and we missed our last lesson too. Today there were seventeen people for geometry, and in the lesson before last – chemistry – there were just seven. It's not exactly proper education. God knows what it is. Tamara wasn't at school today either. I went round to visit her after school, but she wasn't in. She came round to see me later. I wrote Vova a note, which I'll give to Tamara tomorrow. It's very handy that Tamara and Osya live in the same communal apartment, so I can exchange notes with Vova. They're not going to just sell sweets for money at school any more. For every sweet they're going to cut out 10g of sugar coupons.[1] Well, I think that's all my news. I'm going to bed.

The artillery fire was very strong this afternoon. I thought that our windows were going to shatter, but they've been fine so far. It's quite warm in our room. Our 40W bulb is heating it up nicely.

Yesterday I discovered Tamara's 'secret', which she gave to me for safekeeping. I found out that Tamara is in love with Leva Khokom, and apparently something has happened between them. Tamara was too open with him and now she's worried that Leva is laughing at her.

---

1  According to a report issued by the city's department of trade for the period June 1941 to September 1943, '1.XII 1941 saw the introduction of 100% accountability in relation to the amounts of sugar, confectionery and fats issued on food ration cards' (*Leningrad v osade. Sbornik dokumentov o geroicheskoi oborone Leningrada v gody Velikoi Otechestvennoi voiny 1941–1944*, St Petersburg, 1995, p. 268).

# 5 December 1941

New ordeals have begun. It's already the fifth day of the new ten-day period, and we don't have any sweets. Today I couldn't bear it and bought 250g of treacle on my ration card. It's the second day that Aka and I have been unable to get lunch on our ration cards, as we've already used up all our coupons for this ten-day period. It's hardly surprising: our grain coupons are for 12½g, but in other canteens they take one coupon for soup and two coupons for *kasha*, whereas at our canteen they cut out 25g of grain and 5g of butter just for soup. So that's how we've spent all our coupons in four days.

This is the second day in a row that we haven't had any electricity. No one knows when it will come back on. It's horrible not having electricity. It was really frightening last night. You just feel so helpless when it's pitch dark and there's an aeroplane droning, droning terribly, insistently, and then the bombs, one after another, one after another, and nothing but darkness all around, pitch darkness, and it feels as though the whole building is leaning slightly to one side and shuddering after every explosion.

## 7 December 1941

It's the weekend today, and Mama is at home. It's freezing outside. Today we feel full. Yesterday Aka managed to persuade Aunt Sasha to give her a little oil-cake, which we made into a soup with 75g of Canadian canned meat that Aka got this morning. I really liked the oil-cake, it's tasty and very filling. Yesterday I queued for sweets from five o'clock to nine o'clock in the evening and stood there until I got 600g of sweets for 18 roubles 90 kopeks. We shared them out, and each of us got ten and a half sweets. Everyone's saying that there will be extra bread tomorrow. We'll see. For some reason I believe it. Probably because they've started delivering food supplies: white macaroni, Canadian canned goods, American sweets and other items indicate that help is getting through and we won't be allowed to die of starvation.

There was some fairly good news from the front today too. Our troops are continuing their successful advance on Taganrog, in spite of concerted German efforts to stop them. Our troops have successfully counterattacked the Germans outside Moscow, but the Germans have further tightened their encirclement of Tula. Outside Leningrad our troops have seized several villages and settlements and forced the vile Germans back slightly.[1]

I'm wearing my coat and writing these lines by the light of a candle stub. I have part of a sweet and some bread on a saucer in front of me. I'm listening to piano music on the radio and nibbling tiny crumbs of bread, so as to prolong my pleasure. We're going to bed at ten to seven these days. We need to save candles. Tomorrow morning, still lying in bed, I will eagerly await Aka's return from the bread shop. Maybe she'll bring more than 125g – even 150g would be better. I ate four sweets today, though I meant to eat two. Now I've got three sweets left for the 8th, 9th and 10th. One sweet a day. There's a symphony playing on the radio, and bursts of gunfire roaring outside the window. Those damned Germans, firing on Leningrad again. But at night, yet again, the ominous siren will begin to wail, and the building will shudder from the explosion of bombs nearby. Death is hanging over every one of us all the time, and we have grown so accustomed to it that we no longer notice it, or perhaps we simply don't want to notice it. But things are not so bad yet. True, we've had no electricity for three days now, but the lavatory and bathroom are still in good working order. We are able to drink hot water. We still have enough oil-cake and meat for soup to last us two days, and maybe they'll increase our bread rations tomorrow, or perhaps in a few days.

Well, now I must sleep.

---

1  In mid-November 1941 Soviet troops launched their counter-offensive and advanced on Tikhvin; by the end of December they had forced the German army back to the Volkhov River, from where they had begun their attack in October. Many occupied settlements were liberated, including Malaya Vishera on 20 November and Tikhvin on 9 December.

## 8 December 1941

Major events have occurred. England has declared war on Finland, Romania and Hungary, and Japan has declared war on the United States of America. Roosevelt has declared America to be in a state of war with Japan. Mobilization has been announced in America.

So much snow fell here last night, it's simply dreadful. The windows have frozen, the trams aren't running, and everyone is having to walk. We haven't had any air raids for two days – only artillery fire, but that's nowhere near as frightening. They haven't increased bread rations yet, although they did give 100g of butter to adult dependants and white-collar workers, but the word is that bread rations will definitely be increased on the 15th. Never mind, we can manage until the 15th. Yes, December, the last month of 1941, will probably go down in history. We should expect important events to occur before the start of the new year.

## 9 December 1941

The lights came on at eight o'clock yesterday evening. At school today they gave us a bowl of cabbage soup and a cup of jelly off ration. Apparently they're going to give us this every day. I got home and drank two cups of hot water with bread and butter. People are saying they're going to increase bread rations soon. Not by much, only 25g, but that's good. Instead of 125g we'll get 150g.

Thanks to all this good news my mood lifted immediately. Life has improved, become more joyous![1]

---

1   The author is probably quoting a line from a song with the same title, written in 1936 by the poet Vasily Lebedev-Kumach to music composed by Aleksandr Aleksandrov, which was performed by an ensemble conducted by Aleksandrov. This line clearly echoes a phrase used by Stalin in his speech at the 1st All-Union Conference of Stakhanovites on 17 November 1935: 'Life has improved, comrades. Life has become more joyous.'

## 10 December 1941

Hurrah, hurrah! Our troups have retaken Tikhvin and almost broken through the siege ring around Leningrad. Three German divisions were smashed outside Tikhvin. This is a very important victory.

There hasn't been a single air raid for four days.

Mama didn't go to work today. She's going to start looking for another job, because it's impossible for her to walk to the Vyborg Side and back every day when she's so hungry.

What do I wish for now? Only for the days to fly past one after another like telegraph poles glimpsed from the window of an express train. I wish I could make these difficult winter days go by faster, faster, faster. I wish spring, its warmth, its greenery, would come sooner.

I wish events would unfold at the pace of images on a screen.

I wish I could make the hands of the clock turn faster, faster, faster.

## 14 December 1941

One more day and we'll be halfway through the month. There will only be half a month left until the beginning of 1942.

Germany and Italy have declared war on the USA.

The Germans have been completely routed outside Moscow. The second German general offensive on Moscow has been comprehensively smashed. The Germans have begun to retreat. This war is entering a new phase. Everything has been increased for the second ten-day period: grain, meat and sugar. They're going to increase bread tomorrow, apparently. Life is calm at the moment. No air raids. It's hard to believe, but it really does seems as though the most difficult days are behind us.

## 16 December 1941

I was late for algebra today. I didn't have time to finish the test. There were twenty-six of us in the first lesson. Then twenty of us stayed for lunch, and after lunch there were just seven of us for history. Today's lunch was soup for twenty-six kopeks. It was thick soup, with unpeeled potatoes and hard, dark noodles. The soup was hot and tasty, though it needed salt. We'll have jelly tomorrow, which they give us every other day.

They said on the radio today that our troops have retaken Klin and Krasnaya Polyana. We got our literature essays back. I didn't do very well, but Tamara got a 5. She was the only one who did. They read her essay out in class because it was the best. It really was very good – so good that I wouldn't have known it was Tamara's work.

When I got back from school Aka asked me to go and queue for meat. I stood in the queue until quarter to five, all for nothing, because there wasn't enough for everyone.

Maria Nikolaevna Mukhina and her baby daughter Lena.

Sofiya Polikarpovna Mukhina, Lena Mukhina's schoolteacher grandmother, with her children Elena and Nikolai.

Lena's grandfather,
Nikolai Mukhin, with his
daughter Evgeniya.

Lena's aunt, Elena
Nikolaevna Mukhina,
in 1911.

Azaliya Konstantinovna (Aka) with one of her pupils.

Elena Nikolaevna Bernatskaya (née Mukhina) performing Anitra's dance from the Maly Opera Theatre's production of *Peer Gynt*, in the early 1920s.

Lena Mukhina, *c.* 1932.

Grigory Filippovich Bolshakov, opera singer and friend of Elena Bernatskaya, in 1935.

Elena Bernatskaya in 1938.

The design workshop at the Leningrad State Academic Maly Opera Theatre. Sitting at the front is Sergei Viktorovich Senatorsky, and from second left to right behind him: Vera Vladmirovna Milyutina; Kira Nikolaevna Lipkhart and Elena Bernatskaya.

Before the start of the 1941 May Day Parade. Elena Bernatskaya is on the far right, next to her friend Kira Lipkhart.

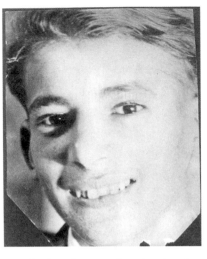

Tamara Artemieva, Lena's friend
and classmate, in 1940.

Volodya Itkinson, Lena's school
sweetheart.

School photograph taken at the end of the eighth grade, June 1941.
Lena Mukhina is third from the left in the back row. Volodya Itkinson
is second from the right in the third row.

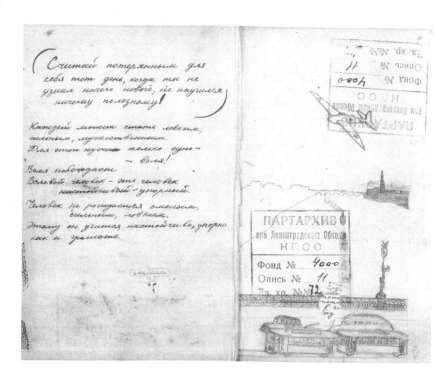

The opening pages
of Lena's diary.

Lena's diary,
22 June 1941.

Mosaic workshop, Leningrad School of Art and Industry, 1947.
Lena is sitting in the centre.

Lena Mukhina in 1955.               Lena in 1986, with her great-niece.

## 17 December 1941

It's already 17 December. We heard some good news today. On the western front our troops, in their continued pursuit of the retreating enemy, have occupied the city of Kalinin and three more small towns. Outside Moscow one of Hitler's armies has been almost completely crushed: about six infantry and three motorized infantry divisions. The remnants of these divisions are retreating in haste, looting whatever they can lay their hands on. They're stripping people in the street, taking everything, even the New Year decorations from the trees. The partisans are inflicting on them defeat after defeat.

Thus, in mid-December 1941 we have reached a critical point in the war between Germany and the USSR. After a six-month offensive German forces have begun their retreat, which will continue for . . . no one knows how long.

Life is very hard at the moment. And studying is very hard. But things won't get any harder, and any changes will surely be for the better.

The harsh winter weather has begun. It's freezing outside. It's cold inside too, because we can't afford to waste firewood, so we only light the stove to prepare supper. And it's dark – most people's windows are boarded up, and those that aren't boarded up are hung with fabric to keep the warmth in. Moreover some people, particularly those who live on the upper floors, are without water. They have to go outside to fetch water. The trams are barely running, because frequent snowfalls are making it harder to clear the streets of snow. One day they're running, the next they're not. But most people relied on the trams to get to work. Now they all walk to work and home again, cold and half starving. They walk, fall, shuffle, drag themselves along, but still they walk. Some of them have to walk a very long way: to the Petrograd Side, or even the Vyborg Side. At least we don't have to put up with any air raids at the moment. There hasn't been one for ages. And the artillery fire never lasts very long. Bread is in short supply: manual workers get 250g, other adults and dependants get 125g. Just 125g, one small piece, it's hardly anything. You have to queue to get other food items on your ration cards. But queuing is like torture these days: your feet and hands freeze, even though the frosts are not yet that severe.

It's very hard to study at school. The school building is not heated, and the ink wells have frozen in some of the classrooms. The only good thing is that schoolchildren get a hot bowl of soup every day off ration.

But never mind. Things will get better soon. It's just a matter of time.

## 18 December 1941

Our troops have seized, or rather retaken, two more towns in the Kalinin sector. Our troops have also forced the enemy back along the Leningrad section of the front, so the road from Tikhvin to Volkhov is completely free of Germans. At school today instead of jelly they gave us soy milk *prostokvasha*[1] – quarter of a litre. It was very tasty. I brought it home and shared it with Mama and Aka. They really liked it too. Today Aka queued for meat and got some lovely American pressed meat, with plenty of fat but no bones. This is the second day that Mama hasn't been to work. She didn't have the energy, and in any case they're going to dismiss them all soon because the hospital is going to be shut down. They've already sent the patients to various other hospitals. Mama will be without a job again. Goodness knows where she will find another one.

---

1   This product was made by adding a small quantity of factory-made *kefir* (fermented cow's milk) or *prostokvasha* (a thicker, milder version of *kefir*) to soy milk, which was then left in a warm place for between twelve and eighteen hours to ferment. Soy milk *prostokvasha* could be used to make a kind of soft soy cheese.

It's already the 19th tomorrow, but we still haven't had either sweets or butter.

The electricity came on at seven o'clock this evening so I'm writing this with the light on, but on the other hand there's no water.

Today we had some tasty soup with meat and macaroni. There's enough cat meat for two more meals. And enough of the American meat for three more, but I don't know what we'll do after that. It would be good to find another cat somewhere, then we would have enough to last us for a long time. I never thought cat meat would be so tender and so tasty.

Frankly, the situation with my schoolwork is awful. I haven't done anything for geometry, and I only got a 2 in the algebra test. I haven't done any drawing. My answer was rejected in chemistry. Well, that's the same as getting a 1. I only got a 4 in German and in history. I'm going to prepare my presentation on the Battle of Gangut this Saturday. Maybe I'll get a 5 in history. I only got a 2 for my literature essay. There were lots of grammatical mistakes, and the essay itself wasn't very good either. I'm allowed to rewrite it tomorrow. I may as well try my luck, on the off chance I might get a 4. Even if I decide not to I won't get a 2 for this term, because I've already got a 4 overall. It was very upsetting to hear the literature teacher say that she was disappointed in me, that she expected better of me. That my attitude makes me one of the most anti-Soviet pupils in the class. No, she's wrong about that. I am a Soviet student at heart, but in fact I'm not acting like one at the moment because I'm so undisciplined, I can't bring myself to make any effort, and all I care about is myself. The fact is that the first term is nearly over and I'm not learning my lessons at all, I'm not paying attention to any of the material, and it stands to reason that I'm not going to get away with it. My poor results are really upsetting

Mama. Of course, it's possible to plead in my defence that it's hard to study at the moment. No one would argue with that. In some ways it would be proof of my patriotism, if in spite of the obstacles I'm facing, in defiance of the circumstances, I applied all my energies to studying well.

Otherwise, how can I justify it? The things I've said, my dreams of earning the right to be called a Soviet citizen – it's all just empty talk. The first ordeals I have encountered on my path have bent me and broken me. I have surrendered. I'm a spineless creature. Intimidated by obstacles. I wrap myself in a hundred layers of clothing, without even earning my daily bread, and I do nothing but whine – it's cold, it's cold.

Yes, it's cold. But is the cold really such an insurmountable obstacle? No, it is possible to conquer cold.

## 19 December 1941

It's ten to nine. We have to switch the light off at nine o'clock. According to the new rules we're allowed to burn a 15W bulb for just three hours a day. Tomorrow I have to give my history presentation, and I've got an oral exam for chemistry. I failed chemistry last time. He gave me a 2. I need to know about silicon and carbon. I'm really worried about history. I've never given a presentation before, it's the first time I've attempted it. What if I forget everything? Today I rewrote my literature essay on Manilovism.[1]

They gave us only one bowl of watery soup in the canteen today. That Adamovich is a strange character.

---

1  Derived from the name of the landowner Manilov, one of the characters in Gogol's *Dead Souls*, this term was used to denote an attitude of sentimentality, smug complacency or passivity.

## 22 December 1941

The weather is milder today. It's quite warm outside. The snow has melted, and it's so slippery that it's impossible to walk. But the fact that it's not cold is reason enough to be happy. Hunger is just about bearable, but when you're cold as well as hungry – that's absolutely unbearable.

This morning I was so hungry that I asked Aka to buy bread for me too when she went to get hers. Mama came home shortly after and made bouillon out of skin. Aka came back with the bread. I drank two cups of hot bouillon and ate more than half my bread. I felt so miserable. I must have been the most miserable person in the world. No wonder, really – I hadn't done any schoolwork for two days. Feeling apprehensive, I eventually resigned myself to my fate: no more than a 2 in any subject. But I was lucky, awfully lucky. The first lesson was physics. I was the first to answer and got the easiest question: from the beginning of the chapter about sound. I think he gave me a 4. In geometry we covered some new material. The next lesson was chemistry, and I got called up to answer again.

'Mukhina, tell us about silicon. The reaction that produces silicon, and the reaction that produces silane.'

I stood at the board for a long time. I didn't care. I knew I would get a 2. By the time he eventually he spoke to me, I had written down both reactions. When I thought hard enough I remembered them. Actually I had learned silicon off by heart for the previous lesson, but he spent the lesson explaining things rather than asking questions, so I thought that I'd learned it in vain. Turns out it wasn't in vain after all. If I hadn't learned it then, I would have been stuck with a 2.

I took my time and calmly told him everything I knew. He didn't ask me anything else, just told me to sit down, and I think he gave me a 4.

We had dictation in chemistry. I'll get more than a 2 for that. Dictation is easy.

We had a test in geography. I had just come from buying flat-breads in the canteen, and he came round with the test papers straight away. I hoped I would get a chance to look at my notes, but I didn't. I got paper no. 1:

1. The population of England.
2. The region of South Wales.
3. British territories in western Africa.

More good luck. It was such an easy paper. I knew almost all of it. I did make a few mistakes, but I was still lucky and fortunately avoided a 2.

After the fifth lesson we went straight to lunch. We had soup with macaroni and meat. I had three pieces of potato and eight medium-sized pieces of macaroni in my soup. I also bought some more flatbreads. I bought four in total today.

I left school feeling full and happy. It was quite warm outside. The trams were at a standstill on Zagorodny, in the middle of the tramline.

*25 December 1941*

What joy, what joy! I want to shout it at the top of my voice. My God, what joy!

They have increased our bread rations! And by a significant amount. Such a difference: from 125g to 200g. White-collar workers and dependants get 200g, and manual workers get 350g.

This is an absolute lifeline for us, for over the past few days we have all grown so weak that we've barely been able to move our legs. And now, now both Mama and Aka will survive. That's reason enough to be happy, but it also indicates that things are starting to improve. Things will improve from now on.

We will celebrate the New Year in good spirits. With bread, sweets, chocolate and wine.

Hurrah, hurrah, and hurrah again. Long live life!

## 27 December 1941

I can't move my hands properly yet, although I got back some time ago. From the theatre. I went to the theatre again today. I went to see a performance of *Home of the Gentry* at the Drama Theatre.[1] I really enjoyed it. I would go to the theatre every day if I could, but I'm not going to go to the theatre again this winter, because the pleasure seems so small in comparison with the torture of returning home. But I will write about it all in more detail later.

Mama went out for bread at six o'clock this morning and brought back some very good bread indeed. It was nice and dry and didn't contain much oil-cake, so 200g was a substantial amount. It was very tasty too. I ate the entire 200g in the

---

1 The Leningrad Drama Theatre was founded by the Arts Administration of the Executive Committee of the Leningrad City Council at the end of October 1941, with a troupe composed of actors who had not evacuated with their respective theatres. The theatre opened at the beginning of November 1941 with a production of *Home of the Gentry*, which was performed initially at the Comedy Theatre (25th October [Nevsky] Prospekt 56) before moving to the Bolshoi Drama Theatre. This particular production was last mentioned in *Leningradskaya Pravda* on 10 January 1942.

morning. They were reporting good news on the radio. Our troops are continuing their offensive and have seized the towns of Belev and Naro-Fominsk.

## 28 December 1941

*Theatre at the Microphone* was on the radio yesterday for the first time after a long break.

It's about twelve o'clock midday. The water has just come back on, so we have been able to replenish our reserves. Water is so rarely available these days that we have to keep a close eye on it. It's very cold in our room. Mama has gone to work at the theatre, and Aka is asleep.

Aka is very poorly. Mama is worried that she won't survive. Aka doesn't get out of bed at all any more. The day before yesterday, when she went for bread in the morning, just after they increased the rations, she fell over three times. On her back and on her face, right on her nose. She broke her nose, and since then she has been getting worse and worse. Now I'm going to have to take over the housekeeping, and Mama will work.

To tell the truth, if Aka died it would be for the best, for her and also for Mama and me. Mama and I could divide everything in half, rather than into three portions as we do now. Aka is just an extra mouth to feed. I don't know how I can even bring myself to write such things. But my heart has turned to stone. The thought of it doesn't upset me at all. I don't care whether

Aka dies or not. But if she is going to die I hope it happens after the 1st, so we'll be able to get her ration card. How heartless I have become.

## 30 December 1941

Tomorrow is New Year's Eve, but it doesn't feel like it at all. There's nothing in the shop. They're only issuing cornflour and sugar on children's ration cards. Everyone was saying that they were going to give us extra chocolate and something else to mark the occasion. But we've not had anything yet. I suppose there's still tomorrow. Maybe they'll give us something tomorrow.

I don't have any bread today. But tomorrow I will welcome in the New Year with 200g of bread. What happened with the chocolate sweets this time was very disappointing. They were giving out chocolate sweets at Mama's theatre yesterday for 22 roubles a kilo. We were entitled to 800g but were only allowed 300g, because I had already bought a kilo of sweet paste for 9 roubles the day before at no. 28. It's supposed to be a sugar substitute, but you can't tell what it's made of. It's like the putty they use to fix windows. It doesn't taste at all sweet but at least it's edible, especially on an empty stomach.

Aka has spent the last five days in bed, but she's feeling better now. Mama is able to get a meal ready remarkably quickly. I prepare the firewood for her, and it takes her just half an hour to prepare a delicious meal. For the past three days we've had two bowls of soup each. Such tasty soup, with a cup of cocoa afterwards too.

Today Mama brought home three bowls of yeast soup and two glasses of cocoa. I hardly brought anything, just the dregs of my soup and one rissole. The soup was very watery today. It was pearl barley soup, but there wasn't much pearl barley in it. They gave us jelly today, but there weren't any oil-cake flatbreads.

Tomorrow is the last day of school, then we are on holiday until the 7th. Back to school on the 7th. There's going to be a New Year's party on the 6th. They're going to hold a New Year's party for local schoolchildren in the building of the Maly Opera Theatre. There will be a show, dancing and a meal – all for 5 roubles. Very interesting. What will they give us to eat? Yes, tomorrow is New Year's Eve. How will we celebrate it?[1]

Apparently the new ration cards are exactly the same as the old ones. They still say 125g of bread for white-collar workers and dependants, even though we're actually going to be getting 200g. And people are saying that they're going to increase it again. But people are saying all kinds of things, and none of it is to be believed. I'm so hungry. Not just for food, but for something else too. I don't know what, exactly. I would like something good to happen, something festive. I would like to see a sparkling, decorated fir tree.

---

1 The Council of People's Commissars of the USSR passed a resolution on 29 September 1929 ('O rabochem vremeni i vremeni otdykha v predpriyatiyakh i uchrezhdeniyakh, perekhodyashchikh na nepreryvnuyu proizvodstvennuyu nedelyu') in which all public holidays were listed, although it was also stipulated that 'on New Year's Day and all religious holidays (formerly special days of rest) work will be carried out on a communal basis'. The Soviet people continued to celebrate the New Year with decorated fir trees and organized entertainment, but 1 January remained a working day until 1947.

## 2 January 1942

I haven't written anything for a long time. So much has happened in that time.

It's 1942. A new year has begun.

Mama Lena and I are alone now. Aka is dead. She died on her seventy-sixth birthday. She died yesterday, on New Year's Day, at nine o'clock in the morning. I wasn't at home at the time. I had gone out for bread. When I got back from the bread shop, I was surprised to see Aka lying so quietly. Mama was outwardly calm, as always, and told me that Aka was sleeping. We drank tea together and Mama even cut me a piece of Aka's bread, saying that Aka would never eat it all. Then Mama suggested that I go with her to the theatre after lunch. I readily agreed, because I was scared to stay alone with Aka. What would I do if she died? I was scared that Mama would ask me to take care of Aka while she was at work. I didn't even want to get close to Aka, because it was very hard for me to see her dying. I was used to seeing Aka bustling about – such a dear, sweet old lady, she was always busy with something. But suddenly here was Aka lying helplessly in bed, as thin as a skeleton and so weak that she couldn't even keep hold of anything.

I didn't want to see Aka like that, so I gladly went with Mama. Mama locked the door behind us and took the key to Sasha's room.

'Mama, why have you locked Aka in? What if she suddenly needs something?'

But Mama said that Aka would never need anything again. She told me that Aka had passed away.

'When?'

'While you were out getting bread. That's why I asked you to come with me.'

'Really, Mama! I wouldn't have stayed alone in a room with a dead person anyway. Did she say goodbye to you?'

'No, she wasn't aware of anything.'

That was how I found out that Aka no longer exists, that Aka has gone.

She died very peacefully, according to Mama. She simply became still. She wheezed once, then again, and then she fell silent. The night before, on New Year's Eve, she had been in a bad way, and Mama had to keep going to her. I was asleep, but in my dreams I heard someone groaning in agony.

Aka is dead.

It's just Mama and I left. I've got no one else but Mama Lena, and she's got no one but me.

Now I will have to take care of Mama more than ever. She's everything to me. If she dies, I am lost. Where will I go? What will I do? But Mama is living on little more than the strength of her spirit. Her spirit is strong. She knows that she can't give up, because she has me.

Now I can continue writing. I went to school to get lunch. Today there was soup for 15 kopeks off ration. It was good soup. Made with pearl barley, and plenty of it. Then I took one portion of pearl barley with butter and four oil-cake flatbreads.

I wonder what Mama will bring. If Mama brings a lot, we won't eat it all at once but will save some for tomorrow. I can get lunch at school again up to two o'clock tomorrow. It's very good that we can get a bowl of soup during the holidays without using our ration cards.

So the New Year has begun, and we have received our new ration cards. There has not yet been any improvement in the food situation. Bread rations are the same as before: 200g for dependants and white-collar workers, 350g for manual workers. There's nothing in the shops, and whenever anything does appear they're still giving out rations for the first and second ten-day periods. They haven't said anything about the third ten-day period yet. The only thing we haven't taken for the third ten-day period is butter.

Yes, butter. That's what we need. There's enough bread, more or less, but no fats. The fact is that many people are living on nothing but bread at the moment.

But we're still living, somehow. We have no electric light – they didn't let us turn the lights on even at New Year. We have no water – for that we have to go down to the *zhakt* on the ground floor. The radio hardly works either. Every now and then it suddenly comes to life and speaks or sings, then falls silent again.

If only we had light we could carry on with some semblance of normal life. We could read, sew and so on. But without any light we go to bed at six o'clock whether we want to or not. Why would anyone want to sit in absolute darkness? At least it's warm under the blanket.

This is how we're living. The trams haven't been running for some time now, so Mama and I are faced with the additional pleasure of dragging ourselves on foot to the Vyborg Side. It's such a long way, but we have no choice. We need the money. I can't let Mama make such a long journey alone. My heart would break if she went alone. But fortunately I'm on holiday from school at the moment so we can go together. We'll crawl there somehow.

Mama really needs to get a permanent job at the theatre if she can. She might be able to arrange it. Then she'll get a worker's ration card and be entitled to use the canteen, where she can get two portions of soup a day. The canteen there is very good.

Now Aka isn't here Mama and I will be able to live more economically. We'll divide everything in half, not into three portions like before, and that will make a big difference. Whereas there used to be two dependants living on Mama's wages, now there's just one. It used to be the case that 600 roubles a month was barely enough for the three of us, whereas now the two of us, as fate has taught us, can easily live on just 400 roubles.

So even the death of someone as dear as Aka can have its positive side. As the Russian proverb says, 'it's a blessing in disguise'. Now Mama will be able to get 400g of bread a day, which is quite a lot. And we can get more at the canteen too. We'll be able to carry on like this for a whole month. And next month our situation is likely to improve.

It's extraordinary, really, how one thing leads to another. If we hadn't killed our cat, Aka would have died earlier, and we wouldn't have this extra ration card, which in turn will save us now. Yes, it's all thanks to our dear puss. He fed us for ten days. Our cat kept us alive for a whole ten-day period.

Never mind, there's no point being downhearted. Everyone says that the worst is behind us. And indeed – the blockade around Leningrad has already been breached in one place.[1]

---

1  Although it had no factual basis this was a widespread rumour at the time, not only in Leningrad itself but also further afield.

## 3 January 1942

Nothing remains for us but to lie down and die. It's getting worse and worse every day. The only thing keeping us alive lately has been bread. We've never been denied bread – I mean, up until now bread has always been available. We've never had to wait at the bread shop for it to be delivered. But it's already eleven o'clock and there's no bread in any of the bread shops, and no one knows when it will arrive. Stumbling and staggering, hungry people have been scouring the bread shops since seven o'clock this morning but, alas, everywhere they have found nothing but empty shelves.

It's good that Mama and I saved some *kasha* and one oil-cake flatbread for today, otherwise I don't know what we would have done. Instead of tea this morning Mama and I had two and a half bowls of hot soup, and because of this we are just about able to endure the lack of bread.

But it bodes ill if we're even having to 'hunt down' bread now.

When, oh when, will things start to improve? It really is time. People are so exhausted, I don't know whether many will re-main alive in Leningrad if the current food situation continues for another month. Many will not survive.

I don't know whether or not I will survive. I feel so weak today, for some reason. I can barely stand up, my knees keep giving way, and my head is spinning. But I was perfectly fine yesterday. And I'm not even that hungry. Why this sudden loss of energy? Perhaps it's the effect that Aka's death is having on me.

Mama is really worrying me. She has been so energetic lately. She's always rushing about, forever on the go, but at the same time swaying from side to side like a drunkard. I'm so worried that this unusual burst of energy will be followed a sharp decline. But what can I do? How can I prevent it? I don't know.

Perhaps it's nothing to worry about, and everything will be fine. Please, God, let it be so.

I wish we could get this business with Aka over sooner rather than later. She's still lying in the kitchen. We can't get hold of Yakovlev, and we can't do anything without him. He has to register the death. Then Mama will have to go somewhere else, and then we'll put Aka on a sled and take her to the hippodrome.[1] It's not far from here.

Oh yes, I forgot to say, the radio is working today, and we heard a Sovinformbyuro bulletin. Our troops have seized the town of Maly Yaroslavets.[2] They didn't even mention the Leningrad front. What does that mean? Probably that things have temporarily taken a turn for the worse. Here we are, dying like flies of hunger, while yesterday in Moscow Stalin hosted

---

1  Lena is referring to the Semenovsky Hippodrome, which was located within the Semenovsky parade ground. The hippodrome itself housed an anti-aircraft battery during the war, but during the first Siege winter an adjacent two-storey barracks building was used as one of the city's makeshift mortuaries.

2  The town of Maloyaroslavets, to the south-west of Moscow, was occupied by German troops on 18 October 1941 and liberated on 2 January 1942.

another dinner in honour of Eden.[3] It's simply disgraceful, the way they're stuffing their faces like devils, while we're being deprived of our basic human right to bread. They're holding all kinds of ostentatious meetings, while we're living like cave dwellers, like blind moles.

When will it ever end? Are we destined never to see the tender, young, green leaves of spring? Will we really not see the May sun? This terrible war has already been going on for seven months. More than half a year.

Yesterday Mama and I sat by the stove after the fire had died down, holding each other close. It was such a nice feeling. The warmth from the stove wrapped itself around us, and our stomachs were full. It didn't matter that the room was dark and deathly silent. We held each other tight and dreamed of our future life. And what we would cook for dinner. We decided that we would fry lots and lots of pork crackling and dip bread into the hot fat and eat it straight away, and we also decided to eat more onion. We decided that we would buy the cheapest types of *kasha* and serve them with plenty of fried onion, golden and juicy and sizzling with butter. We decided to make *blini* out of oats, barley, fine-ground barley and lentils, and many, many other things too.

But I must stop writing now before my fingers become numb from cold.

---

3   Stalin and Molotov's negotiations with Anthony Eden took place in Moscow on 16–20 December 1941, although there was a noticeable delay before this information was released officially.

## 4 January 1942

We finally took Aka away today. It feels as though a weight has been lifted from our shoulders. Everything went incredibly smoothly. Once the dead have been registered they are handed over to porters, loaded straight onto lorries and transported to the Volkovo cemetery. A long line of sleds bearing the bodies of the deceased leads up to the reception point. On some of the sleds there are two or even three bodies. Yes, many people are dying.

This morning I went out for bread at quarter past seven. The bread shop at no. 28 had none. I went to the bread shop behind the Pravda cinema and queued in the street for one and a half hours. My reward was some delicious bread – soft, fragrant and still warm, and I ate almost all of it as soon as I got home with a hot cup of tea.

After that we took Aka away, and now we are home again after acquitting ourselves of this unpleasant duty.

We had to hand in Aka's ration card after all. Comrade Yakovlev wouldn't register the death without it. It was very disappointing, but what could we do? We had no choice.

Now Mama and I have 200g of bread each a day. Perhaps she

will manage to find a job and get a worker's ration card. They might increase bread rations, but for the time being things are going to be very hard. Never mind, there's no point being down-hearted, and the devil is not always as black as he's painted.

## 8 January 1942

Mama and I are in a very difficult situation at the moment. There are still two days left until the end of the first ten-day period, but our canteens are not giving out anything more on either of our ration cards. So all we will have to live on for these two days is the soup I get from school. We are entitled to three rissoles as well, but there's no way of knowing when they will be available.

Today I begged a second bowl of soup, but I won't be able to do that tomorrow. My conscience won't allow me to beg every day.

Mama came back from the theatre with two cups of coffee, a portion of jelly and one horse-meat rissole. Mama and I are now drinking coffee and eating jelly, and we will have a bowl of soup at about five o'clock this evening. We're going to save the rissole for tomorrow. Somehow we have to hold out until the end of the first ten-day period, and then we will work everything out carefully for the second ten-day period.

Such a nuisance: I queued in the street for wine from three o'clock this afternoon, but when there were just eight people left outside the shop the wine ran out. I had frozen in vain. My feet were so cold that I walked home howling. I just couldn't stand up any longer. I felt that if I had to stay on my feet I would keel over and die.

Our school holidays have been extended indefinitely. Some people are saying it will be until the 12th, but others are saying the 16th.

There's nothing in the shop. Today they were issuing flour for the third ten-day period. But our shop hasn't got any butter yet for the third ten-day period. I heard that in another shop they were issuing jam instead of butter. Admittedly it's not as useful, but it's better than nothing.

## 9 January 1942

Mama and I are still alive. There hasn't been any kind of improvement yet. We have 200g of bread today. It's good bread, very tasty, and we were able to get it without queuing. We also have running water, and the radio is working.

Yesterday after two bowls of soup Mama and I also ate the rissole we were saving for today. And we didn't eat it straight away: we grilled small pieces one at a time on a fork over the coals. Oh God, it was so tasty. It was sheer pleasure. If Mama is able to bring two rissoles today, we will enjoy them in the same way.

On 6 January I went to a New Year's party at the Gorky Theatre.[1] First there was a performance of *Home of the Gentry*, which was followed by lunch, dancing around the decorated fir tree and a series of sketches performed by actors. There was a very pleasant and festive atmosphere. I thoroughly enjoyed it.

I was a little late getting there, and when I arrived I was given a pink coupon with the number 3 on it plus a ticket that

---

1  New Year's parties for those studying in the seventh to tenth grades were held at three Leningrad theatres: the Pushkin Drama Theatre, the Bolshoi Drama Theatre and the Maly Opera Theatre.

said '2nd Gallery Circle, no. 31'. I sat in the stalls until the first interval, then found my seat. At the next interval I went into the foyer. Here stood a beautiful fir tree, richly decorated and sparkling with multicoloured lights. There was music playing, and people were dancing round the tree, which was illuminated from above by coloured light from a projector. Crackers were exploding, showering the dancers with confetti rain, and multi-coloured paper streamers were rustling and entwining themselves around all the party guests. There were so many people that I only just managed to force my way through the crowd to find my friends.

At the beginning of the next interval, I met Leva Savchenko on the stairs.

'Lena, where is everyone?'

'Hi Leva, so you're here too? I don't think any of the other boys are here. I haven't seen them, anyway.'

'All right, then, I'll come and find you later.'

'Are you going to eat now?'

'Yes.'

With that he ran down the stairs to catch up with his friends. I stayed there for a long time, letting the children from the special school past. The whole of the Levkin special school was at the New Year's party on 6 January. And they were taken in to eat first. There were four different sittings for lunch. I was in the third sitting, and most of the people I knew were in the fourth.

During the next interval I spotted Tamara in the foyer. Leva was standing next to her. The three of us stood there talking for the entire interval. Leva told us how things were for them. They were getting very well fed.

'For breakfast today, before they brought us here, they gave us a plate of buttered noodles, this full, right to the edges, and a plate of millet *kasha*,' said Leva.

'Leva, what did you just have to eat? Was it nice?'

'Yes. The first course was *rassolnik*,[2] the main course was rissoles with buckwheat *kasha*, and the third was some kind of mousse. It was all delicious, but the portions were tiny, hardly more than a mouthful.'

'Leva, how's Dima? Do you ever hear from him?'

'No, nothing. I don't understand it. Not a word.'

'And Tamara, how's Emka?'

'I haven't heard anything from her either. I don't know anything.'

'What devils they all are. They've gone off and forgotten all about us, the beasts!'

Seeing Leva and the brief conversation we had gave me great pleasure. It turns out that Leva doesn't know anything about the other boys. They don't go and see him, and he doesn't go and see them. He hasn't seen Alka either. He also told us that their school might be evacuated. Then he promised to call in on Tamara to say goodbye.

While the second sitting were eating, those of us in the third watched the actors. They performed individual scenes from the life of Chapaev. At long last it was my turn to go to the canteen. At the entrance we were given a spoon, then we all sat down at a long table. They gave us a piece of black bread and a small clay pot of *rassolnik*. The soup was quite thick, with buckwheat *kasha* mixed in.

I ate most of the soup, but just as I had begun to transfer the solids into my jar the electricity went off. I managed nevertheless to successfully transfer all the solids and then, making use of the darkness, used my fingers to wipe the inside of the pot

---

2 A traditional Russian soup made with pickled cucumber, pearl barley and either beef or pork.

clean. We sat there in the dark for about an hour. I had already eaten my entire piece of bread and was dozing off by the time the lights eventually came back on.

Then they served the main course. We each had a small plate with just one rissole, though it was a fairly decent size, and no more than two tablespoons of buckwheat *kasha* with sauce. It was completely cold. I put it all into my jar, then used my finger to wipe every trace of sauce from the plate.

For the third course they gave us some soy milk jelly on a saucer. It was really unappetizing. I put it into a different jar. And that was all they gave us. I thought they would at least give us a sweet or a biscuit each. But no, nothing. It was quarter past six when we finished eating. I rushed home, because my hungry Mama was waiting for me there, because we had decided that we would make dinner out of whatever I brought from the theatre. I had expected to be home no later than four o'clock, but I didn't get back until half past six. I ran as fast as I could, although I couldn't feel my legs under me. As soon as I got back we made a soup out of everything I had brought, two bowls each, and we shared the jelly. Then we sat by the stove, warmed ourselves up and went to bed.

So that's how it went, this day that I had been dreaming about since last year, when we first heard that we were going to have a New Year's party with food. I had been so looking forward to it. I thought they were going to give us real party food and some kind of special treat.

I heard that at the New Year's party for the seventh grade, which was held in a different theatre, they had a different menu: meat soup with lentils, baked macaroni, jelly and various treats, such as chocolate, gingerbread, two biscuits and three soy sweets.

I don't know whether it's true or not. It's probably just nonsense.

## 10 January 1942

It's the end of the first ten-day period, but the shops are just as empty as before. Some people still haven't been able to get their rations from the second and third ten-day periods at the end of last year.

We're growing weaker every day. Mama and I are trying to use as little energy as possible and spend most of our time sitting or lying down. It's a good thing we're not back at school yet. Studying's the last thing on your mind when there's barely a flicker of life left in you.

School holidays have been extended to the 15th, but people are saying it will be even longer. I don't know why, but whatever the reason it's the most fortunate timing.

I'm very worried about Mama. If I'm so weak that it's making me unsteady on my feet, I can't imagine how she must be feeling. Truly, I'm not exaggerating – when I try to stand up after sitting down for a long time, I have to really exert myself. And when you get out of bed to use the chamber pot, your legs give way beneath you. When I go out I try to walk quickly and complete my journey without stopping, because as soon as you slow down your legs start to falter.

To make matters worse, it's still freezing. Temperatures are no worse than usual, but we're feeling the cold more than ever this year. The frosts are not that severe, but we're suffering as though it were −40°C. This is another symptom of the lack of food, of systematic malnutrition and extreme emaciation. It cannot continue for more than a month. One of two things will happen – either they will give us more food, or we will all turn up our toes.

It might sound strange, but we're not actually that hungry. When Mama and I go to bed we often feel full, but our bodies have been deprived of essential nutrients like fats and sugar for a long time. They are the two things we need the most. We are consuming food, and our stomachs are full, which tricks us into believing that our nutritional needs are being satisfied, but not much of this food is absorbed – most of it passes through the body as urine. We use the chamber pot a lot. We're eating little more than soup, hot soup. It fills us up because it's hot and there's plenty of it, or rather there's plenty of liquid. The actual nutritional content must be less than 10g. The soup they serve in the canteens is watery enough to begin with, and then we dilute it with more water at home. That's why we're growing weaker every day.

Yesterday Aunt Sasha told us about her new discovery, for which we might even owe her our lives. I had better explain.

Mama went to visit her yesterday for some reason and returned happy and cheerful. Apparently Aunt Sasha let her taste some meat jelly that she'd made out of good-quality carpenter's glue, then gave her a sheet of it so that we could try making our own. Mama started straight away. She boiled some water, enough for about two bowls, and put the sheet of glue in. Then she boiled it up again and poured it into bowls that she had already set out on the windowsill. We woke up at about six o'clock and were astonished to find that our jelly was ready. We both liked it. I really liked it. And when we added a little vinegar, it was simply delicious. It tastes like meat jelly, and you really do feel as though you're about to bite into a piece of meat. And it doesn't smell like glue at all. This jelly is quite harmless – on the contrary, it's very nutritious. Good-quality carpenter's glue is made from the hooves and horns of various animals. And of course some people buy the legs of young animals with the hooves attached specifically in order to make casseroles and meat jelly. By using this method, Mama and I will have a ready supply of extra food without using any coupons.

They have the same kind of glue in the theatre where Mama works. As it happens, she recently signed out 4 kilos from the storeroom when she needed them for work. That's about twenty sheets, and one sheet makes about three full bowls. Mama will try to sign out more glue, and then we'll be able to have a tasty, nourishing bowl of meat jelly every day for a month.

According to an old Russian proverb 'necessity is the mother of invention', and I've already worked out more ways to use this jelly. If you add fruit purée or syrup or wine or anything like that to the solution when it's still warm, as it cools it will make a lovely fruit jelly. And if you add a little more fruit purée, or better still jam, then you can make jelly sweets – essentially a stiff, sweet jelly that you can cut into individual pieces with a knife and eat with a cup of tea.

I'm sure we'll think up other possibilities once we start experimenting. If Mama brings rissoles today, for example, we are going to make jellied meat: we'll chop the rissoles into smaller pieces and boil them in the glue, and this will make a jelly that not only tastes of real meat but actually has pieces of meat in it.

I'm so glad that we worked out how to use this glue. I think it will help to make us stronger, particularly Mama.

The radio was working this morning, but now it's not. It's very cold in our room. I'm sitting here wrapped in a blanket as I write this diary. I'm waiting for Mama. It's already after three o'clock, and she said she'd be back at two. She's going to bring something today. Maybe that's why she's taking so long, because she's queuing for sweets. They gave sweets out at the theatre for New Year – maybe they're giving them out today as well, seeing as it's the last day of this ten-day period. I doubt it. But perhaps they're giving out syrup or coffee that we could have with our jelly?

I had two portions of soup today, as Lida promised me yesterday. It was watery soup, made with spinach, but it was still soup – two whole bowls full.

A new ten-day period starts tomorrow. We'll be able to get two 25g soups or one main course per coupon. Where Mama works, they sometimes give out oil-cake flatbreads filled with fruit purée in exchange for 50g worth of grain coupons. I think it's a good idea because you get two flatbreads for a 25g coupon, so 50g is worth four little flatbreads. We can share one flatbread between us and mix the fruit purée with glue to make some of the jelly sweets I mentioned yesterday.

It's getting too dark to write any more now.

Mama's just arrived home!

## 12 January 1942

It's already 12 January, but nothing has improved. They haven't increased bread rations, the shops are empty, the lights don't work, the radio doesn't work, there's no water, and the lavatory won't flush.

All we had yesterday was jelly made from carpenter's glue. Last night we ate one and a half bowls of jelly each. It's so tasty and filling. Very enjoyable. I was still so full this morning that I didn't eat anything but asked Mama to take my bread with her, to look after it for me. So that's something to look forward to this evening.

It's the afternoon now, the hardest time. It's cold. I'm sitting here in my coat, and my hands and feet are like ice. It's 5°C in our room now, and it's freezing outside again. It was −31°C yesterday, and it's the same today. It's impossible to stay outside for long. I went out for water earlier. We have water for two days now, thank goodness. I fetched two buckets. I'm going to school at twenty to two for some soup. I wish this day would hurry up and be over. But Mama will come home just after four o'clock and she'll bring noodles and rissoles. We'll start a fire, draw the curtains, warm the soup and make some meat jelly.

While the jelly is cooking, I mean while it's boiling up, we'll toast the rissoles, bread and noodles over the fire. That's how we always eat these days. We put little pieces of whatever we can on a fork and hold it over the fire. It's more economical, and besides it passes the time and is more agreeable. We'll have meat jelly again in the evening. It only takes two hours to cool. So much to look forward to today! But for now I have to sit here freezing and thinking of ways to pass the time.

The day before yesterday, when I wondered whether Mama was late because she was queuing for something tasty, I wasn't wrong: she came home with 100g of raisins, which she got with my ration card instead of sweets for the first ten-day period. It's awful – just 100g of confectionery. White-collar workers get 150g and manual workers get 300g.

Mama used my ration card because she's hoping to get a new ration card soon, an employee's card or possibly even a worker's card. Then at the end of the second ten-day period she'll be able to use her card to get rations for two ten-day periods at once. For example, if Mama gets a worker's ration card, then at the end of the second ten-day period we'll get: 100 + 300 + 300 = 700g of confectionery in total. Mama and I have already decided that if there are no sweets we'll get a 600g jar of jam and 100g of raisins. We can use the jam to make jelly sweets.

## 17 January 1942

We're still on school holidays. The days are crawling by, remarkably similar to one another. This is the way Mama and I
have been living for the past three days: we get up at about ten
o'clock in the morning. We don't know the exact time any more,
because the radio is not working and our clock keeps stopping.
Mama gets up first, then I get up. We eat a bowl of meat jelly and
drink hot water or, if Mama has been lucky, coffee. Then Mama
leaves. This is the worst part of the day. While I'm at home
on my own I occupy myself with housework: I fetch water if
necessary, prepare firewood, wash the dishes, and so on. Before
I know it, it's time to go to school. I get myself ready and make
sure I'm at school by twenty to two, but the eighth grade classes
are always still eating their lunch. I talk to one or two people
while I'm waiting, and then it's time to sit down at the table. I
wait to be given a bowl of soup. That's all they've been giving
us recently, just a bowl of soup, nothing else, and they don't
put any salt in it at all – it's just water, thickened with flour. It's
quite tasty, though. I pour mine into my jar and go home again.
By this time it's about quarter past two. The nicest part of the
day is approaching. I try to keep myself busy while I'm waiting

for Mama. This makes the time pass more quickly. Eventually Mama arrives, bringing bread and lunch and sometimes even coffee. We divide it all up between us, and then we begin our meal some time before six o'clock. We enjoy what God has sent us, we toast our cherished morsels and if there is coffee we drink it. Once the last embers have died away, we prepare our bowls of meat jelly and go to bed. We eat our jelly at about five or six o'clock in the evening, then sleep until the following day.

All being well, Mama will bring 300g of jam today. This will be for the second ten-day period on both ration cards and for the first on one ration card. Mama has arranged to share a 600g jar of jam with a man she knows. When Mama left the theatre yesterday this man was still standing in the queue, and if he managed to get the jam Mama will bring it home with her today.

I wonder what will be on the 'menu' for Mama and me today. Yesterday we each had 200g of bread, two bowls of *borshch*, 6g of bran *kasha* (three tablespoons), two bowls of flour soup, two cups of coffee and one bowl of meat jelly. Not a bad 'menu', all in all. I have to say, I went to bed yesterday feeling quite full, and so did Mama. Mama has been promised a worker's ration card for the third ten-day period.

I

I'm all alone, master of the whole apartment.
Mama has gone to the market, so I'll put the samovar on,
Split wood chips and boil them up for tea.
Although there's no food yet, I will prepare dinner.
It doesn't take long to make soup,
Soup, soup, shoe-polish soup.
Five fried loofahs will make a tasty main course.

'Miaow, miaow, miaow, miaow,' laughed the cat in the corner,
'I'll gladly eat pork and dip my whiskers in noodles,
But you can't tempt me with your shoe-polish soup.'


## II

People in riding breeches frequent the theatres and cafés.
In order to look like a grown-up,
I need to make myself some riding breeches too.
Dima took his trousers off there and then,
And chopped them up with scissors.
What a fun game! Oh, how the needle pricks.
The cat narrowed his eyes slyly:
'Miaow, a new distraction.'
And the clock, mouth agape, laughed to see him sew.
Tick, tock, tick, tock, how funny he looks.


## III

I'm a mucky little piglet,
I need to do some washing.
The mischief-maker scrubbed his dolls thoroughly with soap:
Tanya in the basin and Kutka in the bucket.
The cat rolled on the floor, choking with laughter.
Dima left the tap on and the water overflowed.
There's a puddle on the floor, oh dear!
The kitten got its paws wet, better wipe them with a cloth.
Pussy cat, pussy cat, let's run away! Together they climb onto the bed.
The cockroaches are startled, they weren't expecting such a bath.
The table floats about the room like a raft, carrying poor Kutka.
The flood draws nearer.
Dima looks for a dry place . . .
Hop, out of the window and into a puddle, giving the piglets an
    awful fright.

## IV

Grandma runs in with a bucket, Pyotr the caretaker brings a mop,
But the cook, carrying a poker, trips the boy up.
He lies on the floor and cries: 'What was that for?
Why did you smash my head and break my nose?'

## V

Mama won't catch me, I'm leaving on the tram.
I'll jump on the footboard, without paying for a ticket.
Oh, the square is so busy, but there's so much to see.
Ouch, some scruffy mongrel is ripping my shirt!
Doggy, doggy, don't bite,
The tram will go without me.
Doggy, doggy, oh, oh, oh,
Dima's lying in the road.

## VI

A man drove past, transporting a barrel of tar.
Black tar, sticky tar,
Horrible to touch.
The man had a beard and looked angry.
His horse was huge and shaggy.
Pulling a face at the man,
Dima grabbed the horse by the tail.
The man lost his temper with Dima,
He didn't drive past after all,
But grabbed Dima by the collar
And stuck him in the barrel of tar.

## VII

All the boys teased Dima:
Dima's black, Dima's dirty.

We don't want to play with you,
We don't want to soil our hands.
Poor Dima cried bitterly.
Instead of teardrops, tar-drops fell.
They spent two whole weeks washing Dima
And only just managed to get him clean!

I've just been to school. All they had was watery soup for 11 kopeks. They told us not to come to school on the 19th. There's no firewood.

### 20 January 1942

No matter what I try to do, everything seems to go wrong. At night under the blanket I make so many plans for the day, but nothing ever comes of them. As I said, everything goes wrong. And it's all because of the cold. In the afternoon it's only light in our apartment by the window, but it's so cold by the window that your hands freeze and you just can't do anything. You want to be able to think the same way as during the night, but you can't think at all. The cold is completely debilitating. Not only are your fingers incapable of holding anything, contorted as they are from the cold, but your thoughts seem to fly away out of reach. At night, on the other hand, the thoughts in my head replace one another with such feverish haste that I lie awake half the night, tossing and turning, and it's impossible to clear my mind. You want to stop thinking, but you can't. Whereas in the daytime your head is empty and you can't think of anything. Even crying is too much effort. You don't feel like doing anything. You don't even feel like going to bed. So you just stand there staring into space, because that's the only thing left to do.

I never realized that cold could have such a devastating effect on the human body. For example, I'm standing up to write this, my frozen fingers slowly forming letter after letter. I could sit down, but I'm loath to make any unnecessary movement. My feet have barely thawed out at all this past month. But it's a cruel winter out there. The winter sun is lighting up the roofs of the buildings.

Tomorrow is a day of mourning. It's the anniversary of Lenin's death. Everyone persists in believing the rumours that bread rations will be increased tomorrow. I want to believe it too, but I daren't. We've been getting such splendid bread lately, the likes of which we never had even before the war. It contains only wheat flour, so it doesn't even resemble black bread. It's so tasty. Simply delicious. Nice and light, with a golden crust, it doesn't break or crumble, and you can easily cut it with a knife, but 200g of this bread is not enough to fill you up. It's as though they're teasing us with a taste of luxury. So frustrating.

They say that bread rations will be increased tomorrow, and they say that butter will be available. They say that we've survived the hardest, that the worst is now behind us, that things can only get better. They say that they will give us lots of food. They say that we will get sanatorium rations. They say so much, people never stop talking, and you don't know whether to believe it or not. You want to believe it, you really do. We're all so tired, so completely fed up, that we're more and more sick of living.

I'm in an uncommonly bad mood today. I'm sick of everything. I feel so wretched, my heart is so heavy, I just want to let go, to close my eyes, to sleep. The cold, the feeling of permanently unsatiated hunger. The cold. That's the worst thing. If we could only be warm, then all our sufferings and deprivations would be halved.

The situation on the fronts hasn't changed. Our forces are attacking and overwhelming the Germans at every step. As they retreat, the Germans are turning everything into a barren wasteland. Everything is being ransacked, burned, demolished.

It's terrible to think what atrocities the Nazis are committing. They're turning the areas that they're leaving into lifeless wasteland, and this is being done systematically, on special instructions. Heaps of debris, piles of ash, mountains of corpses – this is what our troops are finding in the territory they have won back from the Nazis. It makes your hair stand on end and the blood run cold in your veins to think that it's not just a bad dream.

## 25 January 1942

They increased bread rations yesterday. This is how things stand at the moment:

|          | Dependants | White-collar workers | Manual workers |
|----------|------------|----------------------|----------------|
| Before   | 200g       | 200g                 | 350g           |
| Now      | 250g       | 300g                 | 400g           |

But everyone is very upset, because they had hoped for more.

It's impossible to imagine how Mama and I are living at the moment. This is the second day in a row that we've had a severe frost combined with clear, sunny skies. We have hardly any firewood left, just enough for a few bits of kindling a day to heat up our food. It's terribly cold in our room. We are living under our blankets.

This morning I ran out to get bread – no, that's not right, I wanted to run out for bread but ended up having to queue for half an hour, and it was even colder today than yesterday. The blood turns cold in your veins, your brain freezes, and the cold gnaws right through to your bones.

For 1 rouble 90 kopeks, the bread today is nothing special. It looks like bread – it's the right shape and it's brown, but it isn't cooked all the way through so it's very heavy. I hurried home, took my coat off straight away and went to bed. Mama put the water on to boil, and we drank a cup of hot water each and lay in our beds. While I've been writing these lines Mama has prepared the firewood to make lunch, and now I'm going back to bed again, because I'm absolutely freezing.

Something happened yesterday. Mama and I agreed that she would buy bread on her way home from the theatre**

## 29 January 1942

I haven't written anything for a while. I couldn't seem to find the time. We didn't have any bread for two days: 27th and 28th. Hardly any of the bakeries had bread. People are saying that the bread shortage is because the pipes burst at the bread factory, due to the heavy frost.[1]

Whatever the reason, we had to go two days without bread and without lunch, eating only the soup I got from school and meat jelly made from glue. Mama is so weak that she can hardly walk. But, as luck would have it, I got 975g of good-quality wheat flour yesterday instead of bread, and this cheered Mama up no end. We made flour soup and flatbreads straight away. If there's no bread tomorrow either, we can get some more flour. It's warmer today. It's snowing. The water is back on at no. 17. I went there earlier and queued for water. The frosts have been so severe lately, we have been forced to draw water from ice holes in the Fontanka.

---

1   On 27 January 1942 the only source of electricity in the city was just one small generator, with a capacity of no more than 3,000kW. This power shortage resulted in the temporary disconnection of the main waterworks.

I don't know whether we will live through this. The past two days have been so dreadful, they've really taken their toll on Mama. She's very weak, but her spirit is strong. She wants to live, and she will.

## 8 February 1942

Mama died yesterday morning. I am all alone.

## 10 February 1942

I heated the stove up until it was nice and hot. It's about +12°C in the room at the moment. I'll write in more detail tomorrow.

## 11 February 1942

They increased bread rations today. In the morning the care-taker's wife helped me take Mama to Marat Street.[1] We took Mama along the same route that Mama and I took Aka just a month ago. And when we took Mama today, just like last time, there was a snowstorm and then the sun came out in the after-noon. Afterwards the caretaker's wife and I went to the bread shop. I got 600g of bread and gave her 300g. Then I went to school and got a bowl of millet soup and a portion of millet *kasha* with butter. I came home, chopped up some firewood, warmed my lunch, ate some bread and felt that I didn't have the strength to do anything else. I wanted to fetch some water to wash the dishes, but today seems to have worn me out – not so much physically as mentally, and I really don't think I am capable of anything more. Yesterday I sold six sheets of glue for 15 roubles each. I made 90 roubles. Now I have 99 roubles and 60 kopeks. It turns out that they won't give me anything for the room. Ida Isaevna will bring me 100 roubles, no more. I

---

1  During the siege a temporary morgue was set up at Marat Street 76 (about 1 km from Lena Mukhina's apartment building).

will give 50 roubles to Ida Isaeva for the loan of the temporary stove.

I lit the big stove yesterday, and it was +12°C in my room. The stove was red hot, almost right to the top. I will get 600g of bread tomorrow, I can hardly believe it. I'm not going to do anything else now. I'm going to bed. Tomorrow is another day. It's so hard being on my own. After all, I'm still only seventeen. I have no life experience. Who is going to guide me now? Who is going to teach me how to live? I'm surrounded by strangers, and none of them care about me. Everyone has their own troubles. Dear God, how am I going to live alone? No, I just can't imagine it. But life will show me what to do, and I also have family – Aunt Zhenya.[2] She will help me, I am sure of it. But first I have to reach her. I should go and see Kira. Perhaps she will give me some money.

Oh, Mama . . .

---

2   Lena is referring to Evgeniya Nikolaevna Zhurkova (1892–1978), her mother's sister.

## 13 February 1942

When I wake up in the morning, at first I can't believe that Mama has really died. I feel as though she's here, lying in her bed, and she's about to wake up, and we'll talk about how we're going to live after the war. But then the awful reality sinks in. Mama has gone! Mama is no longer alive. Aka has gone too. I'm alone. It's just incomprehensible! Every now and then I'm overwhelmed by rage. I feel like howling, screaming, banging my head against the wall and biting myself! How am I going to live without Mama? The room is in a terrible state, and there's more and more dust every day. I'm probably going to turn into Plyushkin[1] soon. Will laziness really get the better of me? Am I really turning out to be just like my mother? I love it so much when the room is clean and comfortable. No, no and no again. I'm going to get up now, it's warm enough, and I'm going to tidy the room. Only I don't know where to start. I think I'll hang the curtains first, they'll make it feel cosier straight away.

So, I have 97 roubles. Ida Isaevna is bringing me another

---

1   In Gogol's *Dead Souls,* Plyushkin is a miser. His name was used to denote compulsive hoarders, living in squalor.

100. I need to get a job, but I think that I can make it through February.

Only seventeen days left.

Bread – 17 × (1 rouble 70 kopeks) times (17 × 3) = 857 kopeks = 8 roubles 57 kopeks.[2] The food situation seems to be improving. Yesterday all the shops were giving out grain on the new ration cards. Dependants get 250g, but since I'm using the canteen I get considerably less. Yesterday, without having to queue, I bought 125g of split peas and 200g of millet. I made a delicious millet *kasha*. It was simply wonderful. Yesterday I ate 600g of bread, a pot of lentil soup and a bowl of millet *kasha*, and I felt rather unwell. It's understandable, really – we've been surviving on so little for so long that this amount of food is too much for us now.

My dear, sweet, beloved Mama. You couldn't live just a few more days to see things improve. It's so sad. I feel so sorry for you that my heart aches. You died on the morning of the 7th, and they increased bread rations on the 11th and gave out grain on the 12th.

Dear God, how on earth am I going to live alone? I can't imagine it. I just can't imagine it at all! No, I must leave and go to Zhenya's. All the people around me are strangers. I'm so unhappy! Oh God, dear God! Why! Why is this happening?

---

2  These figures are exactly as written by Lena in her diary.

## 15 February 1942

I sent a telegram to Zhenya yesterday: 'Aka and Mama died. Please advise. Lena'. It cost me 5 roubles 25 kopeks. Yesterday I queued at no. 28 for sugar, but the sugar that had been delivered smelled of kerosene, so they took it back to the depot. They promised to bring more by two or three o'clock today. I met Lyusya Karpova while I was in the queue. She was queuing there for meat and got 125g for me on Mama's ration card. I'm grateful to her. It was a very good piece. Yesterday I brought split pea soup from school and diluted it with water, then added a teaspoon of millet and a little meat, and it made a wonderful soup. A small saucepan full. Then I added a little meat to the glue as well. It made three bowls of meat jelly. I've got enough split peas and millet for a few more meals too.

It's so frustrating, but there's no way I could have known: they were giving out buckwheat for grain coupons yesterday. Real buckwheat. If I'd waited just a little longer I could have eaten buckwheat *kasha* with butter.

Butter should be available soon. I'll get around 300g of butter. These days I'm eating so much during the day that I feel ill at night. Today I got up as soon as it was light and went to no. 28.

I thought they would have sugar and butter, but they only had meat. Then I went to the bread shop. I bought 600g of bread and decided to go to the market to exchange my bread for some sugar or sweets, but then I spotted someone with firewood on a sled and remembered that I was desperately in need of some. I asked for one piece, then another, and ended up swapping 400g of bread for nine boards almost a metre long and two fingers thick. Dragging them home was extremely hard work. But this firewood will last me for a long time. I need to do some washing, because I'll have to start getting ready for my journey soon and I don't have any clean clothes. I'll be leaving as soon as I hear back from Zhenya.

It's a real nuisance that my clock is broken. This is a very good room. It's nice and light and has a marvellous stove – it only takes a few little pieces of wood to make it glow almost right to the top. I've been tidying up a little bit. There's not much left to do. Soon it will be so cosy and warm in the room that it will almost be a shame to leave it. But no, I'm definitely leaving. Once spring comes they'll need extra workers at the *sovkhoz*,[1] so I'll be able to work there and then, when the war is over and I have saved up some money, I'll come back to my room and live here, and then I'll get a job. But there's no point getting a job now. I have enough money to tide me over.

I'm sitting down at the moment and I simply cannot get up. Firstly, dragging the firewood home earlier wore me out. I think I might have over-exerted myself. And secondly, I've just had a good meal. I had a bowl of yesterday's soup, 200g of bread, half a bowl of meat jelly and two cups of tea. I asked Aunt Sasha if I could borrow a teaspoon of sugar, and it went wonderfully well with my tea.

---

1  State-owned farm (abbreviated from *sovetskoe khozyaistvo*).

## 17 February 1942

I'm feeling quite rich. I have millet in one jar, pearl barley in another, buckwheat in yet another, a handful of split peas in a box and 125g of meat on the windowsill. I've had no luck with sugar, though. I still haven't managed to get any. Yesterday for lunch I had: split pea soup to start, followed by buckwheat *kasha* with butter, and then for supper I had pearl barley with butter.

For 1 rouble 25 kopeks, the bread today is nice and dry, very good and very tasty.

I've had the radio on for three days now. It's good because it stops you feeling lonely.

I've got money – 105 roubles. I've got firewood. I've got food. What more do I need? I'm completely happy.

It's cold today. The sun is shining, and there isn't a cloud in the sky.

## 25 February 1942

I'm sitting here after a filling lunch, drinking hot cocoa with bread. Today for lunch I had: two bowls of flour soup and some rice with cotton-seed oil. I'm going to light the stove now, because it's cold in the room: just +6°C.

I've been an orphan for over half a month already. I still can't believe that I will never see Mama alive again, the way she is in the photograph.

The food situation has improved. I've now got a ration card that I can use to get grain in the canteen, and I also have split peas, lentils and dried vegetables: onion, beetroot, cabbage. They haven't taken Mama's ration card away from me yet.[1]

---

1  Lena Mukhina later recalled: 'How did I manage to endure that torment, the removal of all that ice, without dying? Simply because Mama Lena died at the beginning of the month – 8 February. The house management committee felt sorry for me and decided to let me stay alive. So I was allowed to keep her bread ration card. From 8 February 1942 to the end of the month I was able to eat a double portion of bread' (Central State Archive of Literature and Art, St Petersburg, f. 495, op. 1, d. 315, l. 14). In fact ration cards were no longer being taken away at all, following the publication of a circular from Evgeny Grushko, the head of the Leningrad Militia Administration, on 7 February 1942. Representatives of the police authorities were no longer permitted to confiscate food and bread ration cards when deaths were registered at

I go to school at one o'clock every day for lunch. Now they're only giving soup on ration cards and there's no jelly, so relatively few people are there. The only people from our class I've seen lately are Lida Solovieva and . . . Leva Savchenko. Yes, Leva. Apparently their special school has already been evacuated, but he was ill at the time and**

domestic addresses (V. A. Ivanov, 'Osobennosti realizatsii chrezvychainykh mer po podderzhaniyu v blokadnom Leningrade rezhima voennogo vremeni', *Gosudarstvo. Pravo. Voina: 60-letie Velikoi Pobedy*, St Petersburg, 2005, p. 475, footnote).

## 27 February 1942

Things are gradually improving. God, it's such a pity that neither Aka nor Mama lived to see it.

I wish the war would end soon.

No, they weren't right, those who said that our government didn't care about us Leningraders, that 4–5,000 fewer Leningraders would make no difference to them. No, I always knew that it wasn't the case, that our government and Comrade Stalin himself were thinking about us Leningraders all the time and doing their best to alleviate our situation.

To tell the truth, I'm perfectly happy at the moment.

It's now about eight o'clock in the evening. I'm sitting at the table with a little oil lamp, writing my diary and listening to the radio. The room is warm and cosy. I've only just finished eating and I feel full. Today I had noodle soup, followed by a whole plate of noodles, marvellous white noodles and a rissole, and for dessert hot water sweetened with cocoa and some bread. So there you have it.

Lately we have been able to get grain on the fourth coupon, meat, cranberries and 150g of sugar. Furthermore, every ration card holder is entitled to a quarter litre of kerosene – I bought half a litre of kerosene just today – and the word is that we'll be able to get butter this month and dried fish on the eighth coupon. Apparently the new ration cards are a joy to behold too: plenty of grain coupons, and not just 12½g of grain per coupon, as it has been up to now – but 20g. People are also saying that canteens are going to start serving soup without ration cards. Bread rations are also expected to increase.

Moreover, there has been a noticeable improvement in our canteen: every day now there is a first course, a main course and a choice of meat. The soups are nice and thick, there's a good variety of *kasha,* served in large portions, and the meat – little sausages or rissoles – is very good quality. Nobody mentions horse meat any more. It's worth remembering that until quite recently the soup was just water, the *kasha* was nothing to speak of, and meat portions were so minuscule they were hardly more than a mouthful. The days of oil-cake flatbreads are over too, whereas at one time they were virtually the only food we had: soup made from oil-cake flatbreads, then a single oil-cake flatbread to follow.

Yes, so much has changed for the better. The bread shops always have tasty bread these days, but still people are not satisfied. Everyone is moaning, complaining, already dreaming about loaves of white bread and gingerbread. This just seems to be the way people are made, and there's nothing you can do about it: whatever you give them, they just keep wanting more. To begin with there's no black bread so they dream about black bread, and when they've got black bread they dream about white bread, and when they've got white bread they start dreaming about cakes. If there's no oil they dream about oil, but if they're given cotton-seed oil, for example, they'll dream about butter, then if they're given butter they'll dream about *smetana* and *tvorog.* And it's the same with meat: if there's no meat they dream about horse meat, if they have horse meat they want beef or lamb, if they have those they want pork, chicken or goose, and if they have those then they will want grouse, turkey, caviar, ham and goodness knows what else besides. It can't be helped, it's just the way people are.

# 1 March 1942

It's March. March has begun. The first month of spring. March, April, May and then summer. So, it's spring, even though it's snowing outside, and the sky remains wintry and grey. But never mind, March means that spring is here.

Bread rations haven't been increased yet. Yesterday I got 300g of cranberries and exchanged 200g of bread for another 200g of cranberries. I decided it was worth it, since I get bread every day, but they don't give out cranberries every day. I've just said goodbye to Ida Isaevna. She's leaving for Tashkent. She's a very nice person. Mama and I are indebted to her. Yesterday she gave me a pair of boots that are still as good as new. They're made of brown canvas, with a low heel. Just what I needed – I shall wear them this spring.

I wish spring would come sooner. I wish the war would end sooner. Patience, Lena, patience! All in good time. I'm just happy because I have it all ahead of me. So many delights, so many pleasures, so much to look forward to.

I'm going out for bread now. It's a nuisance that I have to save matches. I've only got four matches left, and there's no way of knowing when I'll be able to get any more.[1] They probably won't increase bread before the 5th. Everything is different now. They cut out 20g grain and 10g butter coupons for soup, 400g grain and 10g butter coupons for *kasha* and 50g meat and 10g butter for meat. Having said that, the soup is so thick that the spoon stands up in it and we get a whole plate full of *kasha*. I bought 225g of meat today.

So, I made a very good lunch today. *Kasha* with vegetable oil and sugar, then two bowls of noodle soup with meat and onion. Stewed meat, then fried meat and several pieces of bread fried in vegetable oil, and for dessert cranberry drink with sugar. What a splendid lunch! While I was preparing lunch Valya knocked on the door and gave me a postcard. The postcard was addressed to Mama. It was from Zhenya. It appears that Zhenya never received my telegram. She writes that she's worried about us and wonders whether we're all alive and well, because she hasn't heard from Mama for a long time. I've just written a reply. I'll post it tomorrow.

---

1   At the beginning of March 1942 *Leningradskaya Pravda* published the information that from 5 March manual workers, engineers, technicians and white-collar workers were entitled to two boxes of matches per month and dependants were entitled to one.

## 5 March 1942

Women's Day is coming soon. The weather these days is sunny and cold. Bread rations still haven't increased. When you think how much we have been through it's truly horrifying, yet at the same time heartening to know that the worst is behind us. I lived through it and am the only one of the three of us who survived. If the improvement in the food situation had been delayed by another half a month, then I would have followed Aka and Mama to Marat Street 76 . . . Marat Street 76! Such an ominous address, as so many thousands of Leningraders have discovered. I have managed to stay alive and I want to live. With this in mind, I cannot stay here. I need to find a way to Zhenya's in Gorky.

Yesterday my neighbour Raisa Pavlovna gave me a postcard that had been delivered, along with several letters, from the *zhakt*, where it had been lying around for some time. I don't know how this postcard ended up at the *zhakt*. The postcard was sent by Zhenya on 19 January. Zhenya writes that she's very worried because she's sent us a number of letters and hasn't heard back. She gives her address: Mogilevich Lane, Gorky. What a fool I am! I sent my telegram to her old address. That's why she never received it.

This is my current plan of action: I will send Zhenya a new telegram, and then I will try and make my way to Gorky. I'll go and see Kira and Galya and ask them to help me with this. Life will be very hard for me if I stay here. It's very difficult for me to work at the moment, because I am so weak, yet if I remain an unemployed dependant I will be forced to do compulsory labour duty. Spring will come, it will get warmer, the sewage will melt, and there will be a lot of work to do. They might even send us to the cemetery, to bury the dead and to run us into the ground too. No, I need to go to Zhenya's. Zhenya writes that they are getting by, even living well by today's standards. I could put some weight back on, regain my strength, find work and live with Zhenya or Nyura.[1] They are my relatives, after all – they love me, and of course they won't turn me away.

No, no, I have to go! I will write the following telegram: I am alone now. Aka and Mama are dead. Can I stay with you? Reply soon.

I am the only one left alive. Aka and Mama are dead. I am very weak.

Aka and Mama died of starvation. Life is very hard. I am weak. Zhenya! Can I come to you?

My heart breaks when I start remembering Mama. I keep imagining that Mama has just gone out to do some errands and will be back soon. I'm so hungry. Aren't they ever going to increase our bread rations? I'm so tired of dragging myself through this half-starving existence. As for work, I couldn't bear it at the moment – I'm too weak. I have to get to Zhenya's. Zhenya is my only hope, my salvation.

Mama, Mamochka, you couldn't bear it any longer, and you

---

1   The wife of Vladimir Nikolaevich Mukhin, Lena Mukhina's uncle.

passed away. Mama, my dearest friend, how you wanted to live. God, fate can be so cruel. You died courageously. Your spirit was strong, but sadly your body was weak. Mama, you grew weaker every day and then you died. But still you didn't once complain or shed a single tear. Instead you tried to cheer me up, and you even managed to keep your sense of humour. I remember that you were still up and about on 5 February. While I ran from one queue to another, you prepared the firewood. After lunch you calmly said that you were going to lie down for a rest. You lay down, asked me to put your coat over you and . . . you never got up again.

By the 7th you were unable to get up even to use the chamber pot. But what I found most upsetting was that on these last days – 5, 6 and 7 February – Mama hardly spoke to me at all. She lay there, covered from head to toe, all stern and demanding. When I threw myself onto her in tears, she would push me away: 'Foolish girl, why are you crying? Do you think I'm dying, is that it?' 'No, Mamochka, no, you and I are still going to the Volga.' 'Yes, we'll go to the Volga, and we'll make *blini*. But we'd better start by going to the chamber pot. Help me get this blanket off. Right, now lift my left leg down, and now the right, there we go.' So I lowered her legs from the bed to the floor, but when I touched them it was awful. I knew then that Mama didn't have long to live. Her legs were like a rag doll's – no muscles, just loose skin and bones.

'Oops-a-daisy,' she said cheerfully, trying to force herself to stand. 'Oops-a-daisy, hold me up like this.'

Yes, Mama, you had a strong spirit. Of course you knew you were going to die, but you thought it better not to talk about it.

I do remember saying to Mama, on the evening of the 7th: 'Kiss me, Mamochka. We haven't kissed one another for such a long time.' Her stern face softened, and we held each other tight. We were both crying.

'Dearest Mamochka!'

'Oh Lenochka, we're so unfortunate!'

Then we went to bed, or rather I did. After a little while I heard Mama calling to me.

'Lenochka, are you asleep?'

'No, what's the matter?'

'I just wanted to tell you, I feel so good right now. So comfortable. I expect I'll be better tomorrow. I've never felt as happy as I do right now.'

'What are you talking about, Mama? You're scaring me. Why do you suddenly feel so good?'

'I don't know. Never mind, go back to sleep.'

So I went back to sleep. I knew Mama was going to die, but I thought that she would live another five or six days. I could never have imagined that her death would come the very next day.

In my sleep I heard Mama calling me again. 'Lenochka, are you asleep?' I can still hear these words. Then she was quiet. I fell back into a deep sleep. When I woke up again, I heard Mama saying something, but I couldn't make out what it was, so I called to her:

'Mama, Mama, what are you saying?'

Silence. Then she muttered something else without answering me. 'She's probably delirious,' I thought. Then I fell asleep again.

When I woke up the next time, I could hear snoring. Well, I thought, at last Mamochka has fallen asleep, and I fell asleep again quite calmly. I don't know how long I slept, but suddenly I woke up feeling strangely agitated. My heart was telling me that something was wrong. Mama was still snoring, but it was not the snore of a calmly sleeping person. No. Mama was lying on her back with her eyes closed, breathing heavily through her mouth. Something was gurgling in her throat. I started shaking her, calling her. She opened her eyes and fixed me with a blank stare. 'Mama, Mama, can you hear me?' The same stare, then her eyes wearily closed.

Oh God, I thought – she can't see me, she can't hear me, she's dying. Her forehead was cold, her hands and feet were cold, her pulse was barely there. I ran to call for help. The neighbours came. They lit the stove. Prepared some hot water bottles. Made hot, sweet coffee and some kind of vitamin drink. But it was all in vain. Mama kept her teeth clenched shut. When they forced some coffee past her lips, she didn't swallow it. It was six o'clock in the morning. The neighbours left, telling me that I should try and get Mama to drink. So for the last few hours I sat next to her bed. She never regained consciousness and died quietly, somehow becoming still. I didn't notice, even though I was sitting right next to her. That's what death from starvation is like.

## 6 March 1942

At three o'clock I went to the post office and sent a telegram to Zhenya. Next I went to the Molodezhny,[1] but they weren't selling any tickets for today. Then I went to the Mikhailovsky Theatre and found out that Kira had been evacuated two weeks earlier. Then I went to Galya's. I was so worried that I would find nobody in, but that wasn't the case.

Alik's grandfather opened the door. His eyes were red from crying. It turns out that his wife, Yuliya Dmitrievna, died three days ago. Then Galya arrived. She has lost a lot of weight. Then Kira arrived. Then Galya and I went to collect Alik from nursery.

They welcomed me into their home like one of the family. They were all very happy to see me. Galya held me close and kissed me. It felt so nice.

Today we are taking Yuliya Dmitrievna away.

Galya and her father have kindly suggested that I move in and live with them. They have promised to help me as much as

---

1   The Molodezhny (Youth) cinema reopened on 4 March 1942 (*Leningradskaya Pravda*, 5 March 1942).

they can. And if they are evacuated, they will take me with them like a daughter. I hadn't expected to be welcomed so warmly, to encounter such sympathy, such affection. Shared misfortune brings people closer. Alik's grandfather, a fellow nature lover, is a remarkably kind-hearted person. I immediately felt myself coming back to life. I am not alone. I have found friends. I'm so happy. So happy.

It's such a shame about Yuliya Dmitrievna. She was an exceptionally good, kind person, just like her husband.

Galya is worried that her father won't make it either, but no, I refuse to accept this. I believe that the worst is behind us and that anyone who went through it and managed to survive will remain alive for some time to come. That's what I think.

Fate can be so cruel.

## 7 March 1942

I got up at eight o'clock. Just after ten I packed a few essentials into a shoulder bag, put it on a sled and set off for Galya's. The three of us took Yuliya Dmitrievna to the Kuibyshev Hospital. Galya's sister Kira, Galya and I walked back together. The weather was unusually clear and sunny. The sun was shining brightly, and there was a spring-like warmth in the air. Even the icicles were dripping. Spring, spring is making its presence felt. Galya and I went to my canteen and got four soups, some thick (*), and one portion of salami. Then we went to the shop at no. 8. I was lucky: they had only just started giving out raisins, and the queue wasn't very long. Galya took the soup home, but I stood there until I got my raisins then went back to Galya's. The two of us sawed up an enormous log and chopped it up for firewood. Then Galya went to fetch Alik, and I lit the stove.

Galya came back and put the kettle on for her father. Her father spent the whole day in bed with a weak heart and an upset stomach caused by his anxiety. It must be a tremendous blow, losing your life's companion like that. Then I put my soup on to warm up. I ate at half past six. Galya is so kind – she persuaded me to take a slice of bread, saying that it was all right to do so since they had Yuliya Dmitrievna's bread too.

Then I had a cup of tea with some raisins and bread, and now I am completely full. Tomorrow is 8 March. Women's Day. Galya will be at home. Galya is such a good friend. I'm going to bed now. I really want to sleep.

## 13 March 1942

'Frost and sunshine – what a glorious day!'[1] There are more and more signs of the imminent arrival of spring. The sun already has a spring-like warmth, steam is coming off the snow, and the icicles are weeping, although in the shade the frost still mercilessly bites your nose.

I'm living with Galya for now, looking after her sick father, doing what I can to help with the housework. Her father is feeling better today than he did yesterday, and Galya and I continue to hope that he will recover. He has an upset stomach caused by anxiety, and he is very weak. Galya and Alik leave at eight o'clock in the morning and come home at six o'clock in the evening. I'm alone with her father all day. He sleeps most of the time, so I am left to my own devices and can do whatever I like.

Right now, for example, it's two o'clock in the afternoon, and I'm sitting by the window and writing. The spring sunshine is lighting up the whole of this small room. Everything would be fine, if it weren't for this gnawing emptiness in my stomach. I'm

---

1 From the poem 'Winter Morning' by Aleksandr Pushkin (1829).

so hungry, it's simply unbearable. At the moment I'm living on soup and 300g of bread a day. I eat my bread in the afternoon, then I have two bowls of soup at seven o'clock in the evening. That's all. Over the past few days I have grown noticeably thinner and weaker. I don't know whether I will survive. I really want to live. I need to get to Zhenya's as soon as possible. Then I will be saved.

The evenings are agony. I sip my watery soup without bread (I can't make my bread last until the evening), while there is an abundance of bread on the table beside me and Galya cuts big, thick slices and eats them sprinkled with sugar from a jar. I know that it's wrong to feel envy, but I can't help thinking that Galya could easily give me a small piece of bread a day without depriving herself. After all, besides her own 500g she gets a further 700g: 300g for her mother and 400g for her father (he doesn't eat bread any more). She can't possibly eat that much, and she doesn't make many dried rusks, so this bread must be building up in her cupboard (which she keeps locked). It's a sorry state of affairs when someone is growing weaker every day from hunger, while there's bread going stale in the cupboard.

Of course this bread is nothing to do with me. It's Galya's, not mine, and I'm not family so she's not obliged to share it with me, but . . . but if I were in Galya's place I would offer a little piece of bread out of pity. My heart couldn't stand it. I would never dream of asking, though. I'm too proud and have too much self-respect to beg, but why doesn't Galya offer? She knows how hungry I am. Just 300g of bread for the whole day – it's hardly anything. I'm so desperately hungry. There's such a hollow, gnawing feeling in my stomach. God, dear God, please hear me, I'm hungry, do you understand? I'm starving. Oh, I'm so unhappy.

Lord! When will this end?

## 16 March 1942

It's already 16 March – halfway through the first month of spring, yet we're still getting severe frosts. It's warm in the sunshine but freezing in the shade.

I'm still living with Galya. The old man is getting worse every day. He won't last much longer. He's already struggling to speak, and it's impossible to understand anything he says (like Aka and Mama about three days before they died). He's also showing another sign that the end is nigh (I recall Aka and Mama) – increased thirst.

Yesterday we were almost caught up in a fire. It happened in the evening. The neighbour from apartment 27 came and asked Galya if he could borrow her axe to break his front door open, because he'd already been knocking for an hour and no one was answering and he was worried that something might have happened because his frail, elderly mother was at home alone. Galya gave him the axe, and he smashed the lock and opened the door. The apartment was full of smoke. The half-burned body of his mother lay in the doorway to the kitchen, and the floor was burning beneath her. The sofa and blanket were already on fire. Another minute or two and everything would have gone up in flames. Fortunately the fire was discovered just in time, the fire brigade was called immediately, and water was collected from all the neighbouring apartments. The flames were suppressed and a few burning rags were carried out into the snow, then the fire brigade arrived, took the whole floor up and extinguished it for good.

We had a lucky escape, really, as we might all have burned to death if the fire had spread. Of course, we could have left by the main entrance if necessary, but what would we have done with Galya's father? We wouldn't have been strong enough to carry him ourselves, but who would have helped us? The smoke would have suffocated him three times over before the fire brigade even got to us.

If the old woman's son hadn't come home today, or if he had come even a minute later, it would all have been over. Apparently he was due back tomorrow and he only came back today by chance. Life is full of such fortuitous twists of fate.

Kira wants me to register her as a temporary resident in my room, but I don't want to. I just can't bring myself to do it.

Although I don't feel quite as much warmth and attentiveness at Galya's as I had been hoping to, I'm still not disappointed in Galya. Kira tells me that I should be, but I understand Galya's position. Taking care of a dying parent and worrying about her son, all on her own. (Her sister doesn't help her with any of it.) It must be very hard for her, and she probably can't help being a little short-tempered. But things will soon change. The old man will die, and Galya will immediately feel relief as this heavy burden is lifted like a weight from her shoulders. We will bury him somehow, and then I'll see whether I can live with Galya or whether it's better for me to be alone. I will decide then, but it's not the right time to decide anything just yet.

## 18 March 1942

Galya's father died last night. Such a good man, such a kind man...

I went for lunch a little later than usual today, and there was nothing left for me. After standing in the queue for two hours, all for nothing, I was so upset I could have cried. From school I went to the shop and got 100g of meat, without having to queue at all. Then I went home. There was no telegram for me. I took my copper teapot to the market, but nobody wanted to buy it. On the other hand, I couldn't help buying nine postcards at a price of three for 1 rouble. The weather was lovely and spring-like with a nice warm breeze, and not at all cold even in the shade. I came home, gathered up all my things and went back to the market. I was so hungry that I was determined to exchange my aluminium milk-churn for bread, although I was very sorry to part with it. Suddenly I noticed more postcards. I couldn't help it, I started looking through them but it was so difficult to choose. They were brightly coloured, mainly foreign, all with different views, and they were so beautiful I couldn't tear myself away. I ended up buying fifteen postcards for 1 rouble each. If I had told anyone about my purchase they would have scolded me for all they were worth, and with good reason. It really is an unforgivable stupidity to waste money on postcards in times like these. But it's something that brings me great pleasure and joy. After all you can't buy postcards like these just anywhere – they're antiques, and foreign too. How could I have passed up the opportunity? It's such a pleasure to feel that they are your very own postcards. No, I don't begrudge spending money on such wonderful postcards. I've got a total of thirty-four new postcards now.

So, I bought those fifteen postcards and exchanged my little milk churn for 250g of bread. When I got home, Galya had already used up the fire in the stove. I didn't get the chance to cook my meat, so I went without any supper. I had a cup of hot water and some bread and went to bed. I slept very soundly, and all my dreams were pleasant. I dreamed mainly of Grisha Khaunin. In my dreams he and I were friends and we were riding on a rollercoaster, which was scary and strange, and we were both really frightened but the ride ended well. I woke up this morning to the sound of Galya crying in the next room, saying: 'Papa, Papochka, you're sleeping, aren't you? Please wake up'. I completely understood. I ran to Galya, put my arms around her and kissed her.

## 21 March 1942

Greetings, dearest diary, I am turning to you again. I'm very happy at the moment, and this abundance of pleasant feelings is making me want to write.

So what if there's a war? So what if we're starving? Life goes on. Everything we have to endure is temporary. There's no point being downhearted.

'Begone, melancholy and sorrow,
I look boldly towards tomorrow!'[1]

As soon as the war ends I'm going to exchange my room for one in Moscow. It's so nice to think that I'll be living near Zhenya and at the same time I'll have my own room, where I will be in charge. Everything in my room will be just as I want it. It will be comfortable and cosy. The whole room will be one big nature corner. There will be aquariums standing on a table in front of the window, in which schools of tiny multicoloured fish will swim amongst different kinds of algae and other water plants. In the evenings the aquariums will be illuminated with little

---

1  Lena is misquoting Franz Lehár's 1909 operetta *The Count of Luxembourg*.

electric lamps, which will make them a comforting presence both during the day, when the sunlight shines through them, and in the evening, when the curtains are closed. The rest of the free space on the windowsill and table will be occupied by potted plants. There will be lots of different house plants: geraniums, lilies and various others. And spacious cages will hang above it all, housing my favourites – little birds. There will be bullfinches and siskins and redpolls and canaries and ordinary sparrows. I will gradually tame them, so that they allow me to handle them. A special place will be occupied by a terrarium containing white mice, or maybe not white mice but ordinary grey ones or field mice. And there will probably be some other animals too. I don't need a cat or a dog. I will transfer all the affection that I felt for Mama and Aka to my little house guests. Their affection towards me will replace the maternal kindness and love that I have lost. I will treat them with tenderness and devote my heart to them, and they will repay me in kind. I know it. They are very appreciative, these little creatures, and they know when people treat them well.

It's March. Spring. The snow is melting in the sun, the sparrows are chirping gaily. It's warm in the sun, and the air smells of warmed earth and dung. It smells of spring. The days are cloudless and sunny, though still very cold.

I found volume 1 of Franklin's *Natural History*[2] at Galya's too. They are remarkable books. I'm going to read them and make notes in my diary. I really want to find some little twigs and

2   The Russian edition of *Natural History in Stories for Educated Readers and Young People*, by Jonathan Franklin, was published in two volumes by M. O. Wolf, St Petersburg, 1862. The first volume was about mammals, herbivorous animals and birds; the second was about reptiles, fish and other fauna. A second, revised edition was published by the same publishing company in 1875.

branches, so I can see the first spring leaves as soon as possible. Whenever I start thinking about what I would like to study in future, I keep coming back to zoology. This discipline attracts me more than any other. It is my dearest dream to become a zoologist, and in due course it will become a reality. I will be a researcher in zoology at the Academy of Sciences. I will be sent on expeditions, I will travel to the different corners of the country, and then I will return and add my contribution to the world's treasure trove of knowledge.

In making his observations, Franklin unwittingly encourages the reader to regard animals not as study objects or as machines to be used as we see fit, but as living beings in their own right. He invites us to consider them simply as they are. Everything he writes is permeated by a most genuine love for nature in its broadest sense, by a love of truth and justice.

In order to understand animals, we must first learn to see things from their point of view, to share their feelings, their worries and their joys, and to find pleasure in associating with them.

The study of natural history not only facilitates intellectual development but also serves at times as a comfort to man.

In times of trouble or moral uncertainty it is sometimes enough for a person who loves nature, who has spent time studying it, to rest his gaze on a small flower, to hear the song of a bird or the buzzing of an insect – and his heart is revived with hope.

## 22 March 1942

I'm quite satisfied with the way my day has gone today. Yesterday evening I dried some rusks and kept one little rusk for this morning. I gave it to Galya, and when she was feeding Alik in bed she gave it back to me, thanks to which I was able to wait until this evening to buy my bread. At ten o'clock I went to my shop and got my 200g of sugar and 50g of meat. Then I went home, chopped some firewood, lit the stove, boiled up some glue with meat, ate a whole bowl of hot soup and was completely full. Then I heated up some water and washed the dishes, then washed myself. At four o'clock I went back to Galya's. I walked through the flea market again. Amongst all the odds and ends I suddenly noticed something special, a real treasure – the complete collected works of Brehm in four thick, beautifully bound volumes. It really was an exceptionally rare publication. 'How much for this lovely set?' 'I'm practically giving it away. Only 170 roubles, or 600g of bread.' She showed me the inside of one of the books too. An abundance of photographs and colour illustrations gazed back at me. I got to Galya's at four o'clock, but she wasn't there, even though we had agreed that I would come at three and she would already be there by then. I had to wait for her in the kitchen for more than quarter of an hour. I couldn't get the Brehm books out of my head. When Galya finally arrived I had already decided to go back and get them in exchange for 300g of bread and 100 roubles. But by the time I had got ready, bought bread and run back to the market, the seller was no longer there. I walked around the entire market but I couldn't find her anywhere. So I missed out on Brehm.

Today is the same as yesterday. 'Frost and sunshine – what a glorious day!' I may yet acquire the Brehm books. If she didn't manage to sell them, she might come back.

## 23 March 1942

It's warm today, even in the shade. Towards evening it began to cloud over. The sun disappeared. Galya is rearranging the rooms today. I keep dreaming about birds and about the future, when I will be able to live my life exactly as I please. I dream about warmth, about being able to fling open the window, remove the boarding and bask in the warm sunshine. I dream about summer.

I wish summer would come sooner. Warm days. Grass and leaves, green trees, flowers, birds, insects. God, how I want to see all this. Don't worry, Lena, patience, just a little more patience. Time does not stand still. It moves. Everything has its own time. May will soon be here, and summer will come with its rains and hot days. And everything will be fine.

## 24 March 1942

Yesterday evening I went back to my room, ate some meat jelly, drank a little water, put my postcards into the albums that Galya gave me, then went back to Galya's. It seems that spring has finally arrived. The cold days are over. A sudden warm spell has set in. Yesterday evening the temperature was +1°C. Soft, fluffy snow drifted gently down, and a warm breeze caressed my face, which has become accustomed to frost. There are puddles everywhere, the roofs are dripping and icicles are breaking off with a sharp ringing sound.

Today is the same. On days like these you just don't want to go back inside. The sky is full of clouds, and there's a fine, barely noticeable snow falling. This warmth will soon be joined by sunshine, and then it will be real spring. Everything will be fine.

## 25 March 1942

It's only the second day of the thaw and the snow has almost completely melted. The air is terribly humid. There's a warm wind, but it's very humid. Water is pouring from the roofs. There are little streams, even rivers running everywhere. It's terribly slippery. The tramlines have already thawed out in many places.

I missed Yakov Grigorievich this morning. He usually leaves at nine o'clock, but he left at eight today for some reason. He's not working tomorrow. So the earliest we'll be able to start the registration process is the 27th. That leaves the 28th, 29th, 30th and 31st, which should be just enough time to do everything properly.

I asked Rozaliya Pavlovna for advice regarding my room, because she knows a lot about that kind of thing. It has all come about because of Galya. She has a spare room, which she needs to give back to the *zhakt* since she can't afford to pay for it at the tripled rate, and she's going to sign it over to me.[1] The main

---

1   Rental and other housing payments were regulated by a resolution passed by the Central Executive Committee and the Council of People's Commissars of the USSR

thing, says Rozaliya Pavlovna, is that I need to make sure they open a personal account for me at Galya's *zhakt*. Then once the new room is in my name, I'll just have to sign my room over to my local *zhakt*. That's all there is to it.

To be honest, I am rather fond of the room I have at the moment. It's large, warm and light. There's plenty of space in front of the window. It looks out onto the street, and you can also see a sizeable area of sky. But on the other hand it's too big for me, and during the summer it only gets the sun in the evening.

On the other hand, Galya's room is just right for me. It's 10m². It has a low ceiling and is almost square. It's nice and warm, and the main thing is that it gets the sun all day, which, for a nature lover like myself, is of the utmost importance. My future nature corner will need sunshine more than anything. And anyway, I'll get tired of living on my own. Yes, I'll move in with Galya. This move makes perfect sense to me.

But there is another issue. What should I do with my furniture? I'm the owner of a large and rather handsome sideboard. It's oak, too. I'm reluctant to part with such a splendid item, but I can't see that I have any choice. I'll have to sell it. It would be extremely difficult to move it, and in any case it wouldn't fit in my new room.

---

on 4 June 1926 ('O kvartirnoi plate i merakh k uregulirovaniyu pol'zovaniya zhilish-chami v gorodskikh poseleniyakh'). The standard accommodation allowance was 5.5–5.7m² per person. In Leningrad tenants were charged at the rate of 44 kopeks per square metre (2 roubles per square *sazhen'*, an old Russian measure equivalent to 2.13m). Manual and white-collar workers earning less than 125 roubles a month paid a discounted rate of 25 kopeks per square metre. Students were also entitled to specific benefits, as they were included in the category of those earning less than 20 roubles a month. Payment for living space over and above the standard allowance was levied according to a special tariff. Residents paid for communal services and central heating separately, according to actual use.

I plan to sell the sideboard for at least 600 roubles. I can use this money to buy Galya's table and cupboard, which she is planning to sell anyway. There should be enough left to buy a couch or a small sofa. And perhaps something else too. Yes, I need to think ahead.

## 30 March 1942

'No wonder winter rages, for her time is all but gone – spring, tapping at the window, demands that she move on.'[1]

Heavy snow, strong wind. There's a terrible snowstorm outside. I have to report for labour duty again at two o'clock today. Hopefully the snowstorm will have died down by then. Today is the fourth day of this organized effort to clear the city of snow.[2] It will continue until 8 April. And after 8 April Yakov Grigorievich will arrange for me**

---

1 The first lines of the poem 'No Wonder Winter Rages' by Fedor Tyutchev (1836).

2 The city's clean-up operation began with three consecutive *voskresniki* (Sundays spent by the public doing voluntary community service) on 8, 15 and 22 March 1941. However, results fell short of expectations, so the Executive Committee of the Leningrad City Council passed a resolution on 25 March requiring all city residents capable of work ('men between the ages of fifteen and sixty and women between the ages of fifteen and fifty-five') to continue clearing the streets from 27 March to 8 April. This period was subsequently extended to 15 April. Those participating had to work six hours a day. As Lena Mukhina later recalled, the first days of work did not come easily to her: 'I had no strength at all in my arms, which meant that I was incapable of either breaking up the ice with a crow-bar or even shovelling it from here to there. So I was employed as a "horse": other people shovelled snow and ice into a metal bath that had been dragged from somewhere, and several people

(including me) were attached to a harness made of ropes and hauled the bath to the Fontanka. The path was long and hard. We had to use our last reserves of strength. Basically, we worked ourselves into the ground. At the banks of the Fontanka, opposite the Gorky Drama Theatre (Mama Lena's last place of work!) the stronger ones among us lifted the bath and tipped the ice into the river. We tried to walk back as slowly as possible, to catch our breath and rest a little. But as soon as we reached the courtyard the bath was immediately filled again and we "horses" shuffled back towards the Fontanka, dragging our load. How many of these trips did we make in a day? I can't remember. But I do remember clearly that when this torture finally came to an end and we were released for the day, I no longer even had the energy to walk up to my room on the third floor like a human being – instead I crawled on all fours . . . It was a cruel punishment: people who by some miracle had managed to survive that terrible, hungry winter, people who were more dead than alive, who were barely able to put one foot in front of the other, being forced to do such back-breaking, physical work – breaking, raking, shovelling ice. The only ones exempted from duty were those who were so weak that they couldn't even get out of bed. But those who were able to stand on their feet, however unsteadily, were forced to work, threatened that otherwise they wouldn't be given a ration card for the following month. This clean-up operation 'cleaned up' plenty of people too: they sacrificed the last of their strength to it, and in doing so became so weak that in the end it killed them. I do understand, though: this cruelty was necessary in order to prevent epidemics in the spring.'

## 31 March 1942

I was very lucky today. I went to work at eight o'clock this morning and I was already free by eleven. Our house manager[1] gave us a specific task – to find and clear three manholes – and said that after we had completed the task we could go home. So we did. Such good fortune. As soon as I was free I went to no. 28 and got 60g of sunflower oil, and then I bought bread. I will have enough to eat today.

---

1   The person in charge of the management and maintenance of an apartment building. The Central Executive Committee and the Council of People's Commissars of the USSR passed a resolution on 17 October 1937 ('O sokhranenii zhilishchnogo fonda i uluchshenii zhilishchnogo khozyaistva v gorodakh') abolishing *zhakty* (co-operative rented housing associations) and housing construction cooperatives and transferring the management of individual apartment blocks to local authorities. Direct responsibility for the management of each individual apartment block (with living space of more than 3,000m² or over 500 residents) or group of apartment blocks was given to the house manager, who was to be appointed by the housing management committee of the local council. The house manager was responsible for keeping administrative records and accounts in accordance with budgets established by the housing management committee. He or she was also responsible for ensuring that any material repairs were carried out when necessary and to the required standard and for overseeing the maintenance of the building, its technical and sanitary apparatus and all communal areas in apartments.

# 1 April 1942

March is over. Today is the first day of the second month of spring. April has begun. Greetings, April, month before May. What will you bring me?

For now, nothing has changed. Bread rations haven't increased. I got a dependant's ration card. Yesterday evening Yakov Grigorievich came to see me and said that I should take the no. 10 tram to no. 25 and he would meet me there at eleven o'clock this morning. I left the house at half past nine. I decided that I would buy my bread on the way back, but then it occurred to me that I might need to leave my ration card there so they could issue a new one, so I changed my mind and bought my 300g on the corner of Leshtukov.[1] I had a knife with me and cut the bread in half there and then. I cut one half into slices and decided that I would eat this half on the journey but keep the rest until I got home and eat it before going to work, with vegetable oil. But I ate the first half before I even got to the bridge

---

1  Leshtukov Lane (now Dzhambul Lane) was named after the Frenchman Jean Armand de Lestocq (1692–1767), physician to the Russian court. There was a bread shop on the corner where this lane met Zagorodny Prospekt.

over the Neva. It was such soft, tasty bread that it simply melted in my mouth, and I couldn't help myself. Somehow or other, by the time I got to no. 25 on the no. 10 tram I only had a quarter of my bread left.

Yakov Grigorievich sent me to the directorate so I could fill out an application. But when I got to their office, the boss was there and he said that they weren't going to be accepting any new applications until the 8th. So my journey was completely in vain, except for the fact that at least I know where to go now. I was barely able to drag myself back. I got home at one o'clock and went straight to the *zhakt* to tell them that I wasn't able to work today. I went home and immediately lay on my bed. Rozaliya Pavlovna came at three o'clock and gave me a pass to the canteen on the corner of Zagorodny and Nakhimson Square. Izabella Abramovna had given it to her to give to me, because she had a spare. I went there straight away and bumped into Izabella Abramovna herself. I thanked her warmly. There was no *kasha*, only split pea soup and black pudding. I was lucky enough to get two portions of black pudding and one soup. Generally on one pass you're only allowed one soup and one main course.

Well, now I am saved. I have a pass for a canteen.

It's warm today. The sky has been almost completely clear all day. The snow on the sunny side of the streets has already completely melted. Towards evening the sky turned monotonously grey.

I've got a good room. I particularly like it because a large part of the window is occupied by the sky, and that's nice. Yes, I really like my room, it's so bright and spacious. Oh, I'm going to have a wonderful time living here. Over time, I will establish a splendid nature corner by the window. Fish in aquariums, flowers in pots and little birds in cages. Dear little birds, how long must I wait? I'm never going to have cats or dogs – only little animals, and mainly birds.

## 2 April 1942

It has been overcast all day. A thick snow is falling. It's warm. I went to work at eight o'clock. There were ten people from our *zhakt* to begin with, but after the first hour of work half of them had already left. By ten o'clock there were only two girls, who were no older than me, one woman and me. I went home for quarter of an hour as well. The weather is mild and quite pleasant, although this snow is rather tiresome – you have to keep shaking it off.

I did very well today. My arms feel stronger. One bowl of soup makes such a difference. Admittedly I also ate two portions of black pudding yesterday. I'll go to the canteen again today as soon as I finish work.

It has been snowing all day. Everything has gone white again, like the middle of winter.

Fluffy white snow,
Spinning in the air,
Falls to the ground
And lies in silence there.

All is white again,
Underneath this snow.
It should be spring by now,
But it simply is not so.[1]

At the canteen today they had: noodle soup, split pea *kasha* and meatballs. One pass entitles you to one portion of everything. So that's what I got. Then I mixed my soup, *kasha* and meatballs together to make three bowls of soup. I dried some rusks, tucked myself up in bed and ate them there.

Now I'm completely full. I can rest as much as I want. It's much better to get my work done in the first shift, and then I'm free. What joy! I can lie in bed and read or listen to the radio.

---

1   Lena is quoting the poem 'Winter' by Ivan Surikov, though with significant changes to the second stanza. (Compare Surikov's version: 'The field, turned white / In the morning snow, / Might be wrapped in a shroud / For it looks precisely so.')

## 3 April 1942

I decided to go to work at two o'clock today. There are only five more days of work, not counting today. Now I have more energy and I can work properly. When you concentrate on work, rather than just counting down the hours until the end of your shift, it's over before you know it.

So I'll go to the canteen at twelve o'clock today and have lunch. Then I will go to work, and at eight o'clock I will come home and go straight to bed. I think this is a good plan.

Today is warm but overcast, though it's not snowing. I have planted two peas. It's cold in the room, but I don't want to burn the last of the firewood. I really miss sugar. I hope they give us sugar soon.

I feel like doing something. Perhaps I should read? It's so hard living alone. There's no one to talk to about your thoughts, your worries and your sorrows. Having my diary really helps, though. And another comfort is Mama's picture on the wall. She looks so nice in it, my dearly beloved Mama. Fate can be so cruel!

# 4 April 1942

I went to the canteen at two o'clock yesterday. It appears that they don't start serving lunch until one o'clock. Yesterday I had split pea soup and boiled noodles. I came home, ate and went to work. We worked until seven o'clock. I was responsible for loading and unloading the truck for the first time. It was very hard, but at least I didn't have to walk.

The weather has been fine all day, without a cloud in the sky. There's a light frost. Frost, in April! They're giving out grain in the shop today. Tomorrow they're going to give out sugar. This morning I went to the bread shop and arranged with a boy that he would get me a baby mouse in exchange for 100g of bread. So, I will be sharing my room with another living creature. I won't be so alone. I'll share all my food with it. After all, mice are omnivorous animals. Does a mouse need much food?

Only five days of work left. Never mind, I'll get through it somehow. I wish the time would come sooner when I'll be able to keep little birds.

Apt 6, Marat Street 29. Elizaveta Georgievna Peskova. Vet.

## 10 April 1942

I haven't written for such a long time! Not since 4 April. A lot has happened during this time. So much that I can't even remember everything. All I will say, briefly, is that I would almost certainly have left for Zhenya's by now, but I missed the opportunity by just one day. Evacuation has been suspended[1] and will resume only once Lake Ladoga is free of ice. It would have been possible to leave any day, right up to the 6th, by registering on the same day. But I only found out about this on the 6th. I went to the evacuation point[2] for the first time that day and joined the queue for registration. The queue wasn't very long at all. I decided that I would register for the 7th, so I would be leaving the following day. But then I found out that it was only possible to register for departure the same day, so I would have to register on the 7th to leave on the 7th. So I left the queue, since I was not able

---

1   In fact evacuation across the ice of Lake Ladoga continued for another five days, until 15 April 1942.

2   There were two evacuation points in Leningrad: one at Finland Station and the other in the Zvezdochka cinema building at Kommuna Street 44. There was a shop at the Finland Station evacuation point, where evacuees could buy warm clothes.

to leave on the 6th because I hadn't got my things ready. But I decided that I wouldn't put off my departure any longer and would definitely leave the next day. I decided that I would spend the day selling what I could, then I would pack that night and go and register for the five o'clock train the following day.

I started by dragging my sewing machine to the commission shop, but I didn't have time to leave it there to sell so they offered me 96 roubles in cash. I decided that it wasn't enough. By my reckoning I would have been selling it cheaply at 100–125 roubles, so I certainly wasn't prepared to accept any less. I decided to take it to the market and try my luck there, and on the way a woman stopped me in the street. She looked like an educated person. I told her I was selling the sewing machine for 200 roubles. She wanted to inspect it more closely, so she came back home with me. After looking at it, she offered me 150 roubles. I agreed, since I didn't want to miss the first opportunity to sell it for a reasonable price or to drag this heavy object anywhere else. When she found out that I was planning on leaving and was selling everything I owned, she began to select more things for herself. First books, then dishes, then clothes. She paid me and said that she would be back soon to pick up the sewing machine. She brought her neighbour with her. They didn't leave until later that evening. They bought various things from me for a total of 570 roubles. Then I called in on Yakov Grigorievich, and we agreed that he would give me 550 roubles on the condition that everything that remained in my room after I left would belong to him.

I didn't sleep that night, and by morning all my things were packed. I decided that I would go to the canteen as soon as it opened and use whatever grain coupons there might be**

And it was because of this that I didn't leave. When I got to the evacuation point at twelve o'clock there was already a dreadful queue. Registration was in full swing, but they were only registering people for the 9th. I decided to register for the 9th, but at two o'clock they stopped taking registrations, saying that they weren't going to register anyone else that day. They told us to come back the next day at nine. And that was my second mistake: I believed what they said and didn't go back there that day. As it turned out, they started taking registrations again at five o'clock for the 8th, and the people standing next to me in the queue went back then and registered. I saw them on the 8th, and they had already registered. It was so upsetting. My third mistake was that I got there at eight o'clock on the 8th to find that a big queue had already formed, and when we were given numbers I was 236. But they only registered ten people that day. I stayed in the queue until two o'clock, and then I left. I went back again at six o'clock in the evening and waited around until eight o'clock, but they didn't register one more person that day.

Having learned from bitter experience, I didn't sleep at all on the night of the 8th, even though I'd completely worn myself out over the past few days. I left at first light on the 9th, joined the queue at five o'clock and was given number 78. If they had been taking registrations I would have registered and left the same day, but yet again there was no registration. We queued all day, and then they announced that there would be no registration that day and they didn't know when it would begin again. But those of us who were the most desperate – those who, like me, had already sold everything, packed their things, left work, even handed in their ration cards – decided that we would wait there until the evening come what may, in case a few free places came up on one of the special trains. But then they made a public announcement that all evacuation was temporarily suspended, because due to the warmer weather recently the last special trains had been severely overloaded. We had no choice but to leave.

Reeling, I walked out onto the street and barely made it home. It was a warm, sunny, spring day. The temperature was +13°C in the sunshine. Turbulent rivulets coursed down the streets. The sparrows were chirping gaily, and red-winged birds were flitting about in the clear, blue sky. But none of this made me happy. On the contrary, it made me angry. If only it had been a little colder, I might have been able to leave. It was so upsetting. I had sold everything, I had turned my room upside down, but more importantly I had received the long-awaited telegram from Gorky: 'Come. Zhenya. Nyura.' I was quite ready to bid farewell to Leningrad and leave without a backward glance! And now I'm stuck here with just 300g of bread a day, because my grain coupons have already been cut out.

But what can I do? Such is my fate. I will wait for May.

Yesterday evening I went to see Yakov Grigorievich and told him everything. I asked him to find me a job on his team at work. As it turned out, he had already told them about me, and his boss said he would take me on if I went to see him on the 10th. But after everything that's happened these past few days I'm so worn out, so exhausted that I can barely stand up. It's the 10th today, but I'm in no fit state to go there. I'll go tomorrow. Today I need to go to bed and have a long sleep, especially as it's only two o'clock in the afternoon and I've already eaten all my bread, which was supposed to last me until tomorrow. Tomorrow I will have another 300g of bread, and that's all.

Life is going to be hard for me from now on. This room no longer feels like mine, and the same is true of my remaining possessions. I don't even want to touch them. I've already said goodbye to them, and I'm going to leave them all here.

Meanwhile, no trace of winter remains outside. It has been

overcast all day today, and the first spring rain has been mournfully scratching against my window, inspiring an extreme melancholy. Sleds have disappeared, and carts have appeared in their place. It's spitting with rain. I feel so sad. I look around this empty room and just want to vanish into thin air.

I'm so unhappy, so desperately unhappy. Nobody cares about me. I have been left all alone in this world.

'The shame! The agony! Oh, my pitiful lot!'[3]

'But happiness was so close, so close, so close!'[4]

---

3   Line sung by Onegin in Tchaikovsky's opera *Eugene Onegin*.

4   From Onegin and Tatyana's final duet in the same opera, the phrase is actually: 'Happiness was so possible, / So close! / So close!'

## 11 April 1942

It's overcast. A boring, grey day. I found out from Yakov Grigorievich that I will have to wait another two or three days to hear about work, and I was overwhelmed with dejection and despair. I went to the canteen at three o'clock and got a portion of split pea *kasha*. Then I went to the evacuation point to see what was happening. There wasn't any registration today, apparently, but people were still waiting, still hoping. According to the conversations I overheard, this suspension of evacuation is a temporary state of affairs due to the latest special trains being severely overloaded. On the way back I met two of my friends from the ninth grade class. I told them my sad news, and they comforted me, assuring me that evacuation would begin again, and I would still manage to leave. As we parted they wished me a safe trip.

I feel hope stirring again within me. It might be small, but it is still hope. Maybe in three or four days they will open registration again and then ... goodbye, Leningrad! I will leave straight away. So I must be ready. I need to improve my packing, rearrange my things. Go through everything once more, ruthlessly leaving behind anything I can do without. It would be good to try and pack everything into one suitcase and a shoulder bag, because apparently there's a lot of theft at the station, and as I'm alone there's no one to help watch my things.

No, I would gladly leave everything behind – as long as I don't have to stay in this cursed, wretched Leningrad. All that awaits me here is death. Leaving will be my salvation. So, I will keep my hopes up!

## 12 April 1942

The weather started to brighten up yesterday evening. It's unusually warm and sunny today. The roofs are quite dry.

At the canteen I got a portion each of split pea soup and salami. I bought some bread, crumbled bread and salami into the soup and added water to make a new soup. I'm completely full. But I've already managed to eat all my bread, and it's only three o'clock in the afternoon. I'm sitting by the window, looking out at the blue sky, at the sun-drenched roofs, trying in vain to see a sparrow. There isn't a single one.

My clock has suddenly started working again. Tomorrow or the day after I will start work with Yakov Grigorievich. I'll get a worker's ration card and be able to buy 500g of bread, and evacuation will probably resume in a week, or perhaps a week and a half, and then I will leave straight away. Yesterday I found out from a senior officer that evacuation was temporarily suspended because the ice has become unstable, and the trucks that are currently transporting freight across the ice will be the last to arrive by this route. After this deliveries will be brought to Leningrad by barge. Ice-breakers are hacking a passageway through the ice specifically for this purpose. So barges will be coming to Leningrad loaded with freight, and they're not going to go back empty, are they? So they'll start evacuating people by barge instead of on the Ice Road, which means that registration will start again. And I will leave.

My unhappiness is gnawing away at me, eating me up. Life is miserable. It's hard, it's exhausting. I'm sitting by the window in my cold room and howling, howling, howling in despair.

Mama . . . Ma . . . ma!!

I asked Rozaliya Pavlovna for a pass to the canteen at no. 42. I got two portions of noodle soup. It was thick, tasty soup. My mood improved immediately. Tomorrow grain will be available again, and workers will be able to get sugar. So as soon as I start work I'll have some sugar. When you're full, it's easy to make light of your troubles. Take today, for example, I'm completely full. Well, it doesn't take much. Altogether 60g of grain coupons, which is three soups, and 300g of bread. If I don't manage to arrange things with work tomorrow, I won't drop dead. I still have two grain coupons and one meat coupon that I can use in the canteen. Or better yet, I can buy split peas in the shop, and 300g of bread, and maybe my neighbour will give me 150g of bread in exchange for a few clothes. One way or another I'll survive!

Oh yes, I completely forgot, the newspaper says that the trams will start working again on 15 April.[1] How wonderful! I'll be able to go to work on the tram.

---

1  Passenger services resumed on 15 April on five routes, although freight trams had already been in use since 8 March for the transportation of snow and ice. Elizaveta Agapova, a former tram-driver, recalled: 'We walked to the depot as though we were going to a party – we knew we would be going out on the line. Everyone who could be there came. They said: "Get in and drive!" And just like that, I found myself in the driver's seat. I touched the control handle. Moved it into first position. And suddenly the carriage came to life. I can't explain how I felt at that moment. I drove the tram out of the park. People were getting on at all the stops, laughing, crying with joy.'

How funny life can be. That such an extraordinary fit of despair, an attack of such extreme melancholy should be followed by a surge of new energy, exceptional vigour and high spirits. A short while ago I was sobbing my heart out, yet now I feel like singing and laughing. I feel so good, it's nothing short of miraculous.

*A few riddles:*
White field, black seeds, whoever sows them understands them.
(A letter.)
It burns, it melts, it hides all secrets. (Sealing-wax.)
It walks on all fours, two eyes open wide, twitching at one end and rumbling – but not in discontent. (A cat.)
Under the floor goes a lady with spikes, looking for a lady with a tail. (Cat and mouse.)
Seven brothers, the same age but with different names. (Days of the week.)
What is quicker than anything in the world? (Thoughts.)
When is a field striped? (When it has been ploughed.)
Sometimes I sow, sometimes I gather, I myself am full and I feed others. (A ploughman.)
What creature can feed people and light churches? (A bee.)
A robber came to a strange town carrying a knife and a torch, he didn't set fire to the huts or slay the inhabitants, but he took all their goods. (A beekeeper cutting honeycombs.)
Small, black, sweet – a child's treat. (Bird cherries.)
Dressed by mother spring – in a dress of flowers; dressed by mother winter – in a shroud. (A field.)
What weed can even blind people recognize? (A nettle.)
What has no hands but can build? (A bird.)
It doesn't fade in autumn or die in winter. (A pine tree.)
What has wings but is not a bird? (A butterfly.)

What can go by without any legs? (The seasons of the year.)

Little hump-back dug up the whole field. (A sickle.)

What goes into a field on its legs, but out of a field on its back?
    (A harrow.)

Clothed in a white shroud without being deceased. (Winter.)

What can build a bridge without axe or chisel? (Ice on a river.)

It warms in winter, comes to life in spring, dies in summer and
    rots in autumn. (Wood.)

*The Christmas Tree*[2]

The school is full of noisy children:
Footsteps, laughter ringing out . . .
Do they realize why they are here?
What today is all about?
Not lessons. No, for here today,
Sparkling bright for all to see,
Hung with coloured decorations,
Stands the beauteous Christmas tree.
Children's eyes, drawn to the trinkets,
Shine as they admire the toys:
Horses, wolves, a train, a horn,
Delight the little girls and boys.
See the stars and little lights
That shine like jewels, so clear and bright!
Golden nuts and grapes in bunches –
They will feast their eyes tonight!
May you be blessed, now and always,
You, whose hand so good and kind

---

2  'The Christmas Tree' by Aleksei Pleshcheev (1887) is reproduced here without its
final stanza.

Chose this tree and brought it here
For these poor girls and boys to find.

*Proverbs:*
It is a good deed to give shoes to a man who has none so that he too may celebrate the birth of Christ.
Live generously if you can, and share with a poor man.

*Christmas Tree*
(A traditional tale)
It was a holy night – the night the baby Jesus was born. An angel flew silently past the trees, plants and flowers and told them of the birth of the Holy Infant. All of Nature rejoiced: 'Let us go to Him, let us worship the Holy Infant. We will take Him our most appetizing fruits, we will take Him our most fragrant flowers,' said the plants. So they went, and were guided on their path by a bright star. The humble fir tree followed behind them. When she arrived, she stood sadly to one side and wept, for she had no gift to offer the Holy Child. The angel saw this and felt sorry for the sad little fir tree, so he took the bright star from the sky and cast it towards her. The star landed on the top of the tree, scattering bright sparks all around. The Holy Infant looked up and smiled. Ever since, the fir tree has been decorated every year with lights, and a star has been fixed to her topmost branch.

# 13 April 1942

I copied all that from a book published in 1917, which is called *The Sower (A Child's First Reader).*[1] It belongs to my neighbour, and I happened upon it by chance. It's a fascinating little book. Mama studied from it when she was a child.

I really like the way children used to be taught from a very young age that they should love their parents, nature and all that is good. I would like to learn some of this book by heart. I could ask her to give me the book, but I've already limited myself to taking only what is absolutely essential. The only book I'm taking is a plant identification guide, and I've already taken the cover off. The cover was too heavy. I'm also taking an album of bird pictures and *Birds in the Wild*. I can't take even one more book. That's why I want to copy the bits I like best into my diary. I still have time, and in any case I have to pass the day somehow. I expect I will be able to go and arrange everything

---

1 *Seyatel'. Pervaya posle Azbuki kniga dlya chteniya v shkole i sem'e*, a primary school reader written by Klavdiya Lukashevich (1859–1931). The first edition was published in St Petersburg in 1907.

with work tomorrow. Today is a cloudless, sunny day. The only bad thing is that there's a cold wind.

I can hardly believe it! It's already 13 April. April, spring is here. Nature is waking up. Not that I even notice nature these days. But soon I will leave for Gorky, where it's even warmer than here, and they have the same blue sky and sun. It's hard to imagine that I'm going to see the real Volga. I'll be able to walk along the banks of the Volga. The Volga, yes, the Volga! New sights, new people, new acquaintances, a new life. Oh, I wish I could leave this cursed Leningrad sooner. I can't deny that it's a wonderful, beautiful city and I am strongly attached to it. But I simply cannot bear to look at it any more, much less love it. The city where I have had to live through so much sorrow, where I lost everything I had. The city where I became an orphan. The city where I came to know the full horror of loneliness. No, for the rest of my life I will remember the name of this city with a shudder in my heart. Soon, soon I will leave here, and I hope it will be forever.

I just heard on the radio that Grisha is one of the prize recipients. He will receive 100,000 roubles in prize money. Fancy that! Grisha Bolshakov[2] is a childhood friend of Mama's.

Today I survived on 300g of bread and 140g of split peas. Tomorrow I will have only 300g of bread. Hopefully I'll be able to go and arrange things with work tomorrow.

---

2   Grigory Bolshakov (1904–74) was an opera singer. The resolution passed by the Council of People's Commissars of the USSR awarding him the Stalin Prize in 1941 for his performance as Vakula in Pyotr Tchaikovsky's opera *Cherevichki* (The Little Shoes) (1941) was published in *Leningradskaya Pravda* on 14 April 1942. Bolshakov received the Stalin Prize for the second time in 1950 for his performance as Andrei in Pyotr Tchaikovsky's opera *Mazeppa* (1948). He was awarded the title of People's Artist of the RSFSR in 1951.

I packed my things today. I packed, unpacked and packed again 100 times, and finally everything was as I wanted it. Two items: a suitcase and a bundle, and I can pack the bundle into the suitcase if need be so I'll only have one piece of luggage. I packed into the suitcase everything I'll need for eating on the journey, and there is still some free space. But I'm not going to fill it, because who knows what else I might have to put in. Bread, salami or whatever other food they give us. It really is astonishing to think how everything's turned out, almost unbelievably so. I was the only one of us to survive, and now I'm moving to a different city at the age of seventeen. It's daunting, but at the same time exciting. Exciting because I'm feeling something now that I've never felt before. I feel complete freedom: freedom of thought and freedom of action. I'm not bound by anything or to anyone. I can do whatever I want. I'm aware that this is a crucial moment in my life. I have to choose what to do, which path to take, and this choice will affect the rest of my life. I could stay here, get a job and carry on living alone in my own room. It's very tempting. But I can't bear the loneliness of being surrounded by indifferent strangers who don't care about me. No, no. If I were a little older, perhaps this is the path I would choose. But I don't feel as though I'm grown up enough yet, although of course I'm no longer a child. No, I feel that it's still too soon for me to live completely independently. I still need help and support. And I want someone I can be close to, someone to put their arms around me. I want someone to replace even just a little bit of the love and care I was shown by that beloved person who was so cruelly taken from me by fate.

I know that I will be welcomed as family into Nyura and Zhenya's home. I must be careful not to make them feel awkward, or to make any demands on them. I am very aware of that.

I will be joining their family temporarily, during which time I will earn my own money and contribute towards household expenses.

But in time I must try to arrange a room of my own so that I can live independently, without asking anything of anyone. That will be such a happy time! Whatever happens I must live to see it!

## 15 April 1942

The trams started again today. Such wonderful news!

## 17 April 1942

It's already 17 April. I sold my clock today, for 125 roubles and 250g of bread. This is how I spent the day: at twelve o'clock I went to the canteen and had soup with potato and vermicelli. Then I went to a café and had two cups of tea without anything else. At three o'clock I bought my bread, then sat opposite the little round park on Nevsky in the sunshine and ate it. At five o'clock I went and re-registered my ration cards at the *zhakt*,[1] then I went back to Nevsky and sold my clock. I came home at seven o'clock. The weather has been lovely recently. Sunny and warm. At the moment I am getting around two hours of sunshine in my room every evening. They might increase bread rations on the 20th, and we should be able to get grain, sugar and butter too. I got a box of matches today. All my things are packed, and as soon as evacuation begins I will leave the very same day. I met Iya Osipova in the canteen today. She told me

---

1 Re-registrations took place monthly from October 1941, in order to stop the un-authorized use of food ration cards and to prevent food supplies being issued to holders of counterfeit cards. In April 1942 the deadline for re-registration was the 18th.

that she'd heard at the district council that evacuation would start after the 20th.

The day before yesterday, I sold a rug embroidered with asters to a soldier in exchange for 200g of bread. I had to go home with him, and on the way I found out that he had come from Vologda just two days previously. He told me that evacuees were well fed, and that everything was free for them.

Yesterday a pea shoot sprouted in my pot. Flies have appeared outside. I've already seen a live ant. There are fluffy willow branches for sale. The buds on the trees in the gardens are swollen.

The birds are chirping everywhere. For the time being there are no air raids or artillery fire.

## 18 April 1942

The weather is beautiful. The crows have started to build their nests. I spent the day as follows: at eleven I went to the shop and bought 50g of salami, then I bought 300g of bread and went to the canteen, where I ate two bowls of split pea soup. Then I went to the café where I had two cups of tea with bread and salami. I was very full. I haven't eaten anything else since three o'clock today, but I'm still full. They're going to give out grain tomorrow. I'll be able to get 100g of grain. I also found out that if they have something sweet in the café I can get 50g on my fifth coupon. At eight o'clock I went to see Sofya and asked her to get me some *kefir*. I was lucky – she gave me a half-litre bottle for 75 roubles. It's not proper *kefir* but 'full-fat yoghurt made from vegetable oil', according to the label. Nevertheless, this soy yoghurt is very nourishing.

## 19 April 1942

There are ten days until 1 May. That means I've only got fifteen days left in Leningrad, at most. These fifteen days will fly by. Just fifteen more days, or maybe less – ten or eleven or twelve days – and then goodbye Leningrad, forever.

This is how I spent today: at ten o'clock I bought my 300g of bread, came home and broke it up into pieces. I crumbled the soft part and mixed it with some *kefir*. It made a very filling *kasha*, very tasty. Some time after twelve I went to the café and had two cups of tea with bread and cranberry jam, which I got on my fifth coupon. Then I went straight to the canteen and had a bowl of soup. It was good soup, with some kind of oil, vermicelli, split peas, soybeans and various grains. After that I went to my shop and bought 60g of split peas. Then, feeling completely full, I sat opposite the pet shop in the sunshine. While I was there I sold a medium basin for 21 roubles. At five o'clock I went home, ate a piece of bread with jam and a few split peas, then went to the commission shop. I had my fan valued, and they offered me 70 roubles for it, but they valued my summer flannelette gloves at 100 roubles. I sold them on the way home for 60 roubles, and at the bread shop I sold a small basin for

6 roubles. In the evening, at around eight o'clock, I will go and take Sofya's bottle back to her, and maybe today she will give me another bottle of *kefir*. I want to make the second bottle last a little longer, about three days. By then I will probably have saved up a little more money for a third bottle. And by that time butter and sugar will be available to us dependants. So all being well, I will make it to May. And then . . . goodbye Leningrad!

The weather is wonderful – fine and warm.

This is my plan for tomorrow: I'll leave the house at eleven and go to the café, where I'll buy some bread and have two cups of tea with bread and jam, then I'll go straight to the canteen, where I'll eat a bowl of soup with more bread. I'll take the rest of the bread home and leave it there while I go out, and in the evening I'll finish off the bread with some *kefir* then go to bed.

## 20 April 1942

Today is a truly splendid day. It feels like summer, not April. The sun is hot, and it's 15°C in the shade. There's a warm breeze. After eleven I went to the café, bought some bread and had two cups of hot, strong tea with bread and the last of the jam. Then I went to the canteen. A young girl called Katya works there, cutting out the coupons, and she's got a heart of gold. My coupons are not really valid yet, because the dates on them are too far off, but she still lets me use them. She's very kind, and everyone loves her for it. At the canteen I ate a bowl of soup and took a portion of meat. It was liver, and I really liked it – it was very tasty, and I got quite a large piece. It cost 1 rouble, and they cut out 50g meat and 5g butter coupons as well, but it was worth it because every portion of liver came with a spoonful of real meat gravy. After the canteen I went home, left my piece of liver and the remaining bread there and went out for a walk. I walked all the way to the Koloss,[1] bought a ticket and finally

---

1 From the 1920s the Koloss (Colossus) cinema was based in the former Noble Assembly Hall on Italyanskaya Street, which was built in 1912–14.

saw the film *Champagne Waltz*.[2] What a splendid film. Suddenly I found myself yearning to live in luxury like the stars of the film, to be surrounded with the same splendour and comfort. To enjoy the same music, dancing, endless parties and various other amusements. Imagine living like that! Luxury, beautiful women, women wearing the latest fashions, smartly dressed men with slicked-back hair, restaurants, entertainment, jazz, dancing, glamour, wine, wine and love, love, endless kisses and more wine. Noisy, clamorous streets. Luxurious, sparkling shops, gleaming cars, adverts, adverts, endless adverts. Adverts here, there and everywhere. Glittering, whirling, clamorous adverts. Noise, commotion, shrieking, a veritable whirlwind, all of it held together by a kind of internal rhythm.

This war has deprived us all of any kind of entertainment for such a long time. To tell the truth, before the war began we had started imitating the Americans in many ways. A great many ways. We Soviet people are attracted to anything foreign. The thing is, to be honest, we don't have anything of our own – everything we have is borrowed from other countries. We love noise and glamour, and we dress in the latest fashions, mainly American. Our amusements and various forms of entertainment are also, for the most part, American. And jazz. Our young people are such jazz fans. All those foxtrots, tangos, every kind of love song imaginable. Advertising had begun to assume greater importance here too, particularly of late. They had started playing adverts on the radio that were like little

---

2   This American comedy directed by A. Edward Sutherland, which combined the music 'of Strauss's popular waltzes and operettas' with 'contemporary American jazz', was released in the USA in 1937. The film was originally scheduled to be shown in Leningrad's largest cinemas at the beginning of December 1941, but its premiere did not take place until 23 March 1942 at the Koloss cinema (*Leningradskaya Pravda*, 4 December 1941, 24 March 1942).

poems set to music. And our streets had begun to resemble those of a foreign city. Clean and tidy, policemen on every corner, a constant flow of gleaming, modern cars. Trolleybuses. Sparkling, glittering shops stocked with an abundance of all kinds of goods. This war has thrown us off our normal course. But I am firmly convinced that when the war ends things will gradually go back to the way they were before, and we will once again seek to improve our own way of life by following that of others, particularly the Americans.

After the cinema I wanted to go to the café, but it was already closed. In search of another café I wandered to Ligovskaya Street, but the café there was also closed. I asked whether, by any chance, she (the woman working in the café) would give me my bread for the 22nd. To my despair she agreed, and I took it. It was a fine piece of bread – substantial, soft, fresh and fragrant. I ate all 300g of it this evening. I'll have to go without bread tomorrow. But never mind, I'll get by somehow. The anti-aircraft guns have been roaring all evening, and every now and then a crackling sound erupts nearby, frightening the life out of me.

What will tomorrow bring us?

## 21 April 1942

The weather has been lovely all day. Nice and warm, 16°C in the shade. Then it clouded over. Towards evening the sky became overcast, the sun disappeared, and it started raining. Or rather, drizzling.

At the canteen today I ate two portions of soup with split peas and oats, then I went to the café and drank three cups of tea. I don't know whether I'll be able to get any *kefir* today. I'm going to call in on Sofya at seven o'clock. Oh, but the rain has grown quite bold. Steady, slanting, lashing down so hard. And what's this? Thunder.

Thunder, thunder. Hurrah! The first thunderstorm. The first thunder! Such a welcome sound. Such a heavenly sound. So different from the firing of the anti-aircraft guns or artillery fire.

My soul filled with joy. So I have lived to hear the first thunder. A thunderstorm, a real thunderstorm. I can hardly believe it.

What is this yearning that I feel? I don't even know myself. All I know is that I want something good to happen, something out of the ordinary. I wish May would come sooner. I desperately want to leave, to leave here as soon as possible. For once I want to eat until I'm full. I'm so tired of this half-starving existence. Day after day, I am systematically under-eating. I try to banish all thoughts of food from my mind, but still, every evening I'm so dreadfully hungry. Right now, for example, there's a dull ache in my stomach that won't go away. I could eat anything.

I went to see Sofya, but there was no *kefir*. I bought 300g of bread for 120 roubles, took it to Ekaterininsky Park, sat down and ate almost all of it there and then. All I have left is a piece to take with me to the café tomorrow. But no matter what, I won't buy my bread in advance tomorrow. Never again. I'm going to bed! So, another day is over.

## 22 April 1942

Today I am so unhappy, so sick at heart. Unhappiness is gnawing away at me, eating me up, though I don't even know why.
Lord, I'm surrounded by strangers, strangers, only strangers,
no family or friends. Everyone walks past indifferently, nobody
even wants to know me. Nobody cares about me at all. Spring
is here, we had the first thunderstorm yesterday, life goes on,
and nobody but me notices that Mama is not here. That terrible
winter carried her away. Winter has gone, it won't return for
some time, but Mama will never come back to me. Dear, kind,
beloved Zhenya, please understand how hard it is for me.

I'm standing by the open window as I write this. There is
a gentle breeze caressing me, and I can feel the warmth of
the sun. There is a round jar of water standing next to me.
There is bright green algae growing in it, and dozens of newly
appeared daphnia, cyclops and other tiny living creatures are
darting about. Nearby a young pea shoot stands proudly in
its pot, holding itself up towards the sun's rays. I look around
and, yes, it's still good to be alive. Well perhaps, but only when
your stomach is full. I'm not hungry, but I'm certainly not full,
and this is the worst possible situation. This systematic under-

eating is torturing me. God, if only one of Mama's friends were here. I could ask for a small amount of money, at least. Money would buy me a little bit of bread. Oh, God.

When will I see my family? When will I finally be able to sit at the dinner table knowing that I have the right to be there, that I belong, sharing a meal with others, rather than watching while they eat? Oh Lord, have mercy on me. Let me travel to Zhenya's, let me see Lida, Serezha, Danya[1] and Nyura.

Dear Lord. Do this for me, I beg you!

Today is 22 April. There are eight more days until May: 23rd, 24th, 25th, 26th, 27th, 28th, 29th, 30th. These days will be so hard. The hardest days of my whole life.

I forgot to say, when I was queuing for bread on Ligovka yesterday, I saw a real, live Small Tortoiseshell butterfly.

My dear, precious friend, my diary. You're all I have, my only counsel and confidant. I'm telling you all my troubles, my worries and my sorrows. All I ask is that you remember my sad story in your pages and later, when the time comes, tell it to my family so that they might know the truth. That is, of course, if they want to.

I went to the canteen after twelve o'clock today and got two portions of soup. It was noodle soup, not very thick. I lent a woman my spoon to eat her soup, because she had forgotten her own, and in return she placed a piece of coconut fat on the side of my soup bowl. I fished it out, but it still made the soup a bit greasy. Then I earned myself one grain coupon by letting someone else use my pass. The coupons haven't been cut out for a long time, since Katya never asks for them. Apparently they're

---

1   Lena's cousins; Lida and Danya were the children of Vladimir Nikolaevich and Anna (Nyura) Mukhina, and Serezha was the son of Evgeniya Nikolaevna and Pyotr Nikolaevich Zhurkov.

going to close this canteen completely on the 25th, because people are not happy with it. They are forever cursing it. I have been very satisfied with this canteen, and I think the staff are very good here too. I stayed in the canteen a long time, until two o'clock. Then I went to the café on Ligovka and bought my bread. It's the only place that gives bread two days in advance. That's why there's always a big queue – more for bread than for tea. The bread today was very good, very nourishing. I walked back along Nevsky and went into the food shop. There was hardly anyone there. I found a comfortable spot in the corner and ate two plates of noodles with butter and bread. Eventually I made it to the café on Razyezzhaya. I joined the end of a long queue. It was half past three, and the café opened at four. The queue was not for tea, of course, but because they were giving out 50g portions of sugar. Dependants could claim theirs on the fifth coupon, which I didn't have. I ended up standing in the queue for quite a long time, and when I finally received my two cups of tea I only had a small piece of bread left, which I divided in two, spread with the last of my butter and ate there and then.

I left the café with my stomach full of liquid and the knowledge that I am the most worthless and unfortunate creature in the world. Thus, feeling desperately unhappy, I went to where the evacuation point used to be. It was quiet and deserted. I sat down on a bench and was unable to hold back my sobbing any longer. After I'd finished crying I met a woman at the exit who, in answer to my question about when registration would start, told me to come back at the beginning of May.

So any hope I had of escaping from here before May has disappeared forever.

My God! There are still eight days until May. What terrible, hungry days they will be.

I'm looking at the telegram: 'Come. Nyura. Zhenya.' My tears are falling thick and fast. Nyura . . . Zhenya. They are real people, who know me and don't only know me but also know the extent of my sorrow. They know everything. They love me, and they are worried about me. They are my family, the only ones amongst all these strangers who are reaching out a warm hand to help me. But it is a long, long way away. And at the moment there is no way for me to get to them. That's why I'm choking on my tears.

Everyone who could help me is so far away. If Grisha were in Leningrad, would he help me? Of course he would. He would give me money. He's got plenty of it now. And Kira would help me. But they are all a long way away, too far away to help me. I need their help, though. I need it right now, before 1 May, to help me survive these eight days. But there is no one here to help me.

Come! What marvellous warmth this word exudes. Come! My dear family, when will I see you? These last few days that I'm living here in Leningrad, I'm no longer living but stumbling through them. Dragging every day like a heavy burden. I count every hour, every minute, every second. But unfortunately time goes so slowly, I could scream! What can I do to make time go more quickly? I know I should try to forget about leaving for the time being. But that's impossible! Impossible!

## 25 April 1942

Greetings, my dear diary. I have finally taken up my pencil again. A lot has happened over the last few days. Firstly, the weather has changed. The days are clear and sunny, but there's a strong, icy wind. The Ladoga ice is moving. The Germans reminded us of their presence yesterday afternoon. There was a terrifying air raid, which lasted for about two hours, and dreadful artillery fire going on at the same time. This afternoon there was another air raid, which lasted one and a half hours, and more artillery fire. The canteen on Nakhimson has closed, but Rozaliya Pavlovna, who knew about it in advance, got me a pass to another canteen on Pravda Street. I went there for the first time today. Although there was a long queue they had a good, varied menu.

For example, today they had:

Thick split pea soup – 20g grain
Split pea *kasha* – 40g grain
Soy *kasha* – 20g grain
Soy fritters – 20g grain and 5g butter
Rissoles – 50g meat
Salami – 50g meat

I got one portion of soy *kasha* and ate it there. Next I went to the bread shop on the corner of Ilyich Lane, but they weren't giving out bread for the 27th either. The bread shop on the corner of Gorokhovaya and Zagorodny was also refusing to give out bread for the 27th. At this point I made a firm decision not to leave that shop without bread. Whatever happened, I had to buy 300g of bread. And so I did. By six o'clock I had bought 250g of bread at 45 roubles per 100g.

I'm so happy. It's already half past seven, and I'm completely full, but the bread coupon on my ration card for the 27th remains untouched. My dream of catching up a day has come true. Tomorrow I can go into any bread shop and buy 300g of bread. Isn't that worth celebrating? It certainly is!

There's no news about evacuation for the time being. No one seems to know whether it will begin again in the first half of May or not. I have decided to go back to school until evacuation is announced. Classes are starting again on 3 May,[1] and they're finally going to be taking proper care of those who will be studying and devoting considerable attention to the matter. This is a directive from our dear Stalin himself, the aim being to keep Leningrad's remaining schoolchildren alive. School-children will be fed a balanced diet. Rozaliya Pavlovna showed me the order that was issued by the school administration. She typed it herself on her typewriter.

---

1  This date was given in *Leningradskaya Pravda* on 26 April 1942. Lessons were to start at eight thirty a.m. and finish at four to five p.m., and schoolchildren would receive a hot meal twice a day. In fact, lessons resumed on 4 May (*Leningradskaya Pravda*, 5 May 1942) and were attended by 63,719 students (A. V. Burov, *Blokaka den' za dnem. 22 iyunya 1941 goda – 27 yanvarya 1944 goda*, Lenizdat, 1979, p. 182).

*Food for children who will be attending lessons at school.*

Children will hand in their food ration cards, from which not all
    coupons will be cut out.

Children will receive the following food items:

Meat – 200g

Sugar – 300g

*Breakfast at school*
1. *Kasha*
2. Tea

*Lunch at school*

2–3 dishes

Bread will be provided

Children up to 12 years

– 300g at school

– 100g to take home

Children over 12 years

– 400g at school

– 100g to take home

Daily ration of food items for every child:
1. Bread – 400–500g
2. Meat – 50g
3. Fats – 50g
4. Grain – 100g
5. Sugar – 30g
6. Vegetables – 100g
7. Wheat flour – 20g
8. Potato flour – 20g
9. Soy milk – 50g
10. Tea per month – 10g
11. Coffee per month – 20g

Following a medical examination, children deemed to be particularly undernourished will receive supplementary food rations.

School Administration

What's that . . . the anti-aircraft guns are roaring again. Of course, the devils are flying again. Listen to the way the carrion-crows are droning.

As for lessons, all we are going to be doing is repeating the previous school year. So those who are in the eighth grade will repeat the seventh grade lessons, and those of us in the ninth grade will repeat the eighth grade lessons. There will be no exams in the spring. It's not exactly going to be school, more like a special kind of recuperation clinic for Leningrad schoolchildren. The current school year is no longer relevant. Proper teaching will begin only after the summer break. Oh, and I forgot to say – as I was going into the canteen today, I bumped into Vova. My Vova. He has changed so much. He's terribly emaciated, a shadow of his former self. He's staying at a recuperation clinic at the moment, but he's planning to go back to school.

Dear Vova. It doesn't matter how bad he looks, I still love him.

## 26 April 1942

Everything is white, as though covered in snow.
Snow on the road, on the roofs.
The little garden has turned white again,
But this snow does not belong to winter.

It's just after one o'clock in the afternoon, and the roofs have already dried out. I went to Gorokhovaya for bread today, and I was really lucky. The bread was light and airy, so my piece was larger than usual. I took it home, then went to the canteen. It wasn't very busy today. I got two portions of soy *kasha* and one of salami. Now I'm sitting here with my feet under the blanket, listening to the radio. And I'm wondering what I should do if the Ladoga ice has already melted . . . That means they'll start evacuating by boat at the beginning of May. So should I go straight to Zhenya's, or should I stay here for May, go to school, feed myself up a bit and then leave? I just don't know what to do. On the one hand I would like to be back at school, sitting at a desk with the others, taking out my notebooks and exercise books. It's so tempting. Not to mention the food. When I get to school in the morning there will be hot, sweet tea and bread with butter. Yes, and I almost forgot, there will be *kasha*, hot *kasha* with butter, and then tea. Even studying will be enjoyable on a full stomach. After a few lessons it will be time for lunch. We'll be able to take some of our lunch home and eat some of it there, and it will be the same with bread.

Yes, so far so good. But on the other hand I'll come home to an empty room, strangers all around me, nobody who cares. And the air raids, the artillery fire. Do I want to keep risking my life? I could be killed at any moment. It's terrifying. I want to live. What should I do? My dear diary, it's such a shame that you can't help me decide.

If I decide, on balance, that it's better to leave then I'll be given food for the journey. Eventually I'll reach the city of Gorky. I'll set off straight away in search of Mogilevich Lane. And now I'm walking down the lane, with my suitcase in one hand and my bundle in the other, and my heart is about to jump out of my chest with excitement. Finally I reach no. 5 and knock on the door of apartment 1. I'm among family. I'm no longer surrounded by strangers, but by my own family. Zhenya, Nyura, Lida, Serezha, Danya . . . Everyone sits down at the table together, and I join them as an equal. Hello, my dear family!

Oh God, how happy I will be!

What should I do?

Later on, thinking further ahead, I'll go to work with Lida. She will show me the city. We'll go everywhere together. Summer will come, and it will be lovely. Everything green all around, and the Volga, the beautiful Volga right in front of me. And then the war will end. I will go to Moscow with Zhenya. Hello, Moscow! Greetings, you beautiful city. This Leningrader will become a Muscovite. My Leningrad days will be over.

No, no, of course I must go. How can sweet tea and half a kilo of bread make up for my loneliness? Be gone, be gone, loneliness.

I can't wait to be with you, my faraway family. Zhenya, can you hear my heart beating? It wants to jump out of my chest, it's so desperate to be near you, Zhenya.

In my heart and soul, in every part of my being, I feel as though I am already in Gorky. My only wish, my only aspiration, is to put my arms around you all and kiss you as soon as possible!! To hold you tightly, Zhenya! You're like my third mother. Oh Lord, dear Lord! Hear me, I beg you. Let me make it to Gorky safe and sound. This is all I ask of you.

Gorky, Gorky, Gorky . . . Gorky, I will come as soon as I can!!!!

Tomorrow I will get tea, butter and sugar. Then I will go to the café and have two cups of sweet tea with bread and butter.

## 27 April 1942

Another air raid and more artillery fire. It's already the second air raid today. The sky is cloudless, the sun is shining. I can imagine what things are going to be like from now until 1 May. Such a pity I wasn't able to leave when I tried. They're so lucky, the ones who left. They will live. But as for me . . . my future is still uncertain.

There are only a few days left until the start of evacuation. Is it really my fate to die? It's so awful, living with the fear of being killed at any moment by either an artillery shell or a bomb. These last few days before May will probably be just as terrifying.

How pointless and infuriating it will be to die just before leaving, after surviving the horrors of this winter, starvation and extreme cold. How unfair it will be of fate if I am obliged to part with life, having already survived until the spring, having seen the young green grass, having packed all my things . . .

No, I really don't want to die!

These may be the last lines I ever write. Whoever finds this diary, I beg you, please send it to the following address: E. N. Zhurkova, Apt 1, Mogilevich Lane 5, Gorky.

## 28 April 1942

It's good to have something to look forward to. These past few days, I have been living in a constant state of anticipation. No, I am not weary of waiting at all. I'm in no hurry. I know that everything has its own time. I have an interesting experience ahead of me, a journey to another city. I will go by train, then across Lake Ladoga itself. I've never even seen Lake Ladoga before. Then I will continue by train, with a change in Vologda, then onwards by train to Gorky. It's going to be a very exciting journey. And on the way I'll eat for free and have plenty of bread. I've got all this to look forward to. There are only a few days left until my journey begins.

And then I will start my new life. I am burning with curiosity. So much of what lies ahead of me is unknown, and I want to know what to expect. But patience, Lena, patience, all in good time! It's already the 28th today. Tomorrow will be the 29th, then it will be the 30th. I wonder how I'm going to feed myself over the next couple of days. It won't be easy.

All I had today, for example, was 300g of bread, the last of my 50g of butter, and 150g of raisins. Tomorrow I will have 300g of bread, 100g of salami and 75g of cheese. On the 30th I will have

300g of bread, half a litre (*) and 250g of herring. On the 1st I will be able to go to the canteen again and buy *kasha* and soup, and perhaps bread rations will be increased. And then I will probably leave. In any case I will eat well before my journey, and even better once I leave. Yes, it's so good, so delightful to live in anticipation of things to come.

There have already been two air raids today. One early this morning, and one this afternoon. It's cold and overcast today. No sunshine. But still the sparrows are gaily chirping. In the little garden outside my window, the lawns have turned green with young May grass. My pea shoot is growing not so much by the day as by the hour. It's such a handsome specimen. Well proportioned and perfectly straight, its little green leaves nice and even. The twigs that I had standing in a jar of water will also be breaking into leaf soon. Their buds are already opening. So everything is turning out well. If only it weren't for the Germans. Because of them I'm very nervous about 1 May.

Well, hopefully it will all work out somehow.

Soon, soon I will take my suitcase, get on at the front of the no. 9 tram, buy tickets for myself and my luggage and travel a familiar route through familiar streets to the familiar Finland Station. And then . . . the whistle will blow, and the train will depart. We will cross the bridge I have crossed so many times on the no. 20 tram, both alone and with Mama. Goodbye, Leningrad. People at the tram stop are looking at us. What are they thinking? Some probably envy us, but others are saying: 'Go ahead, all the more bread for us.' We have just passed the buildings of the Clara Zetkin Institute of Maternity and Infancy Protection on the left.

Yes, Mama and I worked here for about two months. There's a girl walking down the path, wearing a white robe and a white headscarf and carrying some papers. I walked along that path just like her many times myself, carrying medical certificates. The only difference being that it was winter back then and everything was covered in snow, but now it's May. Spring. See how the blossom is out on the trees, and the first coltsfoot flowers are raising their neat little yellow heads on the slope of the railway embankment. Goodbye, Leningrad.

The sky is blue, so blue. Aeroplanes circle above us, sparkling in the sun. Our air patrol. The train is picking up speed. Such a happy feeling. I open my suitcase, cut a big slice of bread, look out of the window and eat. I feel full. At the station before departure we were given a good portion of noodle soup. It was thick soup, and we were also given split pea *kasha*, a whole pot. I've still got some *kasha* left. They also gave us 800g of black pudding and a kilo of bread. This has to last us until Lake Ladoga, where we will be given more hot food.

How wonderful it all sounds. In my mind I have already left Leningrad, but in fact I'm sitting here with my feet under a warm blanket. The radio is ticking loudly, the trams are clanking, the occasional car honks its horn. My stomach is not that full. To be honest, I would happily eat anything right now, anything at all. But I don't have anything. Not a crumb, not a single raisin. I've eaten everything. No, it's best not to think about food at the moment.

Lena, you will eat again tomorrow. You have already eaten today, and that's enough. Don't forget, you ate 150g of raisins – a whole pile – in just two hours. Poor, poor girl. Don't despair, even though you have gone without food the past few days. You'll be able to go to the canteen again from 1 May. Ah yes, on that first day I'll get one soup and two portions of split pea *kasha*. I'll eat the soup there and bring the *kasha* home. And then, towards evening, I'll buy my bread. What a joy that will be!

## 29 April 1942

Today has simply flown by. I didn't get up until after eleven, because I was sitting in bed with my embroidery. First I took out the chamber pot, fetched some water and sold a Griboedov book for 5 roubles. Then I took the no. 9 tram to the end of Gorokhovaya and back. I bought bread on Gorokhovaya for 1 rouble 70 kopeks. It was wonderful bread. Then I went to my shop and bought 75g of cheese, wonderful cheese, for 19 roubles a kilo. It was soft and fresh. I started queuing for wine. I took my bread and cheese home, took a container for the wine, returned to the shop and got a quarter litre of sweet red wine for 28 roubles 20 kopeks a litre. I came home, wrapped myself in the blanket and began to eat. By taking little bites, I managed to prolong my enjoyment for about an hour. After five I went to the shop and found out that they would have herrings and salami later. I only had 1 rouble left, so I picked out a few books and managed to sell them quickly on the street. I made 20 roubles. I came home, did some embroidery and ate the rest of my cheese. There's only a tiny piece left. At seven o'clock I went back to the shop and queued for salami for 19 roubles a kilo. I didn't get any salami but I got some little sausages instead, for 11 roubles a kilo. They were very tasty.

I'll get herring and beer tomorrow. They say it will be possible to get white bread instead of black bread on the new ration cards tomorrow. But for now I must sleep. I'm very tired after today. The weather was very warm and sunny today and, surprisingly, there was no sign of the carrion crows. Our anti-aircraft guns have started working very well. I heard on the radio that over the last three days alone the anti-aircraft guns have brought down seventy-one German aircraft just outside the city. Not a bad start.

At last, tomorrow is the 30th. I'm so happy. The day of my departure is drawing nearer with every hour. When I was queuing for salami yesterday, I got talking to an old woman. She lives at no. 7, apartment 5. Mikhailova is her surname. She lives alone, and she needs to get to Vologda. She has an adult daughter there with two children, whose husband is in the army. So she wants us to travel together. I don't mind. It might even be worth my while. She's such a gentle, obliging old woman. She might be useful to me on the journey, and in Vologda I could visit her daughter and drink tea with them, particularly since, according to the old woman, she lives just next to the station. The old woman asked me to call in on her when I go to register. Why not? It won't cost me anything, and she promised to make me a cup of tea.

## 30 April 1942

After eleven Lena went to the *zhakt* to get her ration card, but she wasn't able to get her ration card today. Under the impression that Lena had found a job, the house manager Tatyana Vyache-slavovna hadn't included her in the list of dependants. She was told to call back tomorrow between five and six. Lena went to the shop and discovered to her great disappointment that they had just run out of beer and herring. The manager promised that there would be more beer that evening, but she said that there would be no more herring, so Lena should take what there was. Lena bought 250g of dry salted fish. They only cut the tail off, so she got almost a whole fish.

Lena got home and began to eat the fish with great pleasure. It turned out to have plenty of fat and was unusually tasty. At first Lena decided to eat half of it and save the other half to eat in the evening with her white bread. But once she had eaten the first half she began to eat the second half with even greater relish. It was a thoroughly enjoyable activity, and altogether it took about three hours. Of course, after eating something so salty, and especially without bread, Lena was desperately thirsty and drank almost a whole kettleful of unboiled water. Then she went to the café and had four cups of tea poured into her jar. She came home and had hot tea with the remaining pieces of fish instead of bread. Then she went to bed and slept for an hour or so. When she woke up she went back to the shop for beer, but there wasn't any. Lena got some salt, and on the way home she looked in at the zhakt, but there was a padlock on the door. It was already around six o'clock. Lena joined the queue for beer and waited with everybody else until eleven o'clock. At eleven they announced that if even if the beer was delivered they wouldn't be giving it out until the following morning. Lena walked home, reeling with tiredness. It was a starry, moonlit night. 'I wonder what tomorrow will be like,' thought Lena as she wrapped herself in her blanket.

At twelve o'clock the radio came to life, broadcasting from Moscow, and Leningraders heard the striking of the Kremlin's famous clock. This familiar sound hadn't been heard in Leningrad for such a long time, and it was so nice to hear it again. After the 'Internationale' Lena fell fast asleep and slept through to the morning.

I have decided to write my diary in a new format from now on. In the third person. Like a story. So it can be read like a book.

# 1 May 1942

May Day is here. Lena didn't go for beer at six o'clock, of course. She was sleeping particularly soundly at the time. But she got up a little later and decided that she couldn't let the opportunity pass.

Lena went outside. The sun was shining, and there wasn't a cloud in the sky. The brightly coloured flags made the street look so smart. She half expected a band to start playing and a parade of demonstrators to appear. But no, today is an ordinary working day. In fact, it's an extraordinary working day. This year workers have voluntarily given up their holiday, turning May Day into a day of toil and struggle.[1]

There was no beer in the shop, because it hadn't been delivered from the depot. Lena went home. She no longer felt like lying in bed and sleeping, so she started listening to the radio.

---

1 The following announcement appeared in *Leningradskaya Pravda* on 30 April 1942: 'In accordance with the wishes of the workers, the Council of People's Commissars of the USSR and the Central Committee of the All-Union Communist Party (Bolsheviks) have decreed that 1 and 2 May this year will be working days.' Similar resolutions, also referring to the workers' wishes, had already turned 8 and 9 November and 5 December 1941 into working days.

She was really hungry, but she had no idea when she would receive her ration card. Perhaps only towards the evening. Well, never mind, she consoled herself with the thought that she would have 600g of bread today. And if Rozaliya Pavlovna managed to get her a pass to the canteen before five o'clock then she would only get her bread for today, because she would be entitled to more than usual at the canteen because of the holiday. Lena decided that she would take three portions of *kasha*, one soup and one meat dish.

On the radio they were broadcasting an endless stream of military songs, marches, new slogans and poems.

Lena thought about May Day last year. They had walked to Borodinskaya from school and got stuck there. Then it started snowing, so heavily that for a short time the street became terribly wet, dirty and slushy. The street gradually became more deserted. Many people hurried home. It was hardly surprising, as everyone was dressed for spring – the women and girls in light coats, the men and boys in jackets. Lena was wearing a light coat too, and no boots, but she ran home to change into her fur coat and boots. Lena remembered that when she got home Mama was sewing and Aka was baking raisin buns in the kitchen. Lena was in a hurry to leave again, but Mama persuaded her to wait a while, and Lena ate the first hot buns. Aka also gave her some raisins to take with her. Yes, those were happy days. But Lena didn't appreciate any of it at the time. She used to think that was simply how life was and how it always would be. She didn't think there was anything special about the fact that she had Aka and Mama, that they would do anything for her. Everything was for Lenochka. Whenever there was a spare piece, whose plate was it put on? Lenochka's. But Lenochka didn't notice this at the time.

It is only now, when she has lost both Aka and Mama, that

she has come to truly appreciate her former life. She would give anything to have those days back again. But it's impossible to relive the past. She will never see Aka and Mama again, except in her dreams.

If she makes it to Zhenya's she is determined to treasure every moment that reminds her of family life. Even the right to sit at the table with Zhenya and Serezha and help herself to a plate, this alone will bring her the greatest happiness.

Yes, fate has taught her a thing or two, though rather harshly. And now, contemplating all of this, Lena said to herself: 'Let this be a lesson to you. From now on you will appreciate every crumb, you will know the value of everything and you will find it easier to live in this world.'

'Every cloud has a silver lining', according to the wise Russian proverb. Of course, after this 'school of life' the future will undoubtedly be easier for Lena. And not only for her. Life after the war will be easy, productive and full of joy for all Soviet citizens who have lived through this terrible time.

After ten o'clock Lena went down to the *zhakt* again and finally received her ration card. Then she went straight to the shop and got half a litre of beer without having to queue at all. On her way home with the beer, Lena went to the nearest bread shop – the one inside the shoe shop – and got 150g of white bread and 150g of black bread. The white bread was wonderful, for 2 roubles 90 kopeks a kilo, and for 1 rouble 10 kopeks a kilo the black bread was very substantial, with a thick crust. Lena took her bread to the little garden opposite her building, sat in the sunshine and ate a little of both the white and the black bread. She thought the white bread was tastier than any cake or pastry. This was hardly surprising, as she hadn't eaten white bread for months. The last time she ate white bread was in November, when Mama still worked at the hospital and sometimes brought pieces home. But that bread was grey and sticky, nothing like this. She probably hadn't tasted white bread like this for a long time, even before the war began. They never bought such expensive white bread, except on special occasions. During the months before the war they lived a very frugal life. They didn't have much money, and besides, she and Mama were planning to save up in June and July for their trip down the Volga in August. So even the cheapest kind of white bread was a rare treat for them. They ate black bread instead. Their staple food back then was oatmeal. It was cheap, and you could buy as much of it as you liked. Aka made oat soup for lunch every day for a month, two bowls each. But it was as thick as *kasha*, and Lena eventually got so tired of it that she had difficulty eating even one bowl of it. In the evening Aka would often fry oatmeal for supper and dry black bread to make rusks. And this was called making ends meet. Lena could only laugh bitterly at these memories now.

After eating a little of both kinds of bread, Lena decided to visit the evacuation point. It was still deserted, but she found out from three women who were sitting there that people were saying there would be some news regarding evacuation in four or five days' time. 'In that case, I may as well go back to school for a few days,' thought Lena, and she decided to go to the café. She didn't really expect to find the café open, she just felt like a walk. But the café was open, and after queuing for a relatively short time Lena had two cups of very hot tea, the first with black bread and the second with white bread. She went home, left the rest of the white bread there and decided to go and find some good black bread. She went to all the bread shops she knew, but as if to spite her they all had very good-quality white bread and very poor-quality black bread. Lena wasn't too disappointed, though. She took pleasure in walking slowly along the sunny side of the street, screwing her eyes up against the sun and enjoying the warmth, the sunlight and the cheerful chirping of the sparrows.

I should mention that today turned out to be exceptionally fine, as though in celebration of the holiday. There wasn't a cloud in the sky, the sun shone with all its might, and it was so warm that it would have been oppressively hot even in the shade had it not been for the light, refreshing breeze. The street was ablaze with countless red flags waving gently in the breeze, and the sun made them seem even brighter, more brilliantly red. The little gardens were full of noisy, happy children.

The beautiful spring month of May is here. There was artillery fire in the afternoon. Quite heavy, too. But everyone has grown so accustomed to it that Lena didn't really pay any attention. She took up her embroidery and listened to a May Day concert on the radio.

## 2 May 1942

Yesterday passed without any air raids. Thanks in part, of course, to the efforts of Stalin's Falcons.

Lena got up after eleven today. Before she had even managed to get dressed, two young women from the *zhakt* came to see her. They looked around the room and reproached her for its disorderly state. 'The sanitary committee might come and fine you,' they said. Lena was very embarrassed and said they could fine her if they liked but she didn't have any money. The young woman shrugged and asked Lena about the apartment. When she heard that she hadn't paid for April, the girl said that she had to pay today. Lena promised that she would.

She went and paid 17 roubles 40 kopeks for April. She had 5 roubles left.

Then Lena went to the canteen. She bumped into Yanya Yakubson near the shoe shop. They had barely greeted one another when Vera Vladimirovna, the literature teacher, came over to join them. The three of them stood and chatted. It turns out that Yanya has been studying the whole time and is still studying now. He looked very healthy, plump and rosy-cheeked. Lena was very surprised by his appearance. Vera Vladimirovna had grown very thin, but she hadn't lost her enthusiasm for life.

This chance encounter cheered Lena up. At the canteen she took one noodle soup and two portions of soy rissoles. The soup was watery, nothing special, but the soy rissoles were excellent. Lena decided that soy rissoles were probably the best thing on the menu. For 20g meat and 5g butter coupons they give you two large rissoles, golden brown and remarkably tasty. After the canteen Lena went to the little garden and sat there for a while. Then she went and got half a litre of kerosene. Then Lena started counting her grain coupons and suddenly decided that she should get another portion of curd cheese pancakes today. No sooner said than done. Lena hurried to the canteen, but they had run out of pancakes – and meat too. Lena stood there for a little while, wondering what to do, then took one portion of soy *kasha*. Then she went to Gorokhovaya for bread. All they had anywhere was black bread for 1 rouble 10 kopeks. Lena chose the driest bread she could find. She came home, fetched two lots of water and then went to visit Olya. She found her at home in bed. Lena congratulated her on receiving her ration card, and when Olya mentioned that it was her birthday today Lena wished her a happy birthday too. Lena thought she and Olya could go and sit in the little garden, but Olya had just been diagnosed with active tuberculosis (in her legs) so she couldn't go. Lena sat with her for a while. She didn't like this large, dark room with all its expensive furniture. It was very gloomy and cold. Lena borrowed *In the Mountains of Sikhote-Alin*[1] from Olya

---

1  Vladimir Arseniev's factual account of an expedition led by the Amur Department of the Russian Geographical Society to the Sikhote-Alin mountain range in 1908–10 (V. K. Arseniev, *V gorakh Sikhote-Alinya: Ocherk ekspeditsii Priamurskogo otdela Russkogo geograficheskogo obshchestva, 24 iyunya 1908 g. po 20 yanvarya 1910 g.*, Moscow: Molodaya Gvardiya, 1937; Detizdat, 1940).

and took it to the little garden to read. She didn't feel like going home. It was oppressively hot outside, and the garden was full of young children. Their happy shouts and laughter could be heard all the way down the street.

Lena sat on a bench and tried to read, but she wasn't in the mood. She watched the children running happily about. Lena thought about these children, about how they would be happier than she was when they were her age, and how their childhood in general would be happy and bright. They wouldn't have to live through everything that she had been forced to endure. Their parents wouldn't die. Yes, they would be happier.

The sun disappeared, the air turned fresh. Lena returned home and made some tea on the kerosene burner, which hadn't been lit for a long time. Lena had a cup of hot tea with bread and made some fish bouillon. She placed the leftover fish bones, scales and so on into a tin can, added water and boiled it up. It turned out well, and Lena drank a whole cup of delicious hot fish bouillon. Then Lena cleaned and mended her shoes. She had to look respectable in front of other people. This winter, when it was so bitterly cold, people hadn't given a thought to the way they looked. But it was different now. The warm May days were here and people were beginning to take care of themselves, to pay a bit more attention to their appearance. Particularly the young people. Fashionable hairstyles and hats reappeared, men wore suits and smart scarves, and Lena found herself also wanting to dress better, more elegantly. She herself found it unpleasant and somehow irritating to see people who had let themselves go, who continued to muffle themselves in old rags. But for the most part they were elderly people, sick and emaciated. Whereas Lena, although lately she had been barely able to move her legs, was still a young girl and consequently placed a great deal of importance on appearance. If only I could dress more elegantly, she thought, feeling particularly up-set that her hair grew so slowly. She wished she had long hair. You could style long hair in so many ways. Looking at herself in the mirror at home, Lena noted with satisfaction that her face wasn't as terrible as she had imagined, although her body really had grown thin – she was just skin and bones, and there was nothing left of her ample bust. Once upon a time Lena had dreamed of being as thin as Lida Klementieva. Back then her ample bust had been a source of considerable distress, but now she was even thinner than Lida.

Today was calm – no air raids, no artillery fire.

## 3 May 1942

There has been extensive cloud cover since first thing this morning, and our enemies could not fail to take advantage of the situation. There were two air raids even before nine o'clock. Neither was particularly long or scary. The anti-aircraft guns started firing away immediately after the siren, then they gradually fell silent, and the powerful rumble of our Falcons could be heard overhead. There was no shuddering, no shaking, so clearly no bombs were dropped. Maybe they didn't let the enemy into the city at all.

Lena got up after the second all-clear. She had slept well last night, and all her dreams were happy. She ran out for bread, drank a cup of cold tea and started to listen out for Aunt Sasha so she could ask her for a bucket and a basin. Aunt Sasha still wasn't back by half past eleven, so Lena went to the canteen. The canteen was quite busy, but more importantly they were only giving out lunch to those who had new passes. Fortunately Lena saw a friend in the queue with whom she had been studying recently, and this friend took one soy *kasha* and two portions of meatballs for Lena on her pass. The canteen was also issuing bread for 5 May, and, unable to resist, Lena took another

300g of bread. Then Lena went home, ate lunch, heated some water, washed herself, put on some clean clothes and went to school for the medical exam. It was chilly outside, a light rain was falling, and the sky was heavy with clouds. She had to wait in a queue for the medical exam for about an hour. Finally, bearing a coupon marked 'healthy', Lena returned home, where she made two cups of tea, cut the remaining bread into slices and ate it with the last of her meatballs. It was very tasty. Schools are starting back again tomorrow. But Lena's school won't start until the 5th, although there's a meeting for all students tomorrow at four o'clock. Lena heard a broadcast on the radio for schoolchildren, from which she learned a lot. She learned that the school day was going to be completely restructured. Students would be at school for most of the day, but they would study less than before. For the senior classes the school day would finish at half past five, but lessons would go on no later than five. Lessons would start at half past eight, then they would have breakfast at twelve o'clock. Students would receive hot sweet tea and *kasha*. Then there would be more lessons, then an hour's break. The older students would have their lunch at four o'clock. After lunch they would exercise in different interest groups. They would go home at half past five, and they would be able to take with them 100g of bread, a little butter and some sugar. The programme was built entirely around the repetition of the previous year. Exercises would continue until 1 July. All students would spend the summer at specially built Young Pioneer summer camps, where they would rest, have fun and work at various state farms, growing vegetables.

Lena really liked the sound of all this and she would have gladly stayed at her school, if only she had family or close friends here. She remembered with a sudden pain in her heart that she had no one. No, she would have to leave. Maybe the food situation would be worse for her in Gorky than if she had stayed in Leningrad, but still she had to leave. Even if she no longer had to pay for school or food[1] – and Rozaliya Pavlovna had promised to do everything that she could to help her in this matter – she would refuse it all and leave for Zhenya's instead.

No doubt Zhenya is already worrying about Lenochka and waiting for her to arrive. Meanwhile Lenochka is still dallying in Leningrad. But today is already the 3rd. Evacuation is expected to begin any day now, and this has put Lena in a quandary: should she leave immediately, as soon as evacuation begins, or should she study for a week or so at school, in order to build her strength up a little? Lena has decided that she will travel with Tonya, the girl who got lunch for her in the canteen today. Tonya and her mother are planning to leave soon too. Her father is at the front, and he sent a letter advising them to leave as soon as possible because they will have to endure a great deal more if they stay in Leningrad, so they should leave sooner rather than later. Lena's best option is to leave with Tonya and her mother, because they already know each other and in any case it's better to travel in a group of three. But one thing has been troubling Lena: say, for example, she hands her ration cards in at school on the 5th, and they start distributing grain, sugar and butter on the same day. What if evacuation doesn't begin until the 8th or 9th? For these few days Lena will get less sugar and butter at school than she would have been able to get in the shop if

---

1 According to a resolution passed by the Council of People's Commissars of the USSR on 26 October 1940 ('Ob ustanovlenii platnosti obucheniya v starshikh klassakh srednikh shkol i v vysshikh uchebnykh zavedeniyakh SSSR i ob izmenenii poryadka naznacheniya stipendii') Leningrad schoolchildren in the eighth–tenth grades had to pay 200 roubles each per year. The government reinstated free education for all in May 1956. The food that people were entitled to on their ration cards was sold at fixed state prices, not given out free of charge.

she hadn't handed her ration cards in. But this is not necessarily the case, because whatever happens she is entitled to 200g of butter and 300g of sugar. Perhaps they will let her keep some of the coupons, so that Lena will be able to eat at the school canteen right up to the day of her departure and then get sugar and butter at the shop just before leaving. Or perhaps school will issue some kind of voucher allowing Lena to get her rations of 200g of butter and 300g of sugar in one go* That would be wonderful, thought Lena. If she could eat at school up to her departure, and then receive 200g of butter and 300g of sugar just before leaving, ostensibly for the journey, that would be a dream come true.

But dreams are one thing, reality is another. In the end Lena decided that the situation would resolve itself, and there was no point worrying about the unknown.

Today has been a wet and somehow dreary day, but Lena is in good spirits, whereas she was heavy-hearted on 1 May despite the splendid weather.

## 4 May 1942

It's unusually cold and overcast today. There's a strong, icy, gusty wind. It blows right through you, and its gusts are so powerful that it's hard to walk against it. In weather like this it's best to stay at home and not go outside any more than necessary. Lena only went out briefly to go to the canteen. She had some cabbage soup and millet *kasha*, though she didn't manage to buy bread because staff at the canteen weren't accepting coupons for the 6th. She ran from the canteen to school. The meeting had already started. Lena heard some disappointing news: firstly, lessons would not begin until 15 May, and food would not be given out until the 8th. Secondly, older students would receive only 400g of bread and 30g of butter a day. Lena bumped into Misha Ilyashev, who was completely unrecognizable. It really was quite alarming to look at him. Apart from Tonya, no one else from the ninth grade was there. Lena and Tonya agreed that if evacuation were to begin before 15 May they would leave straight away.

Lena came home, made a small bowl of soup out of the remaining *kasha* and sat down to mend her black silk stockings. She needs to hurry. Evacuation is expected to begin any day now, and she still has lots to do. She needs to sew, darn and wash everything that she's taking with her. During the winter she and Mama neglected their appearance, really let themselves go. But that was winter, and it was freezing cold, whereas it's spring now. It's shameful to go outside with dirty hands, wearing dirty, ripped clothes.

What's more, Lena is a young girl, and a young girl's most important attribute is the purity of her mind and body. That's what Rozaliya Pavlovna said to Lena when the two of them were chatting together yesterday evening in Lena's room. Lena completely agreed with Rozaliya Pavlovna. 'Your Aunt Zhenya will treat you quite differently, even if your clothes are slightly old, as long as they are clean, patched and darned, as long as all of your buttons are sewn on properly and your overall appearance is neat and tidy. She will look at you with respect and she will think to herself: "This girl has managed to preserve her dignity, despite everything she has had to endure."' That's what Rozaliya Pavlovna said.

Lena wanted Zhenya to see her this way and vowed that she would get into the habit, from the very first day, of being neat, clean and tidy in every respect. Lena wanted to dress modestly, but elegantly.

'A good man will never fall in love with a slovenly girl. What real men value above all else in a woman is the purity of her body and mind. A girl's room must be kept tidy and the surfaces free of dust, and everything must gleam. Even if the curtains are made of the cheapest material and patched, as long as they are white and spotlessly clean they will be valued more highly than expensive curtains that are dirty and ripped.' Lena completely agreed with this as well.

Towards evening the sky brightened a little, and the sun peeped out just before it set. The sunset was very beautiful today, as though fiery tongues of flame were licking the horizon.

## 5 May 1942

Lena ate nothing but bread all day today, but she didn't feel her hunger so acutely because she spent the whole day at home sitting on her bed, darning her stockings. She ran out for bread in the morning and ate it at one o'clock, then began to sort out her stockings. She selected the ones that were most intact, those that she would take with her, and set about darning them. She darned for a long time.

The weather today was sunny but cold. It's fairly warm in general, but there's an icy wind that blows right through you. Towards evening the sky became completely clear. In the afternoon, someone came from school to let Lena know that there would be a meeting for the older pupils tomorrow at twelve o'clock. Lena signed her name and looked down the list. Tamara wasn't on it, but Vova was. Lena's spirits lifted at the thought that she would see him again tomorrow.

Lena became quite exasperated by the radio. The interruptions began at around twelve o'clock, then they announced that her district would be coming under fire. After they announced that the firing was over a concert began, but then it stopped abruptly and the radio fell silent. Strangely, while the firing was supposedly going on Lena didn't hear a single volley or a single shot. Admittedly the anti-aircraft guns were firing intermittently, but that didn't really count. It was very odd. Lena is planning to go to the evacuation point with Tonya after school tomorrow, in the hope of finding out more information. Then she will go and buy bread, and then she'll spend the rest of the day sewing, darning and so on. She must hurry, because it's not clear when evacuation will begin, and she has to get everything in order and pack all her things as soon as possible so that she is completely ready for departure. So that she can register and leave as soon as evacuation begins, without wasting a single day. Her only aim is to get to Gorky and to find Zhenya as soon as possible. Lessons won't begin until 15 May. Lena will probably leave before then. Apparently they're going to start issuing food rations on the 8th. That really upset her. She will have to survive on bread alone for two more days. Of course 300g of bread is nowhere near enough to satisfy your hunger, but she has no choice. Lena counted her coupons carefully and came to the conclusion that if she were to get anything else at the canteen over the next two days then she would exceed her grain allowance, and then she would risk going without lunch at school. They were specifically warned about that at the meeting.

If only evacuation would begin tomorrow. Then Lena would be able leave on the 7th, reducing her hunger by one day. But no, it's only a dream. Try not to think about food, Lena told herself, feeling the nausea rising in her throat and a loathsome emptiness in her stomach. But it's so hard not to think about food when she can hear the neighbours' kerosene burner and the rattling of saucepan lids on the other side of the wall. Lena can hear the noise of cutlery and even the crackle of bread being cut.

It's torture to feel this hungry, yet to have nothing to swallow but your own viscous saliva.

## 6 May 1942

It snowed overnight, but the snow melted straight away. The weather was overcast, with the same cold wind, but a little warmer. In the morning Lena ate her bread and read the book she had borrowed. Olya was mistaken, it wasn't dull at all. Lena really liked it. In fact, *In the Mountains of Sikhote-Alin* is exactly the kind of book she likes best. At twelve Lena went to school. The meeting took place in the headmaster's office, and it was for all pupils in the senior grades (eighth, ninth and tenth). There were fifteen of them present in total, of whom Lena knew only Nina (she had been calling her Tonya by mistake), Galya Kuznetsova and Misha Ilyashev. Vova wasn't there. The meeting was conducted by the headmaster himself. He announced that lessons would begin on the 15th and that the responsibility for protecting the school from enemy attack would rest on the shoulders of the older pupils. In other words, they were the sole defenders of the school. He divided them into teams. Lena and Nina were in the communications team. The headmaster announced that they would all be registered as members of the self-defence team from 8 May and that they would be on duty from 10 May, when they would also start getting their food rations. It's not hard to imagine how Lena felt about all this news. They were going to start giving food out two days later than they had promised. And they were expecting her to be a signaller, even though she could barely stand up. Over the past few days Lena really had grown quite weak. These days she found going up the stairs to the fourth floor an exhausting task, which drained her very last reserves of energy. She was barely even capable of crawling up the last set of stairs, clinging on to the handrail. She tried to go outside as little as possible, and when she had to go out she tried to go quickly, almost running, because if she went slowly her legs began to falter and she felt as though she were going to fall.

From school Lena went straight to the canteen. Walking was particularly difficult today. Lena swayed as though she were drunk and frequently stumbled, which probably didn't make a very good impression on passersby. There weren't many people in the canteen. The person standing next to Lena in the queue had a pass and promised to get her some *kasha*, but Nina arrived a few minutes later. Apparently her mother hadn't been to the canteen yet. Lena joined the queue. Nina got two portions of noodles for her. Just as they were about to serve them Lena managed to change one portion of noodles for some split pea *kasha*. Nina got two portions of noodles for herself. From the canteen they ran to the evacuation point, since the people standing next to them in the queue had told them that evacuation would begin on the 10th, or maybe even the 7th, and that they'd already started taking registrations on the 5th. The girls cheered up and ran to the evacuation point, their hearts pounding with emotion. But what disappointment awaited them there. The evacuation point was completely deserted. No personnel, no notices, nothing. Lena came home, ate some cold noodles and split peas, lit the kerosene stove and made a whole

pan of soup. It turned out very well indeed. Lena ate half a panful and decided to leave the rest for the following day. She had
taken two main courses so that she wouldn't have to go to the
canteen tomorrow.

After lunch Lena was overwhelmed by apathy and fell into
a kind of torpor. She didn't feel like moving, thinking or doing
anything at all. She could barely even lift a finger. But Lena
was fully aware that busy days were approaching. If people
had already started talking about evacuation, then it was definitely going to happen. She had to hurry up with her packing
and other preparations. To this end Lena went to see Yakov
Grigorievich yesterday evening, and they agreed that he would
let her know whether or not he wanted to buy her furniture and
other belongings on the evening of the 6th. If he was going to
proceed with the purchase they would arrange everything on
Thursday 7th, because he had the day off work.

Lena will go and see him this evening. She will take her little
stove back and find out what is happening.

Yakov Grigorievich wanted Lena to put everything she was
taking with her to one side, then she was to pack the rest of her
clothes into the trunk and tie any that wouldn't fit into a bundle.
So Lena overcame her apathy and forced herself to move, even
though it was very difficult. Afterwards Lena felt terribly thirsty,
because her soup had been quite salty, and she summoned up
the energy to go down for water. Lena boiled the kettle and, to
reward herself for her efforts, drank her fill of hot, strong tea.
Lena has a lot to do. She has to wash everything, since most of
the clothes that she is taking with her are dirty. Then she must
darn and sew.

10 May – that's the date she's placing all her hopes on now.
She has decided to officially withdraw from school, of course.
Yes, soon, soon she will say goodbye to Leningrad. Lena heard

that they've already announced the availability of butter. 'They'll probably announce sugar tomorrow,' she thought, licking her lips in anticipation. Soon she would be drinking proper tea and eating sweets and bread with butter.

Lena decided to go to the evacuation point first thing tomorrow morning to find out what was happening. After that she would finalize things with Yakov Grigorievich, and then she would fetch two buckets of water, chop some firewood and do her washing. She would go to school at one o'clock on the 8th and notify them of her withdrawal. She would meet Nina there too, and they would agree on a plan of action.

## 7 May 1942

Lena got up at about ten o'clock. First she went to her shop and got 90g of sunflower oil. From there she went to the evacuation point. They told her to come back on the 10th. Lena called into the bread shop, bought 300g of bread and returned home. She was just getting ready to have breakfast when there was a knock at the door, which turned out to be someone from the *zhakt* delivering a summons. Lena had been summoned to appear before a special committee at the military commissariat at eleven o'clock. Hurriedly finishing her bread, so that crumbs flew everywhere and oil dripped onto her coat and the floor, Lena took the summons and went to the military commissariat. She racked her brains on the way there, trying to guess why she had been summoned and what the committee wanted.

At the military commissariat Lena was informed that she was being mobilized into the local air defence organization and told to go into the next room for a medical check-up. Lena was so flustered that she couldn't even give her name and patronymic when asked for them, and despite her best efforts to control herself she ended up bursting into tears. The doctor tried to console her, telling her that it wasn't worth getting upset for the sake of it, that maybe she would be rejected because of her eyesight. Lena replied that she wasn't crying because of that but because she simply couldn't help it. The optician soon arrived, and Lena was the first to be seen by him. She was rejected and told that she was free to go. Lena came home, finished her bread and oil, heated up the soup and ate a bowl and a half of it with great pleasure. It was tasty and rich, but most importantly it was hot.

She went to see Yakov Grigorievich but was told that he was at work. Lena sat down to darn her stockings, when suddenly there was a knock at her door. She opened it and there stood a thin girl of medium height wearing glasses, a brown fur hat, boots, a padded jacket and padded trousers. 'Don't you recognize me?' she asked with a smile. Lena looked at her. Yes, it was Verochka, Vera Milyutina,[1] Mama's friend and colleague.

Lena invited her in and they sat down together on the trunk. Vera didn't stay for very long, but in the time that she was there they managed to tell one another a great deal. Lena briefly told her everything. About the way they had lived during the winter, first the three of them, then without Aka. Then how Mama died. Vera knew exactly what Lena had been through.

'You poor girl. You've had to live through so much. But never mind, you won't have to suffer for much longer. You'll be leaving

---

1    Vera Vladimirovna Milyutina (1903–87) was a Leningrad artist. After graduating from the Academy of Arts in 1932, she worked as a theatrical set designer, created the Maly Opera Theatre museum and became chief designer at Lengosestrada. During the 'Great Patriotic War' she participated in civil defence works, produced sketches and propaganda posters at Lengoroformlenie, created the graphic series 'The Hermitage during the Siege' and together with the artist Anna Ostroumova-Lebedeva took part in the creation of the Leningrad Album, which was presented as a gift to the women of Scotland. After the war she worked primarily as a theatre artist.

soon, and with luck the journey will go smoothly, you'll make it to Zhenya's and a new life will begin for you.'

It was so good for Lena to know that there was at least one person in the whole of Leningrad who meant something to her – a friend of Mama's.

Vera was anxious to know whether Lena would be travelling alone or with anybody else, but she was reassured when Lena told her that she was going with a friend from school and her mother. She asked: 'What does Nina's mother look like? Is she in good health? She's not weak, is she? You need to choose travelling companions you can rely on.' Vera questioned Lena solicitously about every detail. Was she taking many things with her? Did she have enough money for the journey? Did she have friends? Was anybody helping her? She pleaded with Lena not to eat too much during the first couple of days, not to make herself sick with *kasha*.

Apparently many evacuees become ill and some even die because they get carried away and gorge themselves on all the food, which has a harmful effect on their bodies, emaciated as they are from prolonged under-eating.

'It will require superhuman effort but you must restrain yourself, especially when it comes to bread. You will be given a kilo of bread at the station, and some people eat it all on the same day. You mustn't do this. I know someone who died during the journey simply because he ate too much – too much millet *kasha* and too much bread. Restrain yourself, and hold others back too. It's a crying shame, the most stupid death imaginable! To survive bombs, shells and a thousand different deaths, and then to perish from one portion of *kasha* too many.'

Vera's words had a profound effect on Lena. She had no intention of dying such a stupid, pointless death, so she made herself promise that she would follow Vera's advice and shun the tempting abundance of food. No, she wasn't going to let herself be killed by *kasha*. Lena had a feeling it would be extremely difficult, but she knew that this was one more impediment she had to overcome somehow.

Verochka told her that she's working as a painter and decorator at the moment. She has a worker's ration card, but it's not enough for her. At least all the toiling and drudgery earn her the right to eat at a special canteen, with special coupons. She asked whether there were any of Mama's paintbrushes left. Lena gladly gave her all of Mama's brushes, paints and other tools and said she would be far happier for Mama's things to be passed on as treasured mementoes rather than ending up in the hands of a stranger, like Yakov Grigorievich.

Lena also gave her a photo of Mama when she was a grammar-school student, a photo of herself and a copy of the book *The Little Captain*. They parted warmly and agreed to meet again the following day. Vera promised to come at about five o'clock.

Lena was very touched by Vera's interest in her. Vera didn't have much money with her, but she gave Lena 20 roubles and shared a small piece of bread that she had found in her pocket. She promised to help Lena however she could.

'I'll come and see you again tomorrow. I can't promise anything, but I'll try and bring something to eat. At the very least I will share my bread with you.' She kissed Lena affectionately. There was something magical about this kiss. It gave Lena such a warm, happy feeling.

Tomorrow is worth waiting for. Firstly it's one day closer to departure, and secondly there's another visit from a dear friend to look forward to, as well as the canteen. Lena has decided that she will spend either one grain or one meat coupon tomorrow, and on top of everything else sugar and chocolate will be available! Lena will be entitled to 100g of sugar and 100g of chocolate. But Lena has decided to get sweets instead of chocolate: 50g of sugar and 50g of sweets, the rest later. So she will drink sweet tea tomorrow with her fried bread. 'It's already 8 May tomorrow,' thought Lena as she gazed pensively out of the window.

The weather was overcast all day today. It was cold outside. The firing has only just stopped. It was very intensive. The whistling of shells could clearly be heard directly overhead, along with muffled explosions. Lena sat darning her stockings until the evening.

Vera Milyutina's address:
Apt 42, Nizhegorodskaya Street 23a, Leningrad.

## 8 May 1942

Lena got up as usual at ten o'clock. She went to the shop and got 50g of chocolate and 100g of sweets, then bought some bread, came home and prepared a feast. She boiled water and had two cups of tea with chocolate, sweets and bread fried in sunflower oil. Then she went to the canteen in the hope of seeing Nina Katysheva, but she wasn't there. Lena didn't have a pass, and they were only giving food out to those who had passes, but they served Lena without even asking for hers. Lena got a portion of millet *kasha* and ate a little there, then brought the rest home and added water to it so that she could eat it later as soup. Then she went to school and asked to be removed from the register.

(Varvara Pavlovna Zharkova asked her to call in on her friends in Gorky.)

When she got home, Lena warmed up her soup and ate it.

## 9 May 1942

Yesterday turned out to be a very interesting day for Lena. She waited a long time for Vera Milyutina, who didn't come at five o'clock as she had promised. Lena had just begun to give up hope of seeing her at all, when suddenly Vera arrived, and she wasn't alone but had another woman with her, whom she introduced to Lena as her friend. They arrived at around seven o'clock in the evening. Lena was very touched by the fact that Vera had brought her a jar of soup and a tiny piece of bread, and also letters and 30 roubles from Kisa, 10 roubles from Uncle Serezha[1] and 10 roubles from herself. Lena thanked her warmly for everything. Vera said that her friend might be interested in buying a few things from her and would pay her in bread. Her friend – a very pleasant woman of medium height, clearly a member of the intelligentsia – began by asking whether Lena would consider selling her the trunk there and then for 300g of bread. Lena thought about it and decided that she was free to

---

1 Uncle Serezha was Sergei Nikolaevich Glazunov, the second husband of Matilda Vasilievna Milyutina-Gugo – Vera Milyutina's grandmother on her father's side. Kisa would appear to be either a relative or a friend of the Milyutins.

do as she liked, that Yakov Grigorievich had no claim to any of her belongings if she had a better offer from someone else, and that given the circumstances she was therefore able to disregard their agreement. So she accepted the offer and began to unpack the trunk, taking out all the clothes that she had packed with such effort a few days previously and putting them all back into the corner.

At this point it became clear that her new customer was a real rag-picker. It was quite something to see how enthusiastically she began rummaging through the piles of clothes, picking out things that Lena considered quite worthless. Lena's pillagers worked away all evening, and by the time they were finished they had each amassed a whole pile of things – to the great surprise of Lena, who believed that she had already sold everything of value long ago. As a matter of fact, Lena was very happy that so many things would not be ending up in the hands of Yakov Grigorievich, whom she had never really liked. Verochka chose three of Aka's hats for herself and tried them on. They all really suited her. She managed to select a considerable number of items for Kisa too. Lena gave Vera her Orlik print as a keepsake, and Vera also took the rest of Mama's paints and artist's mannequins. In the end Vera's friend decided to take the little cupboard too, because she liked it so much, and in return for this 'robbery' Lena's reward was the right to go to the bread shop and buy half a kilo of bread. This was a real treat for Lena, and she went straight to the bread shop behind the Pravda cinema and bought the whole amount at once. It was good bread, too – soft, dry and fluffy. On the way there she met Olya, who was wearing summer clothes and chewing on a large hunk of bread. Olya asked why Lena hadn't been to see her. She promised to call in on Lena and asked if she could borrow something to read. Lena told her that evacuation would be starting soon and asked if she would be leaving. Olya said that she wasn't planning on leaving this month, because she'd already bought her bread in advance. She gave some other reason too, which Lena didn't quite understand.

Lena's guests didn't leave until late in the evening. They agreed that Verochka would try and come the following day, but if she wasn't there by seven o'clock then Lena would go to her house instead. Vera drew a detailed map to help Lena find it. She gave Lena two letters addressed to friends of hers who lived in Gorky and entreated Lena to visit them in person and tell them about life in Leningrad. She said that some of her friends were influential people who might be able to help Lena in some way. In any case, she promised that they would treat her kindly and take her under their wing.

Lena agreed with Vera's friend that she and her husband would come the following morning before ten o'clock to collect the things she had bought.

Worn out by the day's events, Lena ate a little bread with sunflower oil and salt and went to bed. She slept soundly, and the first thing she did when she woke up this morning was to reach for her bread. She had eaten almost all of it by the time yesterday's new acquaintance and her husband arrived, leaving only a small piece to eat with her soup. It's funny the way time plays tricks on you sometimes. Lena thought that they had come later than they agreed, at eleven o'clock, so imagine her surprise when they told her that it was in fact only nine o'clock. She found this very upsetting. Her new friend and her husband took the trunk, saying that they would be back in an hour for the shelves. Lena tried to go back to sleep but she couldn't, so she tried to read, but that was equally futile. All she could think about was the pot of soup on top of the cupboard. Lena reluctantly got up, lit the kerosene burner and warmed up the ill-fated soup, after first diluting it with water. It was oat soup, with a small piece of meat, and it was so rich and thick that even though Lena had added quite a lot of water it still made two and a half satisfying bowls full. There was only just enough kerosene left to heat the soup, and the wick was already starting to burn. It goes without saying how Lena enjoyed this hot meat soup, the like of which she hadn't eaten for such a long time.

Afterwards she began to read, then she reluctantly put her coat on to go to the bread shop, but just as she was closing the door her new friend arrived to collect the shelves. They talked for a while, and from what Lena could gather she seemed to be married to an inspector who worked at the dance school.[2] Lena learned that she and her husband had saved Vera's life, because they had found a place for her in a recuperation clinic and arranged for her to be able to eat at a special canteen without using her ration card, and that they themselves owed their life to their dog, which had fed them for a whole month. Like Lena and Mama they had also resorted to eating carpenter's glue, and a lot more besides.

Lena asked if there was any way she could get her a canteen pass, and she promised to talk to her husband about it. She also offered to take Lena to their canteen at the dance school, but Lena declined. From what she said it became apparent that she was indeed the wife of the inspector of this school, that they were living there temporarily as their apartment had been bombed, that the school would be evacuated as soon as the first train left, so therefore her husband would definitely know about it, and that evacuation wouldn't start until after the 10th. Then she said she might be able to talk to her husband and

2   Andrei Andreevich Bartashevich (1899–1949) was deputy director of the Arts Administration of the Executive Committee of the Leningrad City Council.

arrange for Lena to travel with the school, which would be better for her. She made a lot of promises, all in all, so Lena is confident that she can count on her support.

Before leaving, she said she would let Vera know what she had managed to find out and arrange for Lena when she next saw her. After she'd gone Lena went to the shop, where she bought some bread and exchanged her last remaining coupon for 50g of sugar. When she got home she used some plywood to make a fire in the stove, boiled the kettle and had five cups of sweet hot tea with bread. Then she started reading, and it was such a pleasure reading on a full stomach, all the more so because it was an extremely interesting book. While she was reading Lena broke off little pieces of bread, dipped them into sugar and ate them one by one. When the bread ran out Lena finished off the remaining sugar and felt pleasantly 'full'!

Lena decided to count her money. She found that she had the grand total of 250 roubles. Tomorrow she would have to pay for her room for May, and then perhaps she could call in on Sofya to see if she could get a small bottle of *kefir*. She did something else for a little while and then decided to go and find out what the time was. And once again her assumption was incorrect. She had been under the impression that it was already six o'clock or thereabouts, but in fact it was only four o'clock.

Lena was feeling drowsy so she decided to have a nap, but then she changed her mind. She tucked her legs under the blanket and fell to thinking. She spent a long time looking at the map, studying the route of her planned journey and wondering how it would all turn out. It really would be good to leave with the ballet girls. She might even get to meet Galya Chernoyarova[3].

---

3  Galina Aleksandrovna Chernoyarova was a soloist at the Bolshoi Opera and Ballet
   Theatre of Belorussia and a teacher. As a ballet student she was evacuated from

If this woman's husband was such an important person, then of course he could arrange things in Lena's favour if he were so inclined. They would probably have their own special carriage, or carriages, so she wouldn't have to worry about her things, it would be easier to get food and most importantly it would be more fun to travel with a group of people her own age. Otherwise worrying about her luggage and food supplies could really spoil this momentous journey.

It was so nice for Lena to have reached the point where it was simply a matter of time, the final obstacles were behind her and she was as free as a bird. She had no ties, no obligations and she didn't owe anything to anyone.

It was so nice to feel completely free. While she was waiting to leave she could do whatever she wanted from one day to the next. And she wouldn't have to wait much longer. Certainly no later than the 20th, more likely the 15th or 16th. And she would not be spending these final days alone. She had friends now: Vera and Kisa, this was where she belonged for the time being. As long as she kept her spirits up and looked cheerfully towards the future, everything would be fine.

---

Leningrad to the village of Platoshina in the Perm region, returning to Leningrad in May 1944. After graduating in September 1944 from the Vaganovksy school (renamed in the 1950s the Leningrad State Choreographic Institute), she moved to Minsk.

# 10 May 1942

At exactly seven o'clock yesterday evening Lena put her coat on and took the tram to Vera's house. It didn't take her long to find it. She was welcomed with open arms and given a seat by the cast-iron stove. Lena really liked it there. Vera lives with old Uncle Serezha and Kisa in two corner rooms on the ground floor of a two-storey wooden house. One room has one window, and the other has two. There are trees and bushes growing just outside. Vera's house is one of a group of similar houses arranged around a small courtyard, with a paved path running through the middle of it and grass, shrubbery and trees around the edges. It's lovely here, somehow quite out of keeping with the ruins of the neighbouring apartment blocks. The thing is, Vera lives very close to Finland Station – the railway tracks run immediately behind the building opposite theirs. So this area was badly hit by bombs that were dropped on the station but fell in the vicinity. It may look calm and picturesque, but in reality it's a dreadful place. The apartment blocks on either side of the garden have been reduced to heaps of rubble. One of these buildings, to the right-hand side of their current residence, is where Vera and Uncle Serezha used to live.

Lena felt so comfortable that she didn't want to leave, so she decided to spend the night there. They sat down to drink tea together. Vera gave her a little bit of bread and a spoonful of sugar, and there were also a few grains of citric acid. Then they made a bed up for Lena on a very tall trunk. It was just like a bunk in a long-distance train, and Lena really liked it. She gladly undressed and wrapped herself in the quilted blanket, and as she fell asleep she felt as though she were actually in a railway carriage. She even had the impression that she and her bed were moving, swaying pleasantly from side to side. This was due to the fact that Lena's head had been spinning all day. Thoughts of her impending journey, the proximity of the railway station, the whistles of the steam engines – everything combined to create the illusion that she was already on her way.

Lena didn't get much sleep. The radio was hanging just above her head, and the loud ticking of the metronome clock was impossible to ignore. In the morning, Vera woke her up and she washed her face and hands with real soap. Then Vera chopped some firewood on the doorstep, and Lena ran to the shop to fetch bread and helped carry the firewood inside. Meanwhile Kisa made the tea. The weather was lovely. The wind had torn the clouds apart, and sunshine was lighting up the world once more. Glimpses of blue sky could be seen between the shafts of light, the birds were singing, and the alluring whistles of the steam trains could be heard in the distance. They seemed to be signalling to her, calling: come on, get going!

This morning Lena drank five cups of tea with citric acid and ate some bread and sugar, which Kisa gave her. Then she looked through Vera's children's books. They say that everyone has a 'passion'. For example, Kisa is passionate about collecting embroidery designs, various types of thread and pretty scraps of fabric. Lena has a passionate interest in postcards, birds and other animals. But Vera's passion is very peculiar. She collects children's books, particularly those aimed at very young children. She has a great many of these books. Some are antiques that used to belong to her mother, whereas others are more contemporary, such as *The Silly Little Mouse* and *Terem-Teremok*.

Uncle Serezha went to bed for a little rest, Kisa sat down to write some letters, and Vera got on with her work. She's sketching the rooms of the Hermitage – the Hermitage as it is now, with all the damage caused by bombs and missiles – and then perfecting these drafts at home.[1] What she's doing is making history, recording with her paintbrush evidence of the crimes committed by Nazi thugs. This evidence will become part of our history. Vera is an accomplished artist, and her drawings are very good. Everyone was occupied in their own way, but Lena soon realized with regret that looking through the books was wearing her out so she stopped. She was overcome with apathy and didn't feel like moving a single limb. Her eyes closed, her head was spinning, and she felt nauseous. She really didn't feel very well at all, but she tried her best to hide it. Lena began to put the books back where she'd found them, and while she was walking across the room her knees almost gave way. 'What's the matter with me? I hope I'm not coming down with something,' thought Lena with alarm. She felt miserable and heavy-hearted. The sun disappeared, the sky clouded over, and just at

---

1    Vera Milyutina later recalled: 'Andrei Andreevich Bartashevich came – he looked so gaunt, so yellow! He had come so far to see us! He was trying to save so many people, to find work for all those who had been "forgotten". "Could you walk as far as the Hermitage?" he asked. "Yes," I said. "And home again?" "I'll rest, then I'll manage it." "Well, I already know you can draw," he said confidently. Apparently they needed people to "record" for posterity the "wounds" inflicted on the Hermitage by bombs and artillery shells. This task had been given to the Arts Committee' (Central State Archive of Literature and Art, St Petersburg, f. 495, op. 1, d. 154, l. 19).

that moment came the sinister wail of the siren, announcing an air raid. The raid lasted about an hour, and after the all-clear Lena put her coat on, said goodbye to everyone and left. She got home, collected her jars and went to the canteen. She stood in the queue for quite a long time but still left empty-handed, because the split pea *kasha*, noodles and rissoles had all run out. There was only soy *kasha* left, and that was running out too. There wouldn't be enough left for Lena, and besides the cashier was new and wouldn't have given her any without a pass. So Lena bought 60g of split peas in the shop and made herself some *kasha* at home. The result was neither *kasha* nor soup – God knows what it was. But the split peas swelled and softened so that they were a satisfying consistency and took a long time to eat. Lena ate three peas at a time, and this pleasurable activity occupied the entire evening. Feeling quite weak, Lena went to bed early. There was another air raid that evening, but it didn't last very long. Just before sunset the sun peeped out again and lit up the dismal, cluttered room, the piles of books and other things, the full chamber pot in the middle of the floor. Lena didn't have the energy to carry the waste bucket downstairs. Today was a sad and sorrowful day for Lena. 'Something's going to happen tomorrow,' she thought as she fell asleep.

## 11 May 1942

Lena woke up at around midday but left the house just after (*) She decided to go to the evacuation point first. The idea that registration might already have started was making her extremely anxious. The sun was shining and it was warm outside, but the evacuation point was as deserted as before. Lena asked the man on duty at the entrance for the latest news about evacuation, but he told her that it wouldn't start before the 15th. Lena was plunged into despair and immediately lost her ability to take pleasure in either the sun, or the blue sky, or the warmth.

She went to visit Mariya Fedorovna Bartashevich. As luck would have it she met her on the stairs, carrying a saucepan full of macaroni back from the canteen. She took Lena back to her room. They walked down a long hallway, turning right and then left. Lena would never have found it on her own. Eventually they reached her room. Lena noticed two of her own cushions on the bed – both clean and freshly laundered, with ribbons sewn into the corners. It was nice to see them. Lena's cupboard was there too, its shelves covered with embroidered serviettes and pretty china ornaments, including Aka's blue sugar bowl.

Mariya Fedorovna's room was warm and very comfortable. A mirrored wardrobe, a piano, a writing desk, lots of books, a rug on the floor. Mariya Fedorovna gave Lena's luggage straps back and said that her husband had agreed to her using the canteen there, if she wished. Lena thanked her warmly. They went to the canteen together, and Mariya Fedorovna introduced Lena and told the girl behind the counter that she would be getting her lunch there for the time being as authorized by her husband. Then she showed her how to get in without a pass, signed a pass for her, sent her best regards to Vera, Kisa and Uncle Serezha and asked Lena to tell Vera that she hoped she would come and see her soon. Then she left, telling Lena to come and find her if she needed anything. Lena remained in the queue, which wasn't long – only about seven people. Lena looked around. She was in a small, clean room with two windows. On one side of the room, over by the windows, there were four little tables covered with clean oilcloth. There was a pot of flowers on each table, and flowers on the windowsills too, and the clean windows were hung with white curtains. On the other side of the room there stood an attractive, neat-looking girl wearing a white apron and a red beret. She was surrounded on three sides by tables, and there was a cupboard set into the wall behind her. Everything was remarkably clean and tidy. There was soup, kasha, macaroni, all in spotlessly clean galvanized stock pots covered with lids. The girl was dishing everything out efficiently and precisely. The options were a 250g portion of pure, thick millet kasha, a 200g portion of macaroni and a thick soup made with wheat grain and noodles. There were little sausages for the meat course. Lena took one portion of millet kasha. Then she went home, buying bread on the way, which she ate with her kasha. It made a very filling meal. Then she counted her coupons and worked out that she could use 40g of grain coupons every day and take two portions of meat before 15 May. Then Lena went for water and**

## 16 May 1942

(From 15 May.) The weather is lovely at the moment. It's sunny and warm, 16°C in the shade. The grass is turning green, and the new buds are fit to burst. Spring is in full swing. But the Germans are not idle. We're being fired on every day, and there are air raids several times a day.

There was a terrible outburst of artillery fire just now. Lena was walking along Nevsky Prospekt. She was hoping to exchange 200g of bread that had cost her 90 roubles for some grain. As soon as the firing began Lena crossed the road and took shelter in a narrow trench in Ekaterininsky Park. The shells flew relentlessly overhead, one after another, with a melodious whistling sound. There were incessant, thunderous explosions. It was actually quite frightening. Even the birds, which had been singing constantly, fell silent. During a lull Lena looked out of her hiding place and was amazed by what she saw. It's astonishing, the way people have grown so used to their lives being in danger. Nobody even seemed to have noticed that they were under fire. The trams were still running, cars were speeding by, people were walking about or sitting calmly on benches. Everyone was going about their business, and Lena suddenly felt rather embarrassed. People would think there was something wrong with her, hiding in a trench like that, so she went home. In any case, the firing had already started to die down and eventually it stopped altogether.

The sun didn't make an appearance all day today, but it was warm and rather stifling. Lena spent the night at Vera's house again. Vera and Kisa decided to sleep in a little longer today, but Lena couldn't sleep at all. It was hardly surprising, after the joyous news that Kisa had given her yesterday. As soon as Lena got to their house yesterday evening Kisa asked if she'd had any luck regarding evacuation. Lena imparted the dispiriting news that evacuation would be starting after the 20th, with registration from the 18th, although initially it would only be open to those temporarily registered in the city, soldiers wounded in action and women with children under twelve.[1]

Kisa replied: 'But you're already registered, Lenochka. I submitted an application on your behalf,' and then she went on to explain everything in detail. Apparently she was transferred urgently to the evacuation point today. She's going to be working there again, processing applications. She filled in an application on Lena's behalf and registered her in 60th place on the list. So Lena no longer needs to rush about, or worry, or drag herself to the refrigeration institute[2] every day. All Lena has to

---

1    A resolution passed by the Military Council of the Leningrad Front on 18 May 1942 set out plans for the evacuation of 300,000 people – primarily women with two or more children, those incapable of work, the families of workers who had already been evacuated with their place of work, the families of servicemen, children from children's homes and those who had been wounded or disabled during the war. Evacuation was scheduled to begin on 25 May (V. M. Kovalchuk, *900 dnei blokady. Leningrad 1941–1944*, St Petersburg, 2005, p. 163).

2    Lena Mukhina is referring to the Leningrad Technological Institute of the Refrigeration Industry. During the siege scientists here developed the technology for the

do now is pack her things and wait. Evacuation will begin on the 20th, and Lena will leave in the first few days. This explains why Lena got up so early. She washed herself thoroughly, then sat down to knit. The time flew by. Eventually the others got up too. Lena went out for bread. The bread was undercooked, but Lena made some delicious rusks out of it. They sat and drank tea together. Uncle Serezha treated Lena to some meat jelly, and Vera gave her a piece of butter. Then Lena filled in her application form as dictated by Kisa and resumed her knitting. She took great pleasure in this activity, because it was turning out very well, just the way she wanted it to. Lena had been planning to leave the house at half past eleven in order to get to the canteen on time, but things turned out differently. There was an air-raid warning at eleven o'clock, and the raid lasted nearly an hour and a half. And even though Lena left as soon as the all-clear was given, took the first tram and arrived at the canteen quite quickly, she was still late, and of course there was nothing left.

Lena went up to see Mariya Fedorovna, who was delighted to hear her news. Then she ran to the canteen on Pravda Street, queued for two hours and eventually got some split pea *kasha* and a portion of brains. The *kasha* was nice and thick, and the brains were very rich, tasty and filling, so it didn't matter that they were cutting out 50g of meat coupons for just 30g in weight. Lena met Nina Katysheva in the canteen, who told her that school wasn't starting until the 20th, that they still weren't being fed and that they weren't going to be until at least the 18th. So Lena hadn't lost out at all by taking her name off

---

production of soy milk and soy protein for children and the wounded, as well as the recipe for 'blockade bread'. The institute was evacuated in March 1942, first to Kislovodsk and from there to Semipalatinsk (now Semey).

the school register. On the contrary she was better off because she was completely free, apart from her duties with the local air defence organization. After leaving the canteen Lena went and paid for her room for May, then went home and sat down with her knitting again. At six o'clock in the evening she went down to the *zhakt* and obtained a certificate to prove that she had no debts and that the *zhakt* wouldn't oppose her departure, which was the only document a dependant was required to show at the evacuation point.

This evening Lena went to her new home again, as she had been doing for the past few days. She was looking forward to a cup of hot tea and fried rusks with butter. It was overcast and spitting with rain. She had to wait a long time for the tram, as she always did these days. Eventually two came at once. The first was overcrowded, the second merely full. Lena managed to squeeze on, and it took her all the way to Finland Station. As they went over the bridge Lena gazed in admiration at the beautiful Neva, as she had so many times before. It was so vast, so wide, so colourful in the sunset, with the Peter and Paul Fortress silhouetted above it, the water mirror-calm, warships moored along the bank and the buildings on the opposite side of the river, all reflected in the water in such minute detail. Lena admired everything, unable to tear herself away. She would be leaving soon, and while she had the opportunity to see the beautiful Neva twice every day she wanted to commit this river to memory. She had no way of knowing when she would see it again. Perhaps not for years.

Vera had guests. An artist friend of hers and his wife. They had only just left the recuperation clinic and were on a special diet designed to build up their strength. Being admitted to the clinic had saved them both from certain death, because they had been so weak they could no longer walk, and the artist's wife had scurvy as well as severe malnutrition. But they're recovering now and are planning to leave, hopefully on the 25th or the 27th. They're going to Rybinsk and had come to Vera's to ask Kisa if she could help them.

Lena concluded that they would probably be her travelling companions. Kisa promised to arrange it so that all three of them would be sent together.

The little rusk that Lena had been saving since the morning proved to be far from adequate, and Lena went to bed feeling hungry and miserable. She firmly resolved to go to the bread shop at six o'clock the following morning, although as it happened she didn't wake up until seven and found that she no longer felt so unbearably hungry. She went out for bread at half past eight. At nine the three of them drank tea together. Vera gave Lena two spoonfuls of buckwheat *kasha*, and Kisa gave her a little raw meat. They had just announced that meat was available, and Kisa had gone out early and got some nice lamb for herself and Vera. Like Lena, Kisa enjoyed eating raw meat.[3] Lena spread buckwheat gruel on her bread instead of butter, but after breakfast she was still hungry so she ate the piece of bread she had been intending to save for her evening meal. Lena was in a hurry to leave, because she was worried that there would be another air raid and she would be late for the canteen again. There was no air raid, but the canteen was shut for the day so Lena got her lunch on Pravda. She took a portion of whole-

---

3 Forty years later Lena Mukhina wrote to Vera Milyutina: 'On 1 May, like everyone else, I received the following gift: a slice of white bread, a piece of raw meat and some sugar. I can clearly remember coming out of the shop, crossing the road, sitting in the little park opposite our building and making myself a very strange sandwich. Well, it seems strange now, but it didn't at the time. I put the raw meat on the slice of bread, sprinkled it with sugar and took such pleasure in every mouthful. I couldn't bring myself to eat it now.'

wheat *kasha* and some soup. When she got home she made a whole panful of soup by mixing it all together and diluting it with water. She ate two bowls of soup and a main course (the *kasha* and the dregs from the soybean and split pea soup), then poured the remaining soup into a glass jar to eat later. Now she finally felt full. Lena took up her knitting again and lost track of time. The radio came on at five o'clock.

Then the artillery fire began. Explosions roared like thunder outside, while a children's concert was broadcast on the radio. Their performance was dedicated to the soldiers, their protectors. Their wavering, high-pitched voices were so poignant. They sang, read poems, played the piano and the violin. Meanwhile the weapons continued to roar outside, as the Germans tried to annihilate us and the young performers who were giving their all. This made a profound impression upon Lena. Something else made Lena proud of her homeland and its people, too, and this was the tale of the heroic feat of the five Baltic sailors.[4] They took on a large number of German tanks and fought to the very last bullet, holding the steel monsters in check, but the two sides were not equally matched and the five brave men saw that they did not have long to live. So they said their goodbyes, they hugged and kissed each other for the last time, then one by one, with grenades bound to their bodies, they threw themselves beneath the steel tracks and blew themselves up along with the tanks. These brave men lost their lives, but they stopped the enemy tanks advancing. The motherland will

---

4   On 14 May 1942 the *Krasnyi Flot* newspaper published an article by senior political officer M. Kogut about the heroic actions of political officer N. D. Filchenko and four Soviet Navy sailors – V. G. Tsibulko, Yu. K. Parshin, I. M. Krasnoselsky and D. S. Odintsov – who beat off a German tank attack during the defence of the city of Sevastopol. The article was reprinted in *Leningradskaya Pravda* on 17 May.

never forget their names. They will go down in history, and all the peoples of our motherland will compose stories, songs and epic poems about them. Glory to those men.

> It came to pass that five brave men
> Were forced into battle with enemy tanks.
> They fought bravely and fearlessly,
> But the enemy was stronger. Their death was nigh.
> No! It is not yet their time to die,
> For they must do their duty until the very end.
> They are wearing grenades on their belts,
> Though their hands are useless now.
> Wounded and bleeding**

## 18 May 1942

Today feels particularly hot and sultry, for some reason. Heavy, leaden clouds are crawling across the sky, so there's probably going to be a thunderstorm. At the very least it's bound to rain. It's a real summer's day. The trees and bushes have turned green. The lawns and gardens are full of fresh green grass. Leningraders have already begun making trips outside the city to gather nettles and sorrel. Life is good for Lena at the moment. She goes out for bread in the morning and the birds are singing, the trees are turning green, the trains are sounding their whistles, the trams are clanking, there's an aeroplane droning in the sky . . . It's good to be alive. It's such a pity that Mama didn't live to see these fine days. She was so eager to see the first spring leaves.

Vera says to Lena: 'You're so lucky, Lenochka! You're going to see the Volga, and very soon you'll be a long way away from here. You're starting your life all over again. Just think, your future is entirely in your hands. How exciting!' Yes, it's true, Lena is lucky, but there's one thing preventing her enjoying her happiness to the full – the lack of food. If only she had a little more to eat, the world would be even more beautiful. You may think you're happy, but if your heart is yearning for something this poisons all your pleasure.

Such torment . . . Lena cannot wait until the day she receives her 2 kilos of bread, *kasha* and soup at the station,[1] sits on the train and bids farewell to Leningrad.

This morning Lena had a sweet with her cup of tea. Being workers, Kisa and Vera received 100g of chocolate and 200g of sweets each, and they both gave Lena a sweet and a piece of chocolate. Thanks to the fact that Lena had saved some soup to eat yesterday evening, she felt full after eating just a little bread so decided to leave most of it for later. But just before leaving the house she couldn't help herself and ate it anyway, leaving only a tiny morsel and a few crumbs of chocolate. There's no getting away from it: however much she fights it, however much she tries to convince herself otherwise, the truth of the matter is that Lena is permanently hungry.

I don't care about tomorrow, I just want to feel full today, thought Lena, and she got two portions of wholewheat *kasha* at the canteen. They cut out four coupons. Lena ate just one spoonful of hot *kasha* at the canteen and took the rest home, which she doesn't do very often. She put the *kasha* straight into a saucepan, added water and made it into soup. It was splendid soup, thick and tasty. Lena ate two bowlfuls of it, then some of the remaining *kasha* from the rest of the soup, but she didn't have the feeling of satisfaction that occurs when you're truly satiated. If only she could have had another portion of hot *kasha*

---

1    On evacuation from Leningrad, city residents were required to hand over their food and manufactured goods ration cards to the authorities at their apartment building or place of work; in return they were given coupons for food and travel. Food ration quantities changed several times, but they were given lunch and dry rations at Finland Station, Kobona and Lavrovo (V. M. Kovalchuk, *900 dnei blokady. Leningrad 1941–1944*, St Petersburg, 2005, p. 164).

after her soup, that would probably have filled her up. As it was, her stomach was full but she was still hungry. She wished she had something else to eat.

Kisa said that she would find out about evacuation tomorrow, the 19th. She promised to do everything she could to send Lena in the first day or two.

There was an air raid tonight. The anti-aircraft guns were roaring away so furiously that the whole building shook and the windows trembled. Lena looked out of the window. Countless blue searchlight tentacles roamed the sky, which was lit up again and again by bursts of fire. When did the air raid end? Lena didn't hear, because she had rolled over and gone to sleep, thinking: let them kill me. There was a storm this evening, with a horrendous downpour, and afterwards a terrible outburst of artillery fire. It wasn't clear who was firing, us or the Germans, but it was so loud and so close that the whole building shook and the windows rattled. At first Lena assumed that it was the anti-aircraft guns, but they soon announced on the radio that it was an artillery bombardment.

## 22 May 1942

Lena had an interesting experience yesterday. She left Vera's house at nine o'clock and waited a very long time for the tram. When it finally came it was full to bursting, and the second tram was the same, so Lena decided to take a tram in the opposite direction. 'I'm not in any hurry,' she thought, 'I'll go to the end of the line and get off on the way back.' But halfway there she realized that the tram was going to the park. Lena got off at the next stop and waited for a tram to take her back again, but after a while she gave up and started to walk. She would have to walk 4½ km from 1st Murinsky Prospekt just to get back to Vera's house. And this was after a day when she'd eaten nothing but 300g of bread in the morning and two dried rusks in the evening, which Vera had given her to eat with her tea. But she had no choice. So Lena set off, not walking but running, as quickly as she could. She was in tears at first, and all she could think about was how long it would take her to reach the end of Lesnoy Prospekt. She even tried walking with her eyes closed, so that she wouldn't have to see how far she had to go. But gradually her surroundings caused her to forget her sorrows. It was a beautiful spring evening, with a fresh green smell in the air. It was a remarkably pleasant smell. A warm breeze was blowing. There was a row of bushes with sticky, newly opened leaves along the side of the road, and behind these bushes freshly ploughed allotments stretched as far as the railway embankment. She felt an incredible sense of space and silence all around her. Lena walked along enjoying this spring evening, breathing in the marvellous smell, the fragrance of spring, and before she knew it she was at the railway bridge. She saw a truck idling at the side of the road and its driver doing something nearby. After much persuasion the driver agreed to take Lena to Finland Station in return for a box of matches and 5 roubles that Vera had given her.

Then another citizen came over, and the driver agreed to take her as well in return for a piece of bread that she happened to have. She needed to get to the Five Corners, and the driver agreed to take her to the corner of Liteiny and Nekrasov. The woman got into the back of the truck, and Lena sat in the cab next to the driver. It was warm and cosy. The road was deserted, and they drove along at breakneck speed. Every now and then they overtook a solitary pedestrian. On the way, Lena said that she also needed to get to the Five Corners and asked the driver to take her as close as possible. He agreed. They crossed the bridge over the Neva, and then he changed his mind and turned off Liteiny into one of the side streets. He said that his garage was on Konyushennaya and that he would be going along the Fontanka and past the Summer Garden and the Field of Mars, so he offered to drop them there. Lena agreed, but the other woman asked to get out and started walking along Liteiny. It worked out better for Lena, of course. He dropped her at the corner of the Field of Mars and the Mikhailovsky Garden. Lena thanked her saviour and rushed home along Sadovaya as fast as she could, past the Aleksandrinka theatre, along Rossi Street and down Chernyshev Lane. The streets were deserted, and the footsteps of individual pedestrians rang out against the pavement. The 'Internationale' had long finished playing on the radio by the time Lena got home. She barely managed to crawl up the stairs to the fourth floor, opened the door to her room, took her coat off and collapsed onto the bed, immediately falling fast asleep. She slept soundly, right through until half past eleven this morning. Then she got up and went straight to the canteen at the dance school for lunch, buying her bread on the way. Suddenly there was a terrible outburst of artillery fire. One after another, shells whistled overhead and exploded somewhere on the other side of the Neva. Lena saw Mariya Fedorovna at the canteen and told her about Vera's health, how she had started bacteriophage treatment[1] the day before, how she was terribly weak and in low spirits, how she couldn't go to work and so on. Mariya Fedorovna sent her best regards to Vera, Kisa and Uncle Serezha. Lena asked her for 1 rouble, because she didn't have enough. She got a portion of noodles and 50g of meat.

By this time the firing had stopped, and Lena went back to Vera's house.

Uncle Serezha was just lighting the stove in order to heat up his lunch, so Lena fried her noodles in some fat that Vera gave her and ate them with pleasure, after which she had two cups of hot tea with bread. It was half past two. After lunch Uncle Serezha went to see the doctor, Verochka fell asleep and Lena began to look through the books, selecting the ones she wanted to read. Then she did some washing. When Uncle Serezha came back, Lena went out to fetch water and helped him bring in some firewood from the shed. As she was walking to the shed,

---

1  Bacteriophage therapy was commonly used in the Soviet Union to treat bacterial infections.

she suddenly felt that she needed to leave the city as soon as possible. The weather was warm but wet. A fine drizzle was falling. The air smelled of spring. It was warm, and the birds were singing. There was young greenery all around: on the trees, on the bushes, on the ground. Lena felt happy, and when a steam train sounded its whistle this made her even happier. She wanted to leave on a rainy day just like this, to sit in a railway carriage and travel somewhere far, far away.

After she'd finished helping with the firewood Lena settled down on the sofa at Vera's feet and began looking at books, listening to the radio and talking to Vera. Then Kisa came home. Lena learned that her boss had said the first special train would be leaving on 25 May and that they had spent today sorting all the applications into four directions. Two to the south and two to the east. Lena, Boris Belozerov and his wife Nina had all been allocated places on the second train heading east. Lena was delighted by this news – it meant that evacuation would start on 25 May, not some time in June, which had been a possibility. After a cup of tea and some black rusks, Lena said her goodbyes and went home. She felt happy and cheerful. Tomorrow is already the 23rd. Kisa said that detailed information about evacuation will be available tomorrow, because today her boss went to find out more.

## 25 May 1942

Today is 25 May. I'm leaving any day now. The first special train is going today. Kisa said there's a possibility that I might be leaving tomorrow or the day after. But I'm so weak at the moment that it's all the same to me. My brain no longer reacts to anything. I feel as though I'm half asleep. I'm growing weaker and weaker every day, and my last reserves of strength are ebbing by the hour. I simply don't have any energy left. Even the news about my imminent departure makes no impression on me. It's quite funny, really. I mean, I'm not an invalid or an old man or woman, but a young girl with her whole future ahead of her. I know I'm lucky, I'm leaving soon. But then I look at myself, at what I have become. My apathetic, despondent demeanour, the way I shuffle along like an invalid, hobbling unevenly, barely able to walk up three steps. And I'm not making it up or exaggerating, I genuinely don't recognize myself any more. I feel like laughing through my tears. A month or so ago, whenever I felt desperately hungry in the afternoon my energy would somehow increase to enable me to find more food. I would have walked to the ends of the earth for an extra piece of bread, or anything else edible, but now I'm barely aware of my hunger. I can't feel anything at all. I've grown accustomed to it, but I don't understand why I'm growing weaker and weaker every day. Can a human being really not live on bread alone? How odd.

I got up early today. I bought my bread and went 'home'. Kisa already had the samovar ready. Uncle Serezha was still asleep. Vera, Kisa and I sat and drank tea together. It was nice sitting there at the round table while the samovar puffed away, enjoying the sight of a bundle of young green twigs and a little bunch of white flowers. I left straight after tea, so I still had a small piece of bread. I packed this piece of bread into my suitcase and took it with me, along with my knitting and a copy of *The Garin Death Ray* by Aleksei Tolstoy. Lena took the second tram to the Pravda cinema. She walked to the little garden and started reading her book.

There was greenery all around her. Birds were busy building their nests, little boys were running about, chirruping away. It was lovely. Lena went to the canteen and exchanged the last two coupons on her grain ration card for one portion of split pea *kasha*, tipping it into her round metal can. She went outside, sat on the fence in the garden and slowly began to eat the delicious hot *kasha*. It's funny, but they never used to make *kasha* from split peas before. You could get split pea soup, but none of the canteens served split pea *kasha*, and no one made it at home either. But split peas have always been available to buy in any food shop. They're really cheap. And so filling that two kilos will make you more *kasha* than you know what to do with. I'm definitely going to make split pea *kasha* for lunch in future.

Once she'd finished her *kasha* Lena took a shortcut home through the courtyards, and on the way she noticed some luxuriant vegetation that had sprouted up on the rubbish heap. Lena bent down and saw that they were young nettle shoots. They were about 4 or 5 cm tall, each with three leaves no bigger than a fingernail. Lena collected a bagful of these nettles, brought them home and filled a saucepan with them. She went to ask Aunt Sasha how to make nettle soup, and she just so happened to be making it herself at that very moment. It's quite straightforward. First you have to blanch the nettles, then you chop them finely and boil them up. Lena decided that she would make nettle and meat soup at 'home' later that evening.

*This is Lena's last entry in her diary.*

# Acknowledgements

Sincere thanks to John Dewey for generously permitting me to use his translation of the first two lines of Fedor Tyutchev's poem 'No Wonder Winter Rages' (p. 277). I would also like to thank Natasha Perova in Moscow for her support and advice, on this project and always. Finally, love and best wishes to Svetlana Lepeshkina and family in St Petersburg, who have helped without even knowing it by making me welcome in their home so many times over the past twenty years.

It has been a privilege to translate Lena's diary, and my only hope is that I have helped in some small way to keep her memory alive.